Hadija's Story

Hadija's Story

Diaspora, Gender, and Belonging in the Cameroon Grassfields

Harmony O'Rourke

INDIANA UNIVERSITY PRESS   *Bloomington & Indianapolis*

This book is a publication of

INDIANA UNIVERSITY PRESS
Office of Scholarly Publishing
Herman B Wells Library 350
1320 East 10th Street
Bloomington, Indiana 47405 USA

iupress.indiana.edu

Manufactured in the
United States of America

Library of Congress
Cataloging-in-Publication Data

Names: O'Rourke, Harmony, author.
Title: Hadija's story : diaspora, gender,
    and belonging in the Cameroon
    Grassfields / Harmony O'Rourke.
Description: Bloomington : Indiana
    University Press, 2017. | Includes
    bibliographical references and index.
Identifiers: LCCN 2016034703| ISBN
    9780253023759 (cl : alk. paper) | ISBN
    9780253023834 (pb : alk. paper)
Subjects: LCSH: Hausa (African
    people)—Cameroon. | Hausa (African
    people)—Marriage customs and rites. |
    Women, Hausa—Cameroon—Social
    conditions. | Marriage customs and
    rites—Cameroon. | Islamic marriage
    customs and rites—Cameroon.
Classification: LCC DT571.H38 O76 2017 |
    DDC 306.8108993706711—dc23
LC record available at https://lccn.loc
    .gov/2016034703

1 2 3 4 5   22 21 20 19 18 17

For

MY HUSBAND AND MY SONS

Contents

Acknowledgments

AS A WORK THAT EXTENDS FROM MY DISSERTATION RESEARCH, *Hadija's Story* has been at the heart of my professional life for some ten years, undergoing several rounds of reconceptualization through continuing research and especially from insightful interventions and assistance from individuals at every stage.

This book would have not been completed without the wisdom and calm encouragement of my mentor, Emmanuel Akyeampong. Emmanuel's unflinching support throughout graduate school and his continuing guidance have been central to my development as a scholar. I thank him for instilling in me the value of careful, creative historical interpretation and the perspective required to make meaningful transformations in one's scholarship in light of others' knowledge and criticisms. I also thank him for championing me as I took on the additional roles of wife and mother while completing my graduate work and beginning my career in the academy. Suzanne Preston Blier, Caroline Elkins, Heidi Gengenbach, John Hutchison, Jim McCann, Parker Shipton, and Robert Travers were all essential in shaping my knowledge of African history, Hausa society and language, and European imperial history, and I owe each of them a debt of gratitude for the time, insights, and kindness they offered to me.

Over the years, I have presented portions of this work at conferences and workshops in the United States and Cameroon. I am especially grateful to the following individuals for their constructive comments and encouragement at these events: Idrissou Alioum, Nicodemus Fru Awasom, Edmund Burke, Toyin Falola, Walter Hawthorne, Jan Jansen, Arash Khazeni, Martin Klein, Anthony Lee, Paul Lovejoy, Kenda Mutongi, Afsaneh Najmabadi, Walter Nkwi, Ismail Rashid, Mohammed Bashir Salau, Ahmadou Séhou, Sanjay Subramanyam, Meredith Terretta, and Bruce Whitehouse. Willibroad Dze-Ngwa, Verkijika Fanso, and Christraud Geary also provided excellent advice on researching Hausa communities in Cameroon.

I extend my sincerest thanks to Moses Ochonu and Elisha Renne for their thoughtful and generous readers' reports, which were obtained by Indiana University Press. Their feedback had a transformative effect on numerous aspects of the manuscript, and I cannot thank them enough for their scholarly service. For her sagacity and thoughtfulness, I thank Dee Mortensen at Indiana University Press in guiding me through the publication of this book. Sarah Jacobi, Darja Malcolm-Clarke, Joyce Rappaport, and Paige Rasmussen have also been instrumental, as well as Cyndy Brown, who provided the index.

No historian could complete her work without the assistance of archivists and librarians. I wish to thank the archivists at the National Archives in Yaoundé, the Northwest Region Ministry of Culture in Bamenda, and especially the late Prince Henry Mbain, who had served as head archivist of the National Archives in Buea. Prince's intimate knowledge of and dedication to the documents in his possession were exceptional. I extend my deepest appreciation to the Alkali at Ndop, Alhaji Mohamadu Bello, for trusting me with the trove of historical information on Muslims in the Grassfields. I also wish to acknowledge the late Alhaji Abdu Gidado, who directed me to the Alkali court and its records. Guy Thomas not only guided my research at the Basel Mission, mission 21 archives in Switzerland, but he also introduced me to the basics of Grassfields history. Lastly, I thank Bruno Schelhaas at the Leibniz Institute for Regional Geography in Leipzig for assisting my research on Ernst Vollbehr and his paintings.

I extend my deepest thanks to all of the men and women in the Grass-fields who graciously welcomed me into their homes and into their pasts. I especially wish to recognize Aishatu Ibrahim, whose quilt designs inspired the geometric symbol marking section breaks throughout the book. Hadijah Sali was present with me at nearly every interview conducted for this study. Not only was she a trusted interpreter, but she has also become one of my dearest friends. The support of Sali Buba, Usumanu Buba, Habiba Usumanu, and Elvis "Ismael" Nsaidzeka has also been indispensable over the years.

Multiple funding agencies made this research possible. Long-term fieldwork and archival research in Cameroon, the United Kingdom, and France were funded by the U.S. Department of Education Fulbright-Hays Doctoral Dissertation Award, and supplemented by the Harvard University Frederick K. Sheldon Research Fellowship. Funding from Harvard University's Department of History and Committee on African Studies, as well as Boston University's FLAS program also contributed. Over the past six years, numerous Pitzer College Faculty Research Awards and a Mellon-funded Pitzer College Junior Faculty Research Grant provided opportunities to conduct follow-up fieldwork and made the completion of this manuscript possible.

Some material in this book appeared first in other formats. Text from two articles in *History in Africa: A Journal of Method* are reprinted with permission from Cambridge University Press: "Native Foreigners and the Ambiguity of Order and Identity: The Case of African Diasporas and Islamic Law in British Cameroon" 39 (2012): 97–122, and "Beyond the World of Commerce: Rethinking Hausa Diaspora History through Marriage, Distance, and Legal Testimony" 43 (June 2016): 141–167. The revised reprint of the article, "'I am not his slave': Contesting Marriage among the Hausa on a Cameroonian Frontier, c. 1920–1955," is herein included in this book with the permission of the publisher, Africa World Press, Inc., from the book edited by Toyin Falola and Bessie House-Soremekun, *Gender, Sexuality and Mothering in Africa*, 2011.

A scholar producing her first book never does so without the support, advice, and necessary humor of friends and colleagues. Since 2003, I have benefited from the friendship and wisdom of Sara Byala, Denise Ho,

Adam Ewing, Rob Karl, Betsy More, Vernie Oliveiro, Myles Osborne, Juliet Wagner, and Ben Waterhouse. At Pitzer College, I am grateful to members of the History Field Group—Carina Johnson, Stu McConnell, Daniel Segal, and Andre Wakefield. Their mentorship and commitment to excellence in teaching and scholarship have been essential to my growth as a scholar-teacher. I thank Ahmed Alwishah, Bill Anthes, Brent Armendinger, Will Barndt, Michelle Berenfeld, Tim Berg, Menna Bizuneh, Nigel Boyle, Geoff Herrera, Alex Juhasz, Azamat and Barbara Junisbai, Jessica McCoy, Susan Phillips, Brinda Sarathy, Andrea Scott, Erich Steinman, Emma Stephens, Ruti Talmor, Lako Tongun, Rachel VanSickle-Ward, and Kathy Yep for their friendship and support as I worked through manuscript revisions and the publication process. I also wish to acknowledge two students who directly participated in the successful completion of this project: Jade Finlinson for her research and German translation skills, and Patcharaporn "Nam" Maneerat who created the maps.

This book has been a family endeavor. My sister, Sadie O'Rourke, paid her own way to Cameroon to share my research experience with me: one would be hard-pressed to find an archival research assistant who approached her work with as much alacrity as comedy. Cole O'Rourke, Tricia Luong, John Tyson, and my aunts and uncles have provided moral support during this long writing process. I thank my father, Daniel O'Rourke, for sharing his passion for history with me at an early age and for his ardent support of my work. The encouragement and labor of my mother and my in-laws—Susan Troyer, Nancy Luong, and Jimmy Luong—have allowed me to concentrate on my writing at crucial moments while balancing my commitment to my children and to teaching. For my family's dedication to me as a daughter, sister, and niece, I am eternally grateful.

Ivan Liang has listened to my ideas and meandering thoughts on Hadija and her story over the past ten years, contemplating its resonance with many other family tales. He sacrificed time and energy when I needed it, and he has worked alongside me to create a home for our two young boys, Cy and Asa. It is with great joy that I dedicate this work to them—the grandson and great-grandsons of Lai Tao, a woman whose diasporic journeys as bride, wife, mother, widow, refugee, trader, and grandmother took her from southern China to Vietnam, to Hong Kong, to Toronto, and finally to Maryland where Ivan first introduced her to me as Popo, "maternal grandmother," seventeen years ago.

Hadija's Story

Introduction

IN THE TOWN OF LERE NEAR THE JOS PLATEAU IN NIGERIA, A local ruler promised two young women to a wealthy, Muslim Hausa long-distance trader. This trader maintained social and economic ties to Kano, the historic city-state of Northern Nigeria where he was born and raised. But he was not headed in that direction when he left the ruler near Jos. Now accompanied by the two young women, he instead made his way toward the village of Mme-Bafumen in the Cameroon Grassfields where he had planned to settle among other Hausas in the diaspora. British colonial records refer to him as Alhaji Goshin—*alhaji* being a title of prestige indicating that one has completed a successful pilgrimage to Mecca. However, the name by which his family and friends knew him was quite different: here the Goshin of colonial documentation gave way to Gashin Baki in Hausa circles. His name and place of origin have been written into the historical record, but the same cannot be said for the two young women who encountered him in Lere. One of these women disappeared from the record entirely, or was silenced within it; we know nothing of her other than her transfer to Gashin Baki. But the other woman met a different, more public fate. We will never know her birth name or where she was born, but we know Gashin Baki renamed her as she entered the Hausa diaspora, linked as she now was to this merchant and his network of friends and family, including a senior wife named Talle. The woman would later explain this renaming in her own words: "The [Alhaji] have tied marriage with me before he put this Hadija for me."[1]

Not long after they arrived in the Grassfields, Gashin Baki died, and many people living within the Hausa diaspora world around Mme-Ba-fumen suspected that Hadija had never been Gashin Baki's wife, but his slave, his concubine. To mitigate her heightened vulnerability she married another man. For reasons to be explained, a community patriarch accused her of bigamy, a criminal offense that sent her to the Islamic court where she and her ambiguous status were put on trial. Since Gashin Baki had been wealthy, colonial officials saw fit to intervene in order to ensure the proper transfer of wealth through established Islamic legal practices of inheritance. Through investigations and competing testimonies, the question that the Islamic judge, colonial officers, and Hadija's neighbors wanted to solve was whether Hadija was a widow who could expect an inheritance or a former slave who could be inherited.

These events did not take place in the early 1900s when domestic enslavement, including concubinage, was a recognizable and prominent feature of Hausa households in Northern Nigeria—one that the British both accepted as a cultural norm and tentatively counteracted for decades. Rather, the encounter between Hadija and Gashin Baki occurred in the late 1940s or early 1950s, years after the British formally abolished slavery in the colony in 1936. The nature of Hadija's court case and the colonial documentation that relates to it were rare archival finds in the Western Grassfields, as few records that both Africans and colonial officials produced so explicitly acknowledge a history of enslavement as late as the 1950s. Despite this situation's uniqueness, it nonetheless points to the roles that marriage, enslavement, and community patriarchy played in making Hausa diaspora settlements, as well as how colonial rule, Islamic law, and Hausa cultural mores came together to shape the ways people experienced dispersal and diasporic formation. This story and the way it unfolds figure as a narrative thread for this book, a line of connection and exploration for questions about mobility, settlement, strangerhood, and social capital, for a distinctive cultural and religious minority in Western Cameroon. It also inspires questions about the social dislocation that death and distance can cause, which, when partnered with gendered power asymmetries, shaped the ways individuals searched for the forms of belonging they desired.

This story is also embedded in the history of the Grassfields, a tropical highland region in Western Cameroon known for its pre-colonial economic, political, and linguistic dynamism. Available evidence indicates that Hausa migrants arrived there by the mid-nineteenth century, many of them playing significant roles as commercial agents in the intensified funneling of goods and people northward toward the Benue River and the expanding political domain of the Sokoto Caliphate. In return, they brought various trade items and accompanying Islamic influences. Grassfielders, who successfully resisted Sokoto's militaristic intrusions, perceived Hausas as strangers, and like many other peoples throughout West Africa they would soon come to understand *Hausa* as a recognizable identity distinguished by the Hausa language, Islamic practices, locations of residence, and style of clothing and adornment. Today, many Grassfielders view them as a composite group of Muslims together with the more numerous Fulani—pastoralists who followed Hausas into the area in the twentieth century. Across space and time, however, the meaning of *Hausa* has rejected generalizations, particularly those concerned with shared ethnic markers.[2] Given that Hausa society has been consistently marked by internal diversity and ease of inclusion for new or low-status peoples, for Anne Haour and Benedetta Rossi being Hausa has been a "category of practice" that people have employed and negotiated in different moments "to make sense of themselves and of the society in which they live."[3]

Beginning in the 1960s, scholars usually placed the history of Hausas in the diaspora within the broader framework of African networks across the Sahara and West Africa, focusing mainly on itinerancy, trade, and devotion to Islam.[4] In his landmark study on Hausas in Yoruba towns, Abner Cohen presented Hausa mobility and settlement as a commercial diaspora, a group that had asserted its cultural distinctiveness within host societies in order to maintain exclusive control over long-distance trading networks.[5] The resulting social cohesion within their ranks enabled their economic success while positioning them as what Sanjay Subrahmanyam has called a separate group of "privileged intermediaries," a class in between local "patricians and plebians in imagined constructs

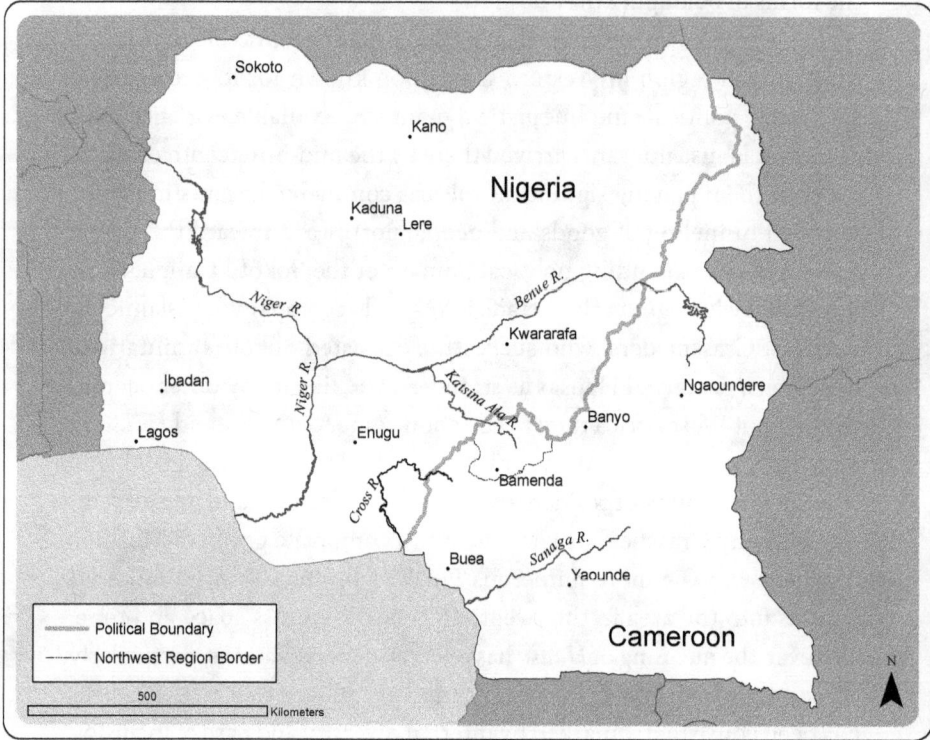

Regional Map of Nigeria and Cameroon

Sokoto

Kano

Kaduna
Lere

Nigeria

Niger R.

Benue R.

Kwararafa

Niger R.

Ibadan

Katsina Ala R.

Ngaoundere

Banyo

Lagos

Enugu

Cross R.

Bamenda

Buea

Sanaga R.

Yaounde

Cameroon

Political Boundary
Northwest Region Border

500
Kilometers

N

The Western Grassfields

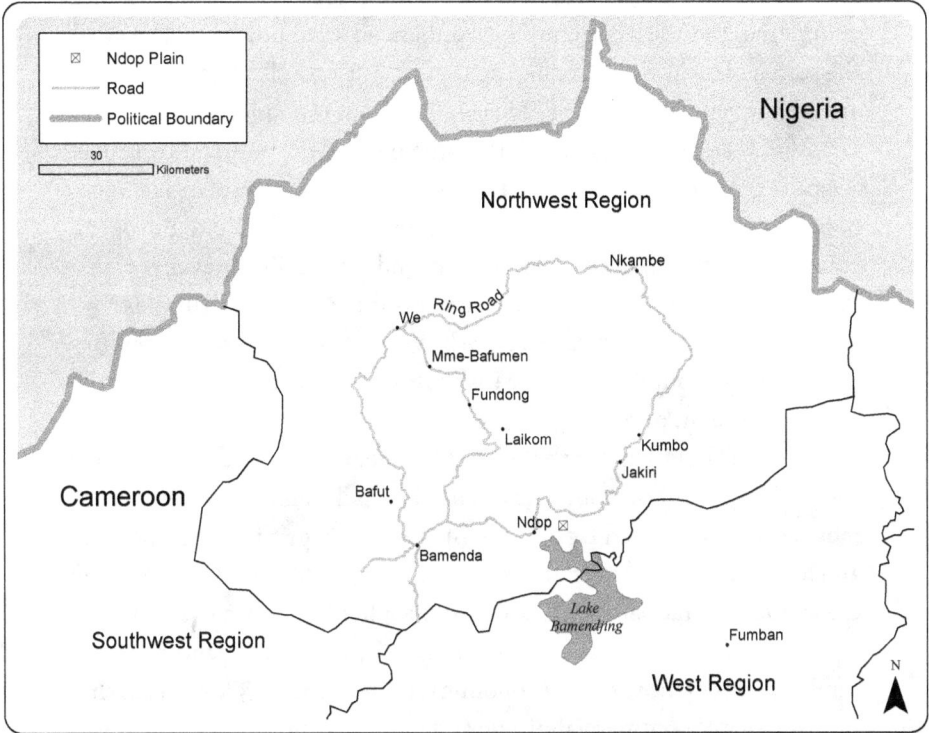

Legend:
- ⊠ Ndop Plain
- Road
- Political Boundary

30 Kilometers

Nigeria

Northwest Region

Nkambe

Ring Road

We

Mme-Bafumen

Fundong

Laikom

Kumbo

Jakiri

Cameroon

Bafut

Ndop ⊠

Bamenda

Lake Bamendjing

Fumban

Southwest Region

West Region

N

of social order."[6] Long-distance trade also influenced political organization: while emerging states in West Africa accorded more security for
commerce, the traders themselves enhanced state power by elevating
the status of local elites in offering them luxury goods.[7] Such dynamics
are largely representative of Hausa relations in the nineteenth-century
Grassfields and other regions within and beyond the political control of
Sokoto's emirate system. Long-distance traders' position of in-betweenness also often meant that they would later come to facilitate European
colonial expansion, both economically and politically, unevenly transforming them from commercial diasporas into colonial auxiliaries.[8]

Alhaji Gashin Baki may therefore be viewed as the twentieth-century
version of the ubiquitous male Muslim traveler, the long-distance, peripatetic merchant or scholar-teacher by trade—a figure that emerged on
West Africa's landscape with the establishment and growth of these vast
trading networks and political systems. He spoke Hausa, his wealth was
most certainly derived from trade in colonial Nigeria and Cameroon,
and he was a follower of Islam as indicated by his title and his renaming
the woman as Hadija, the namesake of Prophet Muhammad's first wife.
His activities may thus fall comfortably in line with the general, structural patterns of movement, economic relations, and religious belief that
the category of commercial diaspora suggests.

But Haour and Rossi, echoing insights from anthropologists Enid
Schildkrout and Deborah Pellow in particular, submit that the sources
most readily available to historians of Hausa society have been biased
"towards issues of manufacture and trade" and therefore obscure other
significant elements of Hausa life.[9] In many locations where Hausas are
present as a minority group, the merchant identity is more an external
ascription.[10] Moreover, such labels rarely encompass the range of a diaspora's activities in all places and times.[11] Such is the case in the Grassfields, where colonial desires to regulate African markets, tax collection,
and geographical boundaries between Grassfields polities influenced
how Hausas integrated themselves into local host communities. Hausas'
role as colonial intermediaries during the first quarter of the twentieth
century eventually gave way to the objectives of Indirect Rule, which
stipulated that where possible the state should govern through indigenous authorities. As a result, Hausas experienced significant political

and economic marginalization by the 1930s and 1940s, especially due to regulations prohibiting trade monopolies and in a few cases because of the loss or decline of their markets.

Viewing Hausas as a commercial diaspora further obscures the fact that traders and Hausa speakers by birth were not the only people to travel into the diaspora, for countless individuals of diverse origins, occupations, and social statuses became Hausa as they joined them in the diaspora—and such patterns would continue into the twentieth century after the onset of colonial rule. Malams (Qur'anic scholars), slaves, soldiers, religious pilgrims, and migrants who might have otherwise identified themselves as Nupe, Fulani, Mossi, or Yoruba often landed themselves in Hausa settlements, assuming a Hausa identity in search of social belonging, sometimes as clients to Hausa patrons.[12] The rationale prompting individuals to migrate necessarily took multiple forms, from a search for wealth or belonging to, in the case of the infamous *yawon dandi*, a desire for "liberation from social constraints" at home.[13]

Categorizing Hausa dispersion in terms of commercial pursuits also presents a deeply masculinized narrative that reflects both colonial and dominant community discourses, which have together reinforced a focus on male activities, particularly roles where diasporic men represented the position of colonial intermediary most clearly—as community leaders, long-distance traders, and soldiers. In fact, these roles were the primary ways colonial officials in the Grassfields wrote Hausa men into their archives. Such tendencies point to a patriarchal reliance on perceptions of the past that involve erasures of women, children, and lower status or socially nonconforming males.

Many of the oral traditions that Nehemia Levtzion collected in Ghana's Middle Volta Basin exemplify this masculinization. According to Levtzion's sources, it was common for a local African chief or king to "bind a Muslim" to his court in order to maintain his access to rare goods of the long-distance trade—and the ruler's "generous gift" of a woman often served this purpose.[14] Equally for local Muslim rulers, like those in Lere where Alhaji Gashin Baki acquired Hadija and the unknown woman, cultivating relationships with wealthy traders ensured one's economic influence and local political control, especially if that power entailed maintaining a reservoir of slaves or persons of servile status to be sold or gifted at will.[15] This then might be the beginning and end of Hadija's historical role within the commercial diaspora narrative: the ruler near Jos cemented his relationship with the Hausa trader by transferring to him his rights and wealth in her and the other woman, and in exchange he enhanced his local power through acquired wealth and prestige. In this narrative, the two women simply perform as familiar items of exchange, as props in a story about the encounter of men from two distinct lands seeking to fortify economic and political relations through patronage. They become, as Edwin Ardener might have put it, "lay figures in someone else's play."[16] This story is a familiar one, not only in African history but also in the many histories of imperial and long-distance trading networks over land and sea in which women's work is overlooked due to the common portrayal of "crosscultural sexual relationships . . . as forces that 'connect' or 'anchor'" men to their new communities.[17] This narrative subordination directly relates to the ways people experienced subordination in their daily lives, as it supports the hierarchical structures that have derived local power and purpose from the ability to enforce an idealized patriarchal order.[18]

Women, though fewer in number, were among the Hausa migrants, and they traveled into or joined the diaspora as wives, daughters, sisters, slaves, and slave-concubines. Some models would characterize their movement as "associational migration," which assumes their mobility only occurred because they accompanied "primary" migrants who were male.[19] Though this model may closely align with the isolating experiences of enslaved women, it overlooks free women's choices in marriage partners and the occurrence of frequent divorce in Hausa history. It also overlooks Hausa women's roles as traders, food producers, craftswomen, spiritual leaders, singers, and dancers—or women who might have had a desire to see worlds beyond their places of birth. Hausa women's diasporic movement can also be viewed as an extension of their broader historical experience as "permanent migrants" in virilocal marriage patterns—"creature[s] of change" who link their families to outside kinship groups both near and far.[20] Should male experiences of movement for economic gain thus be privileged as an outgrowth of Hausa dynamism while women's marital careers are not?[21] And for an enslaved concubine who had no choice but to join a Hausa caravan en route, is there another way to consider her experience that acknowledges but moves beyond its common characterization in West Africa's diaspora narratives as a "banal occurrence ... in the genealogies of freemen"?[22] Similar questions have troubled a number of African diaspora scholars. Judith Byfield, LaRay Denzer, Anthea Morrison, and many others have argued that diaspora has "obfuscated women's engagement in the heavy work of traveling, building networks, and imagining the diaspora," and that using gender as a category of analysis is still "something of a challenge for African diaspora studies."[23]

This line of inquiry leads us to ask the question of how we might envision this history from the perspective of Hadija, her co-wife Talle, or the unknown woman who seemed to have lost her tie to Gashin Baki somewhere between Jos and the Grassfields. In so doing, would we still view this history in the same manner, within the framework that the category "commercial diaspora" typically provides? For Hadija, Hausa language or Islam likely did not mark her childhood and her memories of it in the way they did for Gashin Baki. Once she met the wealthy merchant, her life took a considerable turn: she left everything that was familiar to her, she traveled at least 800 kilometers with him and his entourage, she met his friends and neighbors in and around a small Hausa enclave in the Grassfields, she kept his home along with Talle, and then Gashin Baki died, leaving both women to contend with a situation of extreme vulnerability.

This story is very different from, though foundational to, that of the male Muslim stranger. In analyzing the narrative space that connects these stories, it becomes clear that the commercial diaspora framework that has to date dominated historical treatments of Hausa diaspora experience and influence in West Africa is a restrictive, androcentric characterization that overlooks broader cultural idioms and institutions that shaped individuals' aspirations and struggles. Shifting the lens to focus on gender and stories of women in particular demonstrates that the social politics of marriage, enslavement, movement, morality, and belonging were much more pervasive in determining how people navigated diaspora networks and communities. Here, African mobility is intertwined with intimacy, and this pairing not only formed the changing contours of everyday life in the diaspora, but also influenced the regional political economy, local settlement patterns, and transformations under colonial rule.[24]

Mobility and the establishment of diverse diaspora settlements were therefore not solely part of the architecture of expanding markets and commercial networks forged among men, but also involved contested processes of separation and connection—both physical and social. These processes were at work in Hadija's transformation into a woman of the diaspora, a transformation that synchronously encompassed permanent separation from Lere, remembering a known social world as she left it behind, replacing one name with another, and forging new relationships of dependency as social isolation intensified through travel. In this light, the category of commercial diaspora also does a great disservice to Gashin Baki—a man who not only desired wealth, patronage, and prestige, but also household authority and companionship.

This reading of Hausa diaspora history disrupts dominant patriarchal and colonial narratives that have emphasized male activities and projects to construct a cohesive social order based on shared understandings of cultural distinctiveness. Though Hausa diaspora identity in the Grass-fields was not necessarily indeterminate, it was ever changing—its fluid nature arising from anxieties and contestations over gendered politics of inclusion, exclusion, status placement, and meanings of the past. The issues at stake in these conflicts involved concerns for personal and corporate prosperity and well-being, ensuring the continuation of lineages across generations and geography, maintaining patriarchal power in the household and the community, and expectations of Islamic piety, especially abiding by ideal forms of masculinity and femininity. From such contestations—which involved people of varying positionalities—emerged narratives, memories, and moral arguments that did not undermine Hausa identification but instead constituted the very process of making that identification possible. Moreover, women like Hadija and her co-wife Talle were the major agents and subjects of these conflicts, which challenged the ability of colonial, Islamic, and patriarchal institutions to control the terms on which this history was lived and remembered.[25]

The location of many of these conflicts is also significant, as it represents the manner in which social politics among Hausas and other

Muslims caught the attention of colonial officials. In 1947, the British incorporated a peculiar form of Islamic law into their legal regime, a process that unevenly institutionalized religious and household patriarchy within the Grassfields Muslim community. The court of the *alkali* (Islamic judge) signified the colonial state's attempt to bring order to an increasing population of Grassfields Muslims, as well as to appease Hausa and Fulani patriarchs who issued complaints regarding their lack of control over women. With the colonial state's support, the alkali institutionalized marriage as the ideal site of belonging for women and criminalized sexual transgressions that challenged this ideal. Controlling women became the foundation of the alkali's moral and political authority, as well as the primary means the colonial state used to rule its Muslim subjects. Numerous case records indicate, however, that the stability created with the court's establishment was illusory, for it became the site of tremendous debate over Hausa and Islamic values and means of social acceptance.

The diasporic intimacies involved in these conflicts not only reflect historical dynamics that come to light by analyzing court cases or using gender as a category of analysis.[26] They are also a manifestation of the Hausa diaspora concept of *abakwa*, the name for Hausa settlements within and south of the Benue River Valley, including the Grassfields. Its meaning derives from *abakwan riga*, or *abakwariga*, a Jukun word meaning "novices of the robe or gown." It was most commonly used to describe descendants of mixed marriages between Hausa men and local, mainly non-Muslim women.[27] As a mode of social identification and historical commentary, abakwa reinforces patrilineal claims to belonging in the diaspora, acknowledges the roles of non-Hausa women in ramifying networks, and situates unions between men and women as a central component in diaspora narratives—even as it erases the participation of women who were Hausa by birth. Notwithstanding its limitations, abakwa provides possibilities for understanding relationships between Hausas and their hosts in the Grassfields, relationships that emphasized bonds forged through patronage, marriage, friendship, inheritance, and cultural porosity. Gendered relations of power are therefore central to understanding Hausa dispersion and settlement, because abakwa, though embedded in diasporic claims to legitimacy through lines of

Hausa fathers, also acknowledges the cultural syncretism that grew from
social and sexual relationships. British officers would also become involved in propagating the term's usage. But when inscribed with their
pens, abakwa lost its familial undertones, becoming a hollowed-out version that simply came to signify a Hausa settlement or market.[28] Many
Hausas in the Grassfields today are not aware of this term's historical
meaning, even though the term itself is ubiquitous in marking Hausa
communities. However, in interviews they often provided narratives of
travel and settlement that resonated with its original intent—indicating
the extent to which the intimate social forces embedded within it have
survived in memory even though they have become divorced from the
word itself.

〉〉〉•〈•〈〈〈

The chief of Lere's court where Hadija and the unknown woman were
exchanged; the creation and demise of the homestead in Mme-Bafumen
where Gashin Baki settled his family; the Islamic courtroom where Hadija and so many others contested the boundaries of social acceptance:
these spaces and the negotiations within them illuminate how gendered
inequalities, together with the factor of distance, influenced the odds and
probabilities that people achieved the forms of social acceptance and belonging they desired in the diaspora. Diaspora, therefore, does not figure
here as a unitary, cohesive grouping of a deterritorialized people. To the
contrary, and in line with many Atlantic diaspora theorists, diasporas
exhibit mixed historical references that may or may not include a common experience of dispersal or shared homeland.[29] This conceptualization allows someone like Hadija a role in Hausa diaspora history even
though her place of origin and the reasons behind her movement are so
different from those of Gashin Baki.

This is, therefore, a study of diaspora as metaphor, not a study with
or through diaspora as an analytic concept.[30] For philologist Jonathan
P. A. Sell, it is precisely the metaphoric qualities of *diaspora* that facilitate novel ways for people to understand their world, ways that entail
the "mutual transformation . . . of both migrant and indigene." In the
Grassfields, the arrival of the Hausa diaspora necessitated changes in the
meaning of Hausaness, as well as in how Grassfielders understood them-

selves in relation to Hausa social practices, Islam, the regional political economy, and the land around them. "Mutual transformation" brought about fluidity in ethnic identification as individuals sought new forms of relation, but it also generated political struggles to maintain shared understandings of moral and religious stability. Such understandings provided some Hausas and Grassfielders with the means to distinguish themselves from one another and to reap whatever benefits they could derive from colonial hierarchies of power, which themselves relied on constructed ethnic categories. For many Hausa patriarchs, establishing the alkali court was a response to these imperatives, in large part because it reflected how they (and colonial officials) imagined the significance of Islamic law in their homeland, the Sokoto Caliphate. Wrapped within this process of remembering and narrating an ideal homeland was an attempt to shore up the boundaries of identity in the diaspora by controlling women's sexuality. While tendencies to deploy an ideal homeland for political projects manifest in multiple global diasporas, in this particular case these tendencies had to confront the historical significance of abakwa—itself a powerful metaphor that arose from mutual transformations in the Benue River Valley, connected the political and economic with the intimate, and encompassed contested notions of Hausa diaspora ancestry and identification.

My use of diaspora as metaphor is also grounded in the colonial history of the Grassfields, where a Swiss Basel missionary, J. W. Zürcher, deployed the term *diaspora* in much the same manner, albeit in a different, yet overlapping historical context. When he submitted his report from Kishong on January 10, 1936, he opened with this sentence: "I give here a little experience from my work among the Bamum who live in the Diaspora. . . ."[31] British officers writing three years later estimated that just as many Bamums as Hausas settled in the Western Grassfields, most of them entering the highlands from French territory through the Ndop Plain. They migrated as refugees after the French deposed the famously talented King Njoya in 1924 and later exiled him to Yaoundé, where he died in 1933.[32] King Njoya's skillful leadership and his history as an ally to Germans threatened the French administration and Bamum Christians who aligned themselves with the new colonial power after the First World War.[33] Many of the migrants in British Cameroon had been the king's family members and followers while he was in power—a substantial number of them were also Muslim. Using the term *diaspora* in this case, one that emphasizes involuntary migration but that of a specific group of Africans, Zürcher references but moves beyond its common, contemporary association with Jewish history. In so doing, its use as a metaphor to describe African refugees relocating to an adjacent region within Africa predates academic scholars' readiness to apply the term to peoples dispersed through commercial activity or displaced through colonization.

Robin Cohen, a leading scholar of global diasporas, might call Zürcher's usage of the term one of the "earlier casual references" extended to groups other than Jews prior to the 1960s.[34] However, following Sell's vision, this passage should be considered a significant archival inscription that produces empathy in ways that less allusive and less "emotive alternatives" like "migrancy" do not.[35] Zürcher could have used colonial watchwords like "detribalized natives" or a German variant thereof to describe Bamum communities in the Western Grassfields. But instead he chose a term that provided his fellow missionaries with a historical reference to aid them in appreciating certain aspects of life as a Bamum stranger.[36] Sell further argues that the metaphor of diaspora "underwrites the historical process of colonialism."[37] The history of Muslim African strangers within the Grassfields clearly illustrates this relationship, as *diaspora* involves considering the ways pre-colonial experiences of African mobility, circulation, and transformation intersected with colonialism and influenced the colonial boundaries erected around them.

▶▶▶•▮•◀◀◀

Like many African and diaspora histories, this one relies on the collection, organization, and collaborative construction of a wide variety of historical sources, including Islamic court records, oral traditions and proverbs, individual and family oral histories, personal collections, official colonial documentation, missionary reports and photographs, and a German artist's travelogue and paintings—not to mention the substantial body of secondary sources on Hausa and Grassfields societies. Historians have long established how our sources contain biases, as do our interpretations of them.[38] Each court case I analyzed involved its own particular mixture of accusations, locations, and personalities—all diligently, if imperfectly, translated and recorded by court scribes (*mufutai*).[39] I sifted through the dusty law books and selected those cases that involved Hausas. This necessary step in my research is mired in a host of methodological problems that resulted in incomplete solutions: of the hundreds of named Muslims present in these records, how did I know who was or wasn't Hausa?[40] In many instances, participants in the legal proceedings identified themselves or others as Hausa or as people who lived in a particular abakwa. Still in others, I had to rely on my and others' knowledge of specific Hausa names and titles. I then compared the many cases I collected and drew from them the themes that lie at the heart of this book: gendered contestations over meanings of the past and social acceptance in the present.

I produced this history with the assistance and grace of many people in the Grassfields, not only the Alkali of Ndop, Alhaji Mohamadu Bello, who allowed me access to his court's records, but also the elderly men and women I interviewed, their family members, and my friend and research assistant, Hadijah Sali, whose effective interview and translation skills were central to the success of this research. Building on Hadijah's friendship networks, my first interview took place in the Hausa quarter of Bamenda with the 'Kungiyar Matan Musulman (Society of Muslim Women). Hadijah and I went on to interview these women individually and in smaller groups, and from them we gathered memories, stories, and photographs of the past. From the information and insights these women provided, we carried out interviews with individuals they had mentioned as part of their family and community histories—husbands, community leaders, friends, in-laws, grandchildren, and neighbors—past and present. Family members were often present during interviews, especially children and grandchildren who enjoyed listening to and participating in the construction of their family histories.[41] From these gatherings, I learned about people's life stories, family networks, and the ways their community changed over time. Like many scholars of African history, I was also concerned with how people interpreted their own memories, as well as how they interpreted stories passed down to them from earlier generations and those I had gathered from alkali court records.[42]

In combining many different sources for this project, two major difficulties arose. First, my focus on alkali court documents directed me to consider the histories of individuals who identified as Muslims, since the colonial state prohibited the alkali from trying cases involving non-Muslims. The quest for understanding relationships between Hausas and non-Muslim Grassfielders, especially those that preceded the founding of the court, was difficult to fulfill and required some archival luck and focused questioning in oral interviews. As people shared their family histories, they enabled me to reach further back in time—to the turn of the twentieth century—and further through geographical space, to various Grassfields locations, north to Hausaland, and regions in between.[43]

Second, despite the richness of the information and insights gained from alkali records and oral history participants in the Grassfields, it was challenging to manage the dissonance created when attempting to combine these voices and perspectives with the historical narratives that colonial officials, missionaries, and Hausa community leaders produced. The problem was compounded by the fact that written European sources on Hausas in the Grassfields dominate the available evidence from the 1890s to the 1940s, while alkali court documents involve disputes only from 1947 onward. The division of this book into two parts in many ways reflects this disparity and diversity of sources.

Part I analyzes the ways in which, with the onset of formal colonial rule under Germany and later Britain, Europeans in Western Cameroon harbored attitudes toward diasporic Hausas that grew out of the chasm between African realities and European perceptions of Africans. Even though they observed diverse groups of people residing in Hausa settlements, colonial officials organized their policies around the activities of itinerant Hausa men. These interventions influenced Hausa relations with their Grassfields hosts, as well as the region's dominant historical narratives that continue to designate Hausas as permanent strangers. Part I also unearths this history's exceptional moments where we find alternative possibilities for how contemporary observers and participants might have understood their encounters. Chapter 1, "Worthy Subjects," traces the profound historical changes that took place in the Grassfields in the nineteenth and early twentieth centuries, especially state centralization and associated transformations in slave dealing. These changes both prompted the entrance of Hausas into the region as well as influenced the ways they integrated themselves into local and later German colonial political structures. Chapter 2, "People of the North," continues the examination of Hausa diaspora society from the British seizure of the Western Grassfields during the First World War to decolonization. It emphasizes the contradictory nature of colonial policy toward Hausas, exemplified by the legal category *native foreigners* the British used to define them. This chapter ends with a brief account of the Islamic court's establishment in 1947.

Part II is a continuation and recasting of Part I, as it examines oral narratives and records that the Islamic court produced to illuminate the gendered principles upon which Hausa authority and identity were constructed and challenged at household and community levels. It also explores the ways people negotiated social inequalities in both local and long-distance contexts. It begins with Chapter 3, "Slave or Daughter?" which analyzes Hadija's court trial to illustrate how the gender dynamics of kinship, bondage, travel, death, and authority shaped discourses and anxieties over belonging. In enslavement or marriage, in surviving death, and in voicing a legal testimony of the past, Hadija simultaneously constituted and was constituted by diaspora. Artist and cultural theorist John Akomfrah views such experiences as acts of *peripeteia*, dramatic turning points or reversals of fortune that Aristotle examined in his *Poetics*.[44] Akomfrah argues that diaspora itself comes through peripeteia, for it is through this mechanism—through movement, arrival, settlement, and negotiation—that people circulate things and ideas and commit acts of inscription on the course of history.[45] This is how Hadija inscribed herself. Like so many other women and men, it was an act of nonconformity that would influence whether and how her life might illuminate alternative renderings of the past.

The remaining chapters of Part II are organized around the turning points where Hadija's fortunes were reversed, for better or for worse. Chapter 4, "First Reversal: Marriage and Enslavement," explores the significance of unions between men and women—free and unfree—in ramifying Hausa networks and maintaining diaspora communities, focusing in particular on how travel, strangerhood, and isolation from consanguine relations or other cultural resources placed added importance on marital bonds as a form of belonging for women. Chapter 5, "Second Reversal: Death and Survival," highlights the severing of social ties through death, and it traces how distance from kin and gender difference together influenced the strategies survivors could employ in asserting claims on the dead, especially in matters of inheritance. Chapter 6, "Third Reversal: Conflict and Judgment," examines the variety of ways Hausa diaspora men and women formed and contested multiple sites of belonging; and they did so by challenging state-sanctioned community authority, manipulating the coexistence of multiple patriarchies, and navigating distances separating diaspora settlements.

⟫•❮❮❮

The stories that appear here address the significance of social acceptance and social ties in how people understood themselves in relation to others—even if some of these bonds, like Hadija's, were ephemeral. As diasporic subjects, their tale, like the "tale of errantry" for Édouard Glissant, "is the tale of Relation." As such, it "is not apolitical nor is it inconsistent with the will to identity, which is, after all, nothing other than the search for a freedom within particular surroundings."[46] But so often one person's search for freedom—for his or her ideal means of relation, of belonging—collided with and foreclosed that search for someone else. There were multiple structures and persons that had the potential to disrupt individual aspirations, and it was within this nexus of unequal relations of power where contestations over belonging and morality emerged, continuously replenishing the narratives that sustained the Hausa diaspora world. What follows will help us understand how such instances occurred, the ways people responded, and why these relationships are central to the history of Hausa diaspora lives in the Cameroon Grassfields.

Part One

ONE

"Worthy Subjects"

IN 1912, FOUR DECADES BEFORE THE YOUNG HADIJA MADE HER appearance in court, German travel painter Ernst Vollbehr captured an intimate scene of Hausa life in the Western Grassfields (Figure 1). Just a short walk away from the German military station at Bamenda, high on a bluff overlooking the countryside below, Vollbehr created an image of a Hausa village, representing it by the tranquil goings-on of a family compound, neatly swept and enclosed by low-lying grasses and a simple wooden fence. Amidst the earthly hues of green and brown, the colorful clothing of Hausas in the foreground presents a significant contrast. Beautifully embroidered white robes and turbans clothe the two men in the painting, one of whom stands alongside a mat, perhaps to begin a daily prayer. The two women wear cloth wraps that are decidedly simpler in cut and design. One of the women sits on a mat, caring for an infant slung on her back. The other keeps her eye on a cooking pot set across the fire as she pounds grains and spices with a large mortar and pestle.

Vollbehr was quite taken by the Hausas living near the station, spending much of his time observing their way of life. In his *Mit Pinsel und Palette durch Kamerun*, published after his return to Germany, Vollbehr lamented his short stay at Bamenda, writing, "I would have loved to have had weeks to complete the many changing images that surrounded me here at the interesting Hausa area. Nothing more delightful for the painter as the finely shaped, manicured faces of Hausa children with their oriental jewelry, the black-blue painted eyebrows and the colored bodices are rare. The Hausas in their gorgeous, wide, embroidered robes, and with their characteristic, clever heads are worthy subjects for painting."[1] Vollbehr was unique among German colonial travel painters in his desire to create African family portraits, hoping to offer Germany's youth "a taste" of everyday life in the colonies and to show Africa's landscape as an attractive, albeit primitive space.[2] But like many Europeans before and after him, classical Grecian ideas celebrating the lithe body as the most beautiful human form joined with Enlightenment taxonomy to influence how Vollbehr understood Hausas in relation to the majority of Grassfields inhabitants. European travelers generally divided the peoples of Cameroon into three categories—Pygmy, Bantu, and Sudanic—the last of which included Hausas and Fulanis, people deemed more beautiful and in possession of more intelligent minds. In 1893, Captain Curt von Morgen uncouthly mapped this taxonomy onto the new Kamerun colony: "The further from the coast one travels the more beautiful the people become: to put it at is crudest the more they look like human beings. This became even more striking when I encountered the Sudanic peoples of the interior."[3]

Vollbehr's mode of differentiating Sudanic Hausas from Grassfields peoples was arguably just as stark. On one Sunday morning in Bamenda, he arose to observe the hustle and bustle of the large market near the station, later penning: "Thousands of people, often from the most remote villages, had come with their products. Most were in their black and brown nudity. The colored robes of the Hausas brought a lot of life into the mass of dark, moving images. According to my wishes, there were in front of my house about 30 Hausas in robes with cleaned up women and children." For Vollbehr, local Grassfielders were people who seemed to have lost their humanity in the market. The clothed and adorned figures of Hausa men, women, and children, by contrast, were a more perfect representation of African life and provided pleasure to those fortunate enough to look on them. Religion played its part, too. According to Rebekka Habermas, there was general agreement in imperial Germany "that African 'heathens' should be regarded as inferior not only to European Christians, but also the African Muslim population."[4]

As much as Hausas presented "worthy subjects" for art, they were equally worthy of colonization. Vollbehr thought Hausas were like every other African in that they "completely lack[ed] a sense of historical periods," a mode of thought they would need if they were ever to understand the "elements" of Christianity. Colonial travelers before and after Vollbehr would disagree on the nature and impact of the Hausa presence in the Grassfields. Like him they all had a tendency to place Hausas in a state of in-betweenness, of being two things at once. With their attractive appearance, Islamic faith, knowledge of long-distance networks, and occasional role as economic facilitators for the imperial mission, Hausas were civilized but not civilized enough. They were simultaneously agents and competitors, both an asset and a threat, to the cultural and economic goals of colonization. "The government," wrote Vollbehr, was ". . . not quite so enthusiastic about the Hausas as I am, because they always enrich themselves at the expense of the natives. . . . You attract money and values from the German colonies, and in the end they consume what is acquired on English land in their native Northern Nigeria. What the Indians are for the German East the Hausa are for Cameroon and Togo . . . the restless nomads who know only one aim: to get rich as quickly as possible. . . ."[5]

Such views were characteristic of colonialism's contradictory tendencies toward Hausas in the Grassfields, whether under German rule in 1912 or under a British administration that would come to take over the western part of the region, including Bamenda, during the First World War. They relied on Hausas to gather intelligence, establish markets, encourage production of local crops for sale, and earn revenue for the state by insisting that Hausas purchase licenses and by taxing them at a higher rate than any other category of people.[6] But Hausas were strangers to the Grassfields after all, with no political power over Grassfields societies. In order to administer colonies as cheaply as possible, that is without the expenditures associated with military force, the stability of colonial regimes relied on perceived traditional social organization, hierarchies, and paramount authority.[7] Hausas' latecomer status excluded them from consideration as traditional inhabitants of the Grassfields.

Germans' colonial ambivalence toward Hausas was further grounded in their tendency to articulate the very condition of everyday Hausa life in paradoxical terms. "They are everywhere and nowhere," declared Vollbehr, thinking that all Hausas maintained a nomadic existence, "always walking . . . with livestock, arts, and crafts beads and their very high-quality leather handwork . . . to sell." Despite Vollbehr's attention to Hausa settlement and compound life at Bamenda, and despite his interest in the activities and appearance of Hausa men, women, and children, his definition of them as a people rested on male pursuits germane to the occupation of long-distance trade. This characterization belies the fact that the Grassfields of the early twentieth century were home not only to Hausa men who were itinerant merchants but also men and women who were stationary settlers. These settlers earned a living through local trade, the production of crafts and foodstuffs, Qur'anic instruction, musicianship, medicinal and spiritual healing, hunting, and supplying meat, as well as by offering services, lodging, and provisions to peripatetic Hausas.[8] Many of them wished to reside permanently in the Grassfields, people who were not ambiguously "everywhere and nowhere" at once. But the disjunction between reality and perception remained for most Europeans in these early years. Even the compound depicted in the painting lost its sense of dwelling and family life when Swiss Basel missionaries turned Vollbehr's watercolor into a postcard with a caption that read, "They build themselves only very simple huts," those Hausas who "are permanently on the move," those "clever black merchants of Cameroon."[9]

The idea that Hausa bodies constantly dotted the countryside seemed to downplay the fact that members of first-comer Grassfields societies were in motion as well.[10] So fundamental was this perception to the colonial mental map of the region that when a yellow fever epidemic hit the northern part of the Grassfields in 1917, colonial administrative efforts to contain the outbreak centered exclusively on Hausas. The district officer at the time placed the division under quarantine by posting police patrols on "all roads entering the Division from the North" and curtailing "all movements of Hausa."[11] Using his administrative and military contacts, he wrote to officials and chiefs in Banyo, Bafut, Bekom, Bum,

Babungo, and Kumbo, to warn all Hausas either to stay where they were or to turn back north. At Bamenda, he quarantined the Hausa settlement, ordering its leader to turn out four new arrivals from Ibi, Ibadan, and Kumbo, and to burn the houses in which they were living.[12] The officer's understanding of Hausa bodies in motion against Grassfields bodies *in situ* was so deeply held that only Hausas could be fathomed as the human vectors for a disease that was known at the time to be transmitted by mosquitoes.

Europeans thus harbored attitudes toward diasporic Hausas that grew from two related sets of contradictions that together contributed to the masculinization of Hausa diaspora history in the region. First, Europeans defined Hausaness in terms of men, long-distance trade, and continual movement, even though they observed people of different ages, genders, and occupations attempting to carve out permanent spaces for themselves, their friends, and their families. Second, the colonial categorization of all Hausas as nomadic traders positioned them as a singular group of people who had the potential to both advance and destabilize the colonial project. This particular brand of colonial myopia would influence the state's changing political and economic policies toward Hausas in the years to come. Consequently, debates among colonial officials usually ignored the familial aspects of Hausa life at the heart of Vollbehr's watercolor.

While this painting inspires questions about how European categories of knowledge may have shaped Hausa lives in the Grassfields over the course of the colonial period, it also inspires questions about routes and encounters. How and why did the men and women in the painting make their way to the Grassfields and to Bamenda in particular? Did each of them have a home in Northern Nigeria, or did some of them join Hausa corporate groups from other locations? Might some of them have been Grassfielders who sought a new form of belonging in Hausa society? These are some of the questions lying at the heart of this book. This chapter begins the process of exploring them, providing the context for Hausas' entrance and integration into the region in the nineteenth century. It also illuminates how the dominant political and economic objectives of Hausas, Grassfielders, and German colonizers compounded the erasure of African women's work in this history, a factor that has important consequences for the categorization of Hausas as a distinct group of permanent strangers among Grassfields hosts.

▶▶▶•|•◀◀◀

Our story begins in the fifteenth century when most Hausas spoke a variety of Hausa dialects, practiced a polytheist religion, farmed, and produced craft items, cloth, and iron. They lived in the savanna grasslands east of the Niger River—between the Songhai Empire to the west and Bornu to the east.[13] Over the course of the sixteenth century, due to competition over resources and a need for protection from conflict, these Hausa speakers built massive walls encompassing their hamlets and farmlands. These walled towns became places of refuge for groups throughout the region, and eventually the towns' influence transcended the walls that enclosed them. Hausa city-states then emerged, becoming enduring forms of political power and home to diverse groups of immigrants.

With the development of centralized authority came social stratification. An aristocracy (*sarkin 'kasa*, lit. "chief of the land") formed, and below them were fief-holding officials (*masu sarauta*). Most people continued as peasant farmers and found themselves in the commoner class (*talakawa*). Commoners also practiced occupational specialties, working as healers, tailors, leatherworkers, musicians, smiths, and butchers.[14] Slave ownership was ubiquitous, with slave owners drawn from all social classes; inequalities also formed along gendered lines but changed over time with political and social transformation. With the exception of some titled female positions in pre-colonial Hausa society, familial and political organization has generally emphasized patriarchal rule and solidarity among men.[15] Nonetheless, Mary Wren Bivins has reminded us of women's central roles in the cultural and economic life of Hausa society. Linguistic evidence describing women's work and knowledge of food production, for example, demonstrates the significance of women in "the cultural processes so vital to the success of Hausa agriculture and the transformation of a natural environment into a human landscape."[16] Like their male counterparts, women also established craft specialties and participated in trade.

Over time, the vibrant economic activity within Hausas' walled towns attracted the interest of merchants across the trans-Saharan trade network. The Wangara, or Dyula, West Africa's pioneering itinerant merchant group, brought their knowledge of long-distance trade and Islam into Hausas' social and economic world in the sixteenth century. Many Hausas then entered long-distance trading (*fatauci*) themselves, heading south and west to sell textiles, leather goods, cattle, and jewelry, in exchange for slaves and kola nuts, a bitter stimulant found in the forested regions of West Africa and highly sought after in northern markets.[17] In this process, Hausa became "a language of trade and social contact in West Africa."[18] Though many Hausa traders and some aristocrats converted to Islam, most Hausas did not care to, or, if they did, they incorporated Islamic practices into their indigenous belief system, creating a syncretic form of the religion.[19]

The tie between Hausa identity and Islam strengthened over the course of the nineteenth century, however. Muslim Fulani pastoralists had been living in Hausaland, having migrated there from further west. By the late eighteenth century, some Fulanis formed an Islamic clerical class, but one that was politically disempowered. Those residing in the Hausa state of Gobir were especially marginalized, enduring harassment and growing increasingly frustrated with "the godless ways of the Gobir nobility."[20] Near the turn of the nineteenth century, Usuman dan Fodio led the Fulani in a military jihad that conquered all of Hausaland, culminating with the creation of the Sokoto Caliphate. Despite the fact that Fulanis became the political elite in the nineteenth century, and Islam the religion of the state, Hausa culture and language persisted with most Fulanis becoming "Hausaized."[21] Moses Ochonu argues that the terms *Hausa, Hausawa,* and '*Kasar Hausa,* which refer to "the language, the people, and land of the Hausa respectively," likely originated from dan Fodio's writings. It was he who "homogenized the Hausa-speaking but autonomous peoples of the different Hausa states in what he defined as a collective of bad Muslim rulers and syncretistic Muslim masses."[22] With the jihad, Islam became inscribed as an important marker of Hausa identity such that "being Hausa" in West Africa increasingly became "more about Islamic piety and the ability to speak the language" than about a historical connection to the old Hausa states or to Hausa ancestry.[23]

People's references to the Hausa ethnic idiom have therefore varied over time and space as strategies for inclusion or exclusion.[24] Both Ochonu and Steven Pierce note, however, that speaking Hausa and converting to Islam were only "beginning point[s] . . . on the path to becoming Hausa," for being Hausa "also encompassed particular ways of living" both within and outside of the Caliphate—as traders or as farmers with specific approaches to agriculture.[25] Today, northern Nigeria and southern Niger are home to 25 million Hausa speakers, while another 15 million people speak Hausa as a second language throughout West Africa.[26]

Over the course of the nineteenth century, Fulani rule expanded into present-day Cameroon. Hausa traders, malams, and mercenaries in the jihad moved into newly conquered territories in Adamawa. Hausas' commercial operations thrived as they branched out their networks. They acted as scouts and spies, buying up booty and slaves while setting up markets for Fulani administrative satellites.[27] On his tour of the Grassfields, Adamawa, and the Benue lands from 1889 to 1892, the often misinformed German entrepreneur and adventurist Eugen Zintgraff understood the Hausa traders he encountered as people who exploited slaves along caravan routes and who worked as "spies and scouts for the Fulani" as they "point[ed] out new slaving-grounds. . . ."[28] Prior to this period, Chamba, Mbum, Vute, and Tikar groups operated as "buffer states" near the Benue region, shielding the Grassfields from the pressure of expanding states in the north.[29] Beginning around 1820, however, Chamba raiding parties began attacking Grassfields polities. Their mounted bowmen operated in various directions, seeking captives to sell to Hausas and other northern traders.[30] Later in the 1840s, Fulani forces attempted to extend their reach southward from Adamawa and began raiding the northern Grassfields for slaves and to exert political dominance, but the jihadists failed to conquer the Grassfields' powerful northern chiefdoms. Nonetheless, new communication and trade pathways were opened, and by the mid-nineteenth century, Hausas had become integral in linking Grassfields economic resources to the Caliphate and beyond. Only a few thousand Hausas have ever lived in the Grassfields at one time, but their presence was part of the great transformations that occurred in Grassfields economic and political structures prior to and during colonial rule.

As a tropical highland region, the Grassfields could not be more eco-logically distinct from the semiarid conditions of Hausaland. This, of course, was part of the appeal for Hausas: different environments offered new opportunities. In ancient periods, hunters and gatherers inhabited the forests that once flourished in these highlands but have since largely disappeared. Savanna grasses grew in their place, later inspiring German colonizers to call it *Grasland*. Anyone from the north journeying there had to ascend its formidable plateau, situated between 800 and 1400 meters above sea level. Most Hausas arrived through one of two passageways, from the north crossing the Katsina Ala River or from an easterly entrance through the Ndop Plain.

Prior to the entrance of Hausas, regional trade within the Grassfields had developed over hundreds of years. While some low-lying areas are home to tropical climates, others of higher elevation are much more moderate. Such diversity has allowed for the cultivation of both tropical and temperate zone crops, which, along with iron production, prompted a lively trading network that included palm oil, camwood, raffia, kola, livestock, game, hides, calabashes, tobacco, and farm implements. Most of the land is very fertile with the capacity to produce a variety of crops, including yams, sorghum, bulrush millet, cowpea, plantains, bananas, and vegetables. Owing to predominantly female and junior male labor, Grassfields societies have been almost entirely self-sufficient in agriculture.[31]

Anthropologist Jean-Pierre Warnier compellingly made the case years ago that the Grassfields were home to a distinct "culture area," where people shared a common history marked by extensive communications, multilingualism, trade, and intermarriage. Available evidence suggests that the Grassfields have been continuously peopled for several millennia. Over time, the region's populations generated one of the densest and most diverse assemblages of languages that exist on the African continent.[32] Within a 40 kilometer radius around present-day Bamenda alone, people speak more than twenty mutually unintelligible languages.[33] This diversity developed among peoples who experienced significant social intermixing through marriage and trade networks and who developed a specific sociopolitical organization—the chiefdom, which was based on lineages, centered on a hereditary and sacred chief known as *fon* or *mfe*, and balanced by powerful men's societies. By the end of the nineteenth century, chiefdoms ranged in size from those numbering perhaps just one hundred people to very large and hierarchically organized states such as Mankon, Bali, Bafut, Nso, and Bamum, the latter two of which had populations estimated as high as 60,000.[34]

When Hausas arrived in the Grassfields by roughly 1840, they encountered a linguistically and ecologically diverse region but whose peoples were nonetheless similar in modes of technology, commercial exchange, and social and political organization. They observed a common gendered division of labor whereby women and junior men performed the lion's share of agricultural work, while adult men cultivated bananas, raised livestock, and operated as specialists in iron smelting, smithing, medicine, divination, raffia wine production, carving, and commerce.

The Grassfields offered Hausa traders, hunters, and other tradesmen incredible commercial opportunities, given the items produced there and its high population density. Hausas hunted down elephants for ivory, and they were heavily involved in trading kola nuts. With good fortune, the demand in the savanna and regions to the north was highest for the species of kola commonly grown in the Grassfields, *Cola anomala*.[35] High population densities and extensive commercial networks further meant that the Grassfields offered Hausas potential markets for their goods and services. The fact of large populations had a dark underbelly, however, one that many Hausa merchants exploited by facilitating the extraction of people from their highland homes into new worlds of enslavement to the north and to the coast.[36] Those slaves relayed toward the coast were exchanged for items such as umbrellas and guns.[37] Those headed northward trekked alongside donkeys loaded with ivory and kola. These slaves and luxury items were exported so that salt and the Benue region's coveted dyed-blue "Hausa cloth" could make their way into the highlands. These garments were for elite men only, as most commoners and women did not wear textiles until the 1930s (Figure 2 and Figure 3).[38]

Hausas acquired slaves produced by the raids of Chamba and Fulani forces, but they also obtained slaves through their integration within Grassfields polities, which local political, economic, and gendered social structures helped to facilitate. The organization of state power and culturally specific conceptions of wealth, changing dynamics of land tenure, and patriarchal control of marriage together informed the ways in which Hausas established themselves throughout the region. Hausa diaspora pursuits in large part rested on their ability to establish amicable relationships with Grassfields political elites. Regional insecurities and the elites' growing power in the nineteenth century had led to intensified state centralization. As Hausas were accustomed to the hierarchical governance structures of Sokoto's emirate system, integration into the states of Bamum and Nso, for example, was a familiar process. Most Grassfields notables were happy to host these Islamic strangers. Palatine elites achieved their status and power through the accumulation of material possessions of symbolic value, as well as multiple dependents and other social affiliations.[39] As a new set of clients, Hausas therefore enhanced the wealth of the local elite, through the collection of gifts and rents, and through access to rare, luxury goods of the long-distance trade.

A major way Grassfields elites used Hausas and other traders to enhance this form of wealth was by controlling slave dealing in their realms of authority. They achieved this in a variety of ways. According to Paul Nchoji Nkwi, the chief of Nso directly "conferred the privilege of trading for him on those who obtained from him the royal market bag (*kibam ke way ke fon*)."[40] In Mankon, not only the fon but clan heads, too, had the right to handle slave dealing. Only this select group of men could possess the special license known as the slave-rope (in Mankon *nki bu'* or "rope-slave"). According to Warnier, the slave-rope "was usually made of human hair plaited with a black vegetal fiber. It was rather short—50 cm in length at most—and no thicker than the little finger. It was not used to tie the slaves with. Rather, it was supposed to have an amnesic effect on a slave who had been touched with the rope: he or she would forget about his or her own country and become docile to the dealer. The rope was a license. Without it, it was forbidden to deal in slaves."[41]

Regardless of the methods used, Grassfields notables conspired to funnel people out of their polities through what many regard as acts of betrayal; however, these men were also careful to construct a discourse positioning them as guardians of the community. According to Nicolas Argenti, "although the objects of terror in the original Chamba and Fulani raids had been the raiders themselves . . . the local palatine elites who later abducted people by ruse and stealth rather than by organized raiding portrayed those they enslaved as the sources of danger and instability while presenting themselves in paternalistic terms as protectors of the people."[42] Their palaces served both as the centers for this discrete trade as well as sites to demonstrate the accumulation of wealth.[43] To purchase slaves, Hausas had cowries on hand, having brought the currency with them from the Caliphate, especially Kano. Local notables would then display cowries as part of the palace treasury.[44] In return for these new economic and political opportunities, state authorities and village heads permitted Hausas to settle and continue their trade. They also attempted to guarantee the safety of Hausas within their realms of power, even though this could not always be achieved.[45]

With the growth of long-distance trade, the composite states of the Grassfields became increasingly centralized over the course of the nineteenth century. Bamum, Bafut, Kom, and Nso all engaged in wars of capture to incorporate diverse populations into their growing realms of power, turning the losers—sometimes each other—into clients, servants, tributary polities, and even commodities to be sold down the line. Their raids, alongside the predatory wars of Chamba and Fulani warriors from the north, created an environment of intense insecurity, prompting further state centralization as vulnerable groups sought protection from raiding parties.[46] By the end of nineteenth century women had to be accompanied by armed guards, often themselves slaves, in order to work their fields.[47]

With the augmentation of political power, new settlement patterns emerged and some societies shifted from a lineage-based organization to a territorial one based on wards and quarters. Most Grassfields political units had been composite city-states with members of mixed origin. Mankon, for example, consisted of nine large clans and a number of satellite chiefdoms that were interspersed with the settlements of Mankon exogamous lineages.[48] But due to the "spectacular processes of change" of the nineteenth century, lineages lost some of their significance as power came to rest more and more on wealth and membership in palace societies.[49] It is likely that such a change in structures of power assisted Hausas who desired to obtain political rights in land through grants or prestation from local authorities.[50] In Hausaland, the endowment of fiefs was the "condition for eligibility and tenure," but in the diaspora where Hausas were strangers, leadership positions could not be tied to land in the same fashion.[51] According to Abner Cohen, as Hausa settlements grew in population "local chiefs would decide to allot to the Hausa a special Quarter . . . and would recognize one of the Hausa men of influence (always one of the important 'business landlords') as chief."[52] This man would then be responsible for his community's conforming to local laws and demands.[53] As a result, the "chief" of a Hausa diaspora settlement, the *Sarkin Hausawa*, came to function as a village head or sub-chief in a number of Grassfields states, and he was recognized as such by local African authorities.

This situation obtained in Bamum where the settlement of Hausas was the largest in the nineteenth-century Grassfields. In part due to Bamum's location at the eastern, low-lying edge of the region, Hausas had been active there since c. 1840 at the latest, under the reign of Mbuembue. Bamum traded kola nuts and craft items, including exquisite brass castings, and in return they received cloth, garments, beads, and guns. By the turn of the century, the Hausa presence was so substantial that Basel missionaries described the Hausa quarter there as a "colony" whose residents totaled more than a thousand, just over 1 percent of Bamum's entire population.[54] Referencing the political relationship between Hausas and Mbuembe's descendant, King Njoya, Basel missionary Anna Wurhmann noted in 1915 that the Hausa, "are naturally linked to King Njoya, since they live on Bamum soil, and are subject to the laws of the land. If there is a festival the Hausa chief appears with his subjects, and their appearance is always a statement without words of their homage and their acknowledgement that Njoya, although from their point of view a heathen, is greater and more powerful than they are" (Figure 4).[55]

Despite Hausas' small numbers in relation to the Bamum population, Basel missionaries observed the extent to which Hausas and the inhabitants of its capital, Fumban, had influenced one another. In writing the caption for one photograph he took c. 1905, missionary Friedrich Lutz brought together three important elements of Bamum's Hausa presence: "Haussa assembled for prayer in Bamum on the market place in front of the old King's palace."[56] King Njoya initially insisted that Hausas reside within Fumban's town walls, keeping them, their economic activity, and their knowledge within his reach. Every day Hausa men worked in the market located immediately in front of the royal palace. There, merchants traded items from Adamawa, the Benue, the Grassfields, and the coast. Hausa butchers worked at their market corner accompanied by musicians and their drums, migrants who had also made their way southward (Figure 5 and Figure 6).[57] At midday, these traders, butchers, and musicians, along with malams, leatherworkers, and other craftsmen, heeded the call of the muezzin to congregate in the open space in front of the palace to commence their collective prayer, *azahar*.

Earlier in the 1890s, King Njoya agreed that he and his court would convert to Islam and enter into a client relationship with the Adamawa Fulani to the north if Ardo Umaro of Banyo would assist him in quelling a rebellion within Bamum.[58] Many members of Bamum's elite ranks converted, but they only embraced some of Islam's doctrines. They did not, for example, change their traditional form of burial or cease consuming palm wine. But, as Christraud Geary has shown, "Some of the visual aspects of Islam were more readily adopted," including garments—especially robes woven by Hausas—and weapons that were worn as fashion. Such vestments were a "deliberate statement of new political alliances." Njoya also "adopted ideas from the Hausa, [later] the Germans, and neighboring peoples," incorporating new forms of cloth production, namely weaving, dyeing, embroidery, crocheting, and tailoring.[59] He even had Hausa master weavers instruct some of his wives to use the Hausa treadle loom, a significant innovation given that weaving had previously been the sole province of men (Figure 7).[60]

Ernst Vollbehr and Basel missionaries also noticed that elite Bamum women adorned themselves with Hausa amulets (*laya*). One of Vollbehr's watercolors depicts a Bamum girl with an "archaic old-assyrian [*sic*] hair-style," and at the back of her head she wore "small leather envelopes introduced by the Hausa as magical protection" (Figure 8).[61] Hausa malams and others literate in Islamic teachings fabricated these amulets by writing Qur'anic verses on small pieces of paper, which were then sewn into leather pouches and usually tied about the neck as a form of medicine to ward off evil.[62] The distribution of laya would become widespread in the Grassfields, eventually moving beyond the domain of court elites.[63]

By 1915, Njoya had even married a Hausa wife, Nzinzie. According to missionary Anna Wurhmann, this Hausa woman from Banyo had developed a "strong desire" to see Njoya. "She was scarcely adult when she left her father's house, accompanied by a few female slaves, and travelled eight days on difficult trails to reach Fumban and announce her arrival to chief Njoya. Everything which she heard and saw pleased her so extraordinarily much that she forgot her home town and her parents' house, her friends and her relatives, and offered herself to the Bamum king as his wife. Naturally Njoya did not refuse this offer but took her willingly, and presumably because of her high rank gave her honour and made her to be one of his chief wives" (Figure 9).[64]

▶▶▶▪◀◀◀

Available evidence suggests that this Hausa woman's marriage to a Grassfields chief, nominally Muslim at best, was a rare occurrence. More common were Hausa men's marriages with women from the Grassfields and nearby regions, a gendered pattern of expansion reflected in the term *abakwan riga*, or *abakwariga*—"novices of the robe or gown." As noted in the Introduction, these novices refer to descendants of mixed marriages between immigrant Hausa men and local, non-Muslim women within and south of the Benue River Valley.[65] According to Mahdi Adamu, Hausa traders, malams, and craftsmen first settled in the valley within the Jukun kingdom, perhaps as early as the fifteenth century. Some of these Hausa migrants married Jukun women and with them established a Hausa community in the kingdom's capital, Kwararafa. Oral traditions collected among Jukun peoples indicate that it was they, the hosts of the Hausa, that bestowed the name *abakwariga* onto the children of these marriages, "for though [these children] spoke more Jukun than Hausa, they claimed Hausa descent and constantly wore the riga, Hausa gown, to assert this claim." The word *abakwa* then came to be associated with the original male Hausa settlers, while *abakwariga* referred to their descendants, especially sons who wore the riga—people who came to exhibit "tenacity . . . in claiming descent through the father."[66] Other translations of this word have a similar meaning: "a man born of renegade Hausa parents" or "one who has abandoned Hausa customs and has been brought up as a pagan."[67] As of the 1970s, abakwariga near Kwararafa

continued to claim Hausa ethnic identity "simply because their family histories showed that they had Hausa paternal ancestors. Once a
person was Hausa, his descendants could remain Hausa if they wished,
no matter how divorced they might be from the Hausa culture."[68] In the
Grassfields, some people do not view Hausas' exogamous practices in the
same light, especially Fulani elders who remarked that Hausas living in
the diaspora "were not pure" because of marriages with local women.[69]

Despite these external ascriptions, patrilineality did become a significant factor in delineating membership within Hausa diaspora society, a
lived structure and a historical narrative that privileges experiences associated with men, like long-distance trade and wearing the riga, which
have generally not been accessible to women. Such gender bias embedded in abakwa—which most Hausa diaspora settlements came to be
called—mirrors what some scholars have considered the androcentrism
of the term *diaspora* itself. Stefan Helmreich has argued, "Diaspora, in
its traditional sense . . . refers us to a system of kinship reckoned through
men and suggests the questions of legitimacy in paternity that patriarchy
generates."[70] This dynamic is particularly noteworthy, considering that
privileging male social participation in the diaspora through patrilineal
descent contradicts Hausa kinship structures and behaviors that were
markedly bilateral in Hausaland. However, marriage was virilocal, and
at the core of residential units were groups of "males linked by ties of
kinship traced through males," often a father's family combined with
those of his sons. Thus, while bilaterality might have prevailed in kinship affiliation, it contended with a strong patrilineal bias.[71] Through the
diaspora's ramification patrilineality then itself became reinforced and
worked to ensure localized male dominance along the way.

Gayatri Gopinath and Lok Siu have warned that such renderings
of belonging in diasporas deploy masculinity and women in a manner
that echoes the gendered representations associated with conventional
nationalism. According to the "patrilineal, genealogical economy" of
abakwa, a term that is diasporic at its core, local non-Hausa women become symbolically associated with reproductivity, much in the way that
women became "mothers of nations." Women hailing from Kwararafa,
Lere, and other regions outside of Hausaland thus operate as "liminal
but necessary figures" that have allowed Hausa men to become fathers.

They provided a means of establishing kinship relations in the diaspora, permitting this traveling brotherhood of men to metamorphose into a unified family.[72]

These narratives resonate with how a number of diasporic Hausas understood their community history in the Grassfields. For example, when I asked the *limam* (imam) of Bamenda, Alhaji Baba Malam Shuaibu, why Hausas initially decided to settle in Bamenda, he spoke of an intimate relationship between travel, trade, Islam, and fatherhood, which involved silencing women's roles: "If you go to trade, and the place is good for you, then you will stay there. In this compound, our father was from Kano, Nigeria. He fathered twenty-three children in this compound before he died. Hausa chief Malam Baba was also from Kano. Before he died he fathered eighteen children. The other one they called him Malam Hamidu; he fathered twelve children. The other one they called Zakari, thirteen children. All of them fathered here. It was here in Bamenda that they started Islam. Here, before any other place."[73]

Hausa men did not belong in or to society through marriage, per se, but the prestige associated with having multiple wives and children was an integral element in assessing a man's standing in the community. Anthropologist Pamela Schmoll has observed that having many wives, children, and possessions—including slaves—made a man "more desirable as a friend, thus further augmenting his social status and 'prosperity.'"[74] Marital bonds also established and solidified diasporic relations among men, tying Hausa networks together by creating new kinship affiliations.[75] It was common practice among corporate merchant groups, for example, to exchange daughters and sisters.[76] Women could thus turn diasporic men not only into abakwa fathers, but also created alliances between men as brothers, business partners, patrons, and clients.

Yet the ideology of abakwa encompasses more than this. Though it is embedded in claims to legitimacy through lines of Hausa fathers, it also acknowledges the mixed historical references and modes of cultural syncretism associated with abakwariga and the women who gave birth to them, even as the women themselves transformed into Hausa diaspora wives and mothers. In so doing, abakwa ties an unstable, heterogeneous mode of identifying with Hausaness in the diaspora together with demands for a stable, fixed Hausaness that is grounded in essential sex

difference.[77] Though abakwa does trace the origins of diasporic Hausaness almost exclusively through men, it also acknowledges the roles that
diverse groups of women played in the very same history, from negotiat-
ing their own means of identification and belonging to highlighting the
constructedness of Hausaness itself.

This leads to the question of how marital practices in the Grassfields
contributed to Hausa integration. Jean-Pierre Warnier found that Grassfielders' marriages had been predominantly exogamous and virilocal,
facilitating multilingualism and enhancing interchiefdom relations.[78]
Similar to Hausa diaspora conjugal patterns, the exchange of women for-
tified networks of formal trade friendships by transforming traders into
brothers.[79] It should be noted, and is explored in greater depth in Chapter 4, that notables exchanged both slaves and freeborn girls to meet
these ends.[80] Warnier has also written that part of a trading household's
success rested "on its capacity to maintain and increase its linguistic
competence," primarily achieved through intermarriage, adoption, and
likely also by retaining captive slaves.[81]

Marriage and the ability to control it were integral aspects of exercis-
ing economic and political power in the Grassfields. Local ideologies
have historically disempowered women politically while valuing them
for their ability to create and sustain life through their reproductive and
productive capacities. Such a system championed women as creators of
a society that should be ruled by men.[82] According to Miriam Goheen
and her research on gender relations in Nso, this ideology did not mean
that women lacked political importance. Quite the contrary, titled men
who inherited wealth, especially in the region's patrilineal systems,
"had the right to arrange marriages of the women of their respective lineages, and could therefore build up large networks of affinity and power
through their control of women and thus their control of production
and reproduction as a basis of power. . . . Lineage heads controlled, with
few exceptions, the marriage of all female dependents and received the
bulk of the services and gifts which husbands were required to give to
their affines during the course of their marriage. It was through control
of women's reproductive and productive labor, and through alliances
set up through affinal arrangements, that men wielded power."[83] The tie
between patriarchy, political power, and commercial success was there-

fore primarily centered on heterosexual, exogamous marriage and its attendant efficacies of acquiring new knowledge and languages, enhancing regionalized brotherhoods and interstate relations, and assuring the endurance of lineages. It must be noted, too, that the power of lineage heads to control marriage resulted in extensive polygyny within their ranks, while economically, politically, and sexually repressing men who could not acquire dependents, particularly wives and children. Nicolas Argenti has observed that "palatine courtly societies are marked by a stark concentration of wealth among the fons and the few elites gathered around them, and this wealth is measured in the form of people, and in particular in wives, of which the fons of the greatest chiefdoms of the Grassfields possess hundreds."[84]

Though evidence is scarce, Grassfields gendered relations of power mediated through exogamous marriages and the exchange of enslaved girls did play a role in facilitating the settlement of male Hausa strangers who outnumbered their female counterparts in the nineteenth century. As Chapter 4 further demonstrates, local patron–client ideologies could be extended to Hausa men through this exchange of women, providing the men involved a connection to one another's social and economic networks and systems of knowledge.[85] Grassfields traders, including lineage heads, could expect privileged access to Hausa gifts, rents, and trade goods, while the Hausa groom secured an assured local market, access to kola, ivory, or slaves, as well as personal safety. The diverse and murky dynamics of slave dealing in particular tied the northern savanna, the Grassfields, and the coast together in a predatory economic framework that allowed Hausa men to settle in the highlands and in the process acquire women for themselves. The extent to which the women involved acted as cultural brokers is unknown. Most Hausas today believe their forefathers preferred young girls who would more easily acculturate to Hausa ways as they grew up and came of age to marry.

For Hausa men in the Grassfields, the marriage itself was not just a means to an end. It held significance on its own, too. The tie between Hausa husbands and wives, including those depicted in Vollbehr's watercolor, was a primary way for men and women to establish and signify community belonging and local status. Likely oblivious to him, Vollbehr rendered a compound that symbolized the gender dynamics of

Hausa travel and settlement so central to their claims of belonging in the Grassfields. Like the men in the painting, a trader from Kano by the name of Mohamadu Balarabe made a home for himself, his family, and his followers in this very same Hausa village. Years later his grandson would come to understand this original settlement as his "ancestral land"—rather than Kano, the Hausa state where his father and grandfather had been born. Such beliefs are foundational to Hausas' understanding themselves as locals in the Grassfields. This is especially salient given the "logic of strangerhood" in African contexts, which, according to Bruce Whitehouse, "holds that people can only fully belong in places where they can demonstrate some ancestral affiliation."[86] Mohamadu Balarabe's grandson supported his assertion by recounting what his elders had told him: that Hausas were the first people to live on this ground, for it "was all bushes" when they had arrived.[87] The compound with its swept floor, domed huts, prayer mats, and cooking utensils thus signified the clearance and domestication of the bush. As the site of childbirth and where ideal gender roles were played out, the compound also represented the model familial order that men could not have brought to such an "untamed" landscape without the knowledge, labor, and reproductive capacities of the women living alongside them.[88]

The successful establishment of a family compound indicated a significant achievement for members of the diaspora who sought to uphold Islamic values and a hierarchic, moral order grounded in the Hausa concept of lafiya.[89] This term has a number of interrelated meanings. Scholars of Hausa society have defined it as "peace, fecundity, prosperity, and good fortune" and more specifically as an "ideal state of affairs with everything running smoothly, each component of existence in its ordered, assigned, and rightful place."[90] Contrary to Vollbehr's views, Hausa men in the Grassfields did not pursue material wealth on its own. For many Hausa men, such aims were part of a comprehensive bundle of desires and expectations that included adherence to established sociopolitical authority, strengthening corporate networks, and enhancing individual prestige by accumulating wealth in things and in people. Material wealth acquired in the Grassfields enabled men to obtain wives, children, clients, and slaves, whether at "home" in Northern Nigeria or in the diaspora.

In an ideal world, a man would endeavor to produce lafiya through the principle of *mutumin kirki*, being a "good man" who exercised patriarchal authority over dependents and clients in a morally sound and calm manner.[91] Mutumin kirki was the dominant masculinity among Hausas, which, for Robert Morrell, bestowed "power and privilege on men who espouse it and claim it as their own," thereby subordinating women and other masculinities.[92] The ideal Hausa man was therefore one who followed the way of Islam, brought wealth to his community, treated people kindly and honestly, and controlled his household and the people who followed him, all of which were integral aspects of lafiya.[93] Women were also responsible for upholding community lafiya, but their social expectations emphasized shame, respect for others, and acceptance of male authority. These qualities are embedded in the concept of *kunya*.[94] With Hausa men having to integrate themselves locally through patron–client relations with non-Muslim authorities, often cementing that relationship through gifts, rents, marriage and slave-dealing, lafiya in the diaspora was a condition obtained through a hybrid social order predicated on peaceful relations with non-Islamic states and the maintenance of patriarchal, Islamic virtues in the realms of the personal, the familial, and the corporate.

》》》•|•《《《

As the late nineteenth century neared its end, the nature of Hausa relations with Grassfielders would undergo tremendous changes. When the African continent came under imperial rule, Germany claimed Kamerun as one of its new African protectorates in 1884. Five years later, the expedition led by Eugen Zintgraff reached the Grassfields, marking the first direct contact between Grassfielders and their colonizers. Being the well-traveled "culture brokers" they had become, some Hausas found work as guides for European explorers, including Zintgraff and the Royal Niger Company's Lich Moseley who preceded him. Both men were interested in understanding the networks connecting Adamawa and the Benue with the Grassfields. E. M. Chilver has noted that Zintgraff perceived Hausas as resourceful and industrious people, given their long-distance networks and expertise in such areas as leather production and metalwork. At one point, he wondered if "Europeans could ever compete successfully with them."[95] Rather than compete, however, most German officers in Kamerun tried to harness Hausa knowledge and networks for the militaristic and economic advantage of the colony.[96]

Over the next twenty years, they employed Hausa men variously as guides, military spies, carriers, and soldiers.[97] They also endeavored to redirect Hausa commercial activity from Adamawa and the Benue to the German coast, particularly the lucrative rubber and ivory trades.[98] The result of these efforts was a mixed bag. Some Hausas sought their fortunes at the Kamerun coast, while others maintained their pre-colonial networks, to the chagrin of many officers and European traders. Still others established new hamlets in the Grassfields, this time without the permission of African notables. Understanding Germans as a new paramount authority, Hausas increasingly tended to settle where colonial military stations were established. As Vollbehr noted, German opinion of Hausas remained ambivalent; nonetheless, they did enjoy their access to trade items through nearby Hausa markets, especially the availability of beef.[99] Their continued expansiveness and role as colonial auxiliaries probably influenced the Germans' later decision to use Hausa traders as agents in replacing cowry shells as currency with copper and nickel coins.[100]

In the Grassfields, colonial authority spread unevenly as it encountered diverse responses from chiefs and kings who wished to maintain their local power. In the Western Grassfields, Zintgraff and the entrepreneur Max Esser had heightened the regional political power of the Bali-Nyonga chiefdom in the 1890s.[101] German officers had a station built there, hoping it would become an important hinterland entrepôt directing trade to the coast. Relations with Bali also benefited German entrepreneurs, for it became a source of labor for their coastal plantations producing palm oil, cocoa, and rubber. Many Germans believed that highland men would make better laborers than the coastal Duala. The men of Bali, according to Esser, were "proud and brave with a free, open outlook, long-legged sons of the mountains, of the highlands, wiry and muscular in build."[102] What they actually thought, however, was that the Grassfields did not have much to offer but labor. The labor drain from the Grassfields, which had begun in response to northern and coastal demands for slaves, did not abate but was rather formalized as Germans transformed the highlands into an official labor reserve area for their coastal plantations. Historian Denis Fomin has argued that "forced labor recruitment in Cameroon during the colonial era resembled slave business in its economic function. For those recruited through the connivance of traditional rulers, two shillings was [sic] paid per head to him. The German acquisition for laborers was made to the paramount rulers who in turn got them from their vassals. Although freeborn and persons of slave origin were recruited, slaves or their descendants were the first to be sacrificed in any society."[103]

Unlike Bali, other Grassfields polities wished to remain completely independent of the colonial administration, and they paid for it dearly. Between 1901 and 1907, punitive expeditions were launched against Nso, Mankon, and Bafut, with thousands of men killed, imprisoned, or levied as forced laborers.[104] Amidst the mayhem, the colonial military established a new station in 1902. It was situated high on a bluff of the Bamenda plateau, where one could take in an encompassing view of the countryside below. This station replaced the one at Bali, which was abandoned as colonial relations with the fon deteriorated.[105] That same year, German administrators abolished slave trading in the colony, a decree that was barely enforced and ignored their own forced labor policies. Germans also participated in slave trafficking by employing soldiers and carriers without providing compensation. Some German officers further expanded the practice of enslavement during their punitive expeditions, capturing women whom they would then present as gifts to allied chiefs, as well as to those unpaid soldiers and carriers.[106] From Zintgraff's explorations in 1889, when he engaged in Germany's first battle with Bafut, to that chiefdom's submission in 1907, most Grassfields peoples experienced colonial occupation as an era of force characterized by manipulation, misunderstanding, competition, defiance, forced labor, enslavement, and violence.

To what extent Hausas participated in the suppression of chiefdoms like Nso, Mankon, and Bafut is unknown. However, the chiefs of the latter two were reluctant to allow Hausa settlement on their land, primarily because they saw these strangers as allies of their German occupiers.[107] This process and these perceptions varied throughout the Grassfields. For the Mendankwe peoples who claim first occupancy at the site of

the Bamenda colonial station, Germany's possession of land and Hausa
settlement went hand in hand but in a manner that, at least in oral traditions, did not build mistrust between the groups. When German administrators founded their station at Bamenda, they had to first acquire the
land by receiving permission from Fon Abongwa Ndu-Mambo. After
the fon "planted a fig-tree," the Germans presented the Mendankwe with
a "flag symbolizing their ownership of the land on which they lived."
The tradition then states that "since the Germans needed . . . milk, they
asked the Fon to settle them ['the Haussa people'] at up station." Not
long afterward, a small number of Hausas set up a hamlet nearby, bringing their cattle trade, language, knowledge, and modes of everyday living with them.[108] According to historian Nicodemus Fru Awasom, this
initial group of Hausas comprised some thirty bachelors but soon grew
to a community of about one hundred people, including women and
children.[109]

▶▶▶•◀◀◀

A decade after Bamenda became the site of colonial power in the
Western Grassfields, and just as the construction of most buildings at the
fort neared its end, Ernst Vollbehr arrived in Kamerun on his tour of the
German colonies. With his pencil and his brush, not only did he create
one of the only surviving visual representations of Hausa family life in
the Western Grassfields prior to the First World War, but unlike most of
his European contemporaries in Kamerun, he was open to conversing
with Hausa women. These inclinations combined with his talents to
result in one woman's likeness and words uniquely etched into the historical record, albeit through his and an interpreter's mediation:

> I portrayed a dancer modelled standing with her body in rhythmic dance
> movements. In the nose they had put a 5 cm-thick red coral pin. She was like
> all Hausa women, their teeth, hair and nails hand-dyed red with the leaves of
> henna. As I mused on their peculiar nose jewelry, she laughed out loud and
> singing, whirled around, looked at me with twinkling eyes and asked me,
> "Mister, it is true that you are bad against your white women?" "Not at all, if
> our women are nice to us, we are nice to them," I said through her interpreter.
>   Again, she whirled herself around and throwing her head back, she flashed
> me with her eyes and exclaimed, "I do not believe it. I have to say, you treat
> your women badly, you take a liane, peel it off and wrap the fiber straps round

the body of your woman. A white man running hither and thither wraps it (she pointed to opposite directions) and pulls until the ribs are exposed, and the body is very thin. Then they fasten a knot, and so let her run around, your poor women. Anyway you are very cruel to your kind. Against us Negroes you are so good, you only beat us when we deserve it. Among yourselves you torment each other to death."

Determining whether or which sentiments expressed in this passage accurately reflect the intensions of the Hausa dancer is a near impossible task. Though it appears that Vollbehr may have used this encounter to reflect critically upon his society's mistreatment of women through normalized bodily practices, we cannot discount the great possibility that the artist genuinely engaged with and listened to the words of the dancer. He did not paint her as an ethnographic type but rather as the subject of a modern portrait (Figure 10).[110] Unlike other Africans in the colonies, this Hausa woman was to Vollbehr a "worthy [subject]" for art, and therefore, perhaps, her words held enough value to be heard and recorded.

We must consider this passage and the painting as products of a critical colonial encounter in which the individuals involved—the European artist and the African dancer and interpreter—acted to transmit, acquire, and refine knowledge about themselves and their interlocutors in a space marked by unequal relations of power and violence. Here the Muslim Hausa woman is free from the barbaric constraints of European dress, upending imperial indices of civilization based in part on societies' treatment of women.[111] The structural, quotidian violence against white women highlights the cruel and "rude" nature of European society more broadly, but it also, as a mode of dark humor, creates a discursive opening through which to confront endemic, racialized violence in the colony.

With the First World War not far off in the distance, it is tempting to turn the dancer into a fortuneteller, a *mai duba*, and to characterize her commentary on torment and death among Europeans as prophetic. The great irony would be that war among European nations would lead to African death and extensive dislocation in the Grassfields, even on the very spot where this historic encounter took place. In another two years, this woman and the family scene that Vollbehr captured on his Kamerun journey disappeared entirely as the effects of the war ramified across the colony.[112] The divisions among European nations that positioned

Germany against the Allies caused great political and economic up-
heaval in the Grassfields, which was both reflected and exacerbated by
massive social displacement.

British colonial forces invaded the Western Grassfields from Nigeria
in 1914, employing mainly Hausa, Fulani, and Yoruba troops. In their
takeover, British and French authorities interned Swiss missionaries
of the Basel Mission. Some of these missionaries commented on the
Anglophone Muslim soldiers that led them toward the coast, and in
one specific instance, a missionary characterized them as "fantastically
dressed Hausa people."[113] The German military was mainly comprised
of local men from Bali and a few other Grassfields chiefdoms, but it also
employed some Hausa carriers.[114] Men of the Hausa diaspora thus found
themselves on both sides of the conflict. Initially, German forces held off
British advancement into the region, but by October 1915 officers abandoned their post at Bamenda and retreated southeastward toward the
more secure capital of Bamum.[115] People in small villages and bands left
the region out of fear.[116] This included nearly all Hausa communities, including the one at Bamenda. Many fled to Nigeria while others followed
the German military to Bamum, seeking refuge under King Njoya.[117]
Some chose to stay in the region but paid for it greatly. In September
1915, German-employed soldiers from Kumbo captured a Hausa trader
named Moma-Boyjoga. Suspecting he was a spy for the British, they tied
him up and as a result he lost one of his arms.[118]

As for the Hausa dancer, we know nothing about her other than her
encounter with Vollbehr and the certainty of her displacement from
Bamenda. We can only wonder how she may have understood what ultimately caused the violence and disruption. The one clue we have is
found in her response to Vollbehr's final question in their recorded exchange. He had asked her why she thought Europeans so tormented one
another. According to Vollbehr, "She pointed to an image of a white man
representing the crucified Christ on the cross." Because of this Hausa
woman's actions, Vollbehr seemed to have internalized a new and invaluable way of thinking. "I felt," he wrote, "like I learned that each image
performed differently for each person."[119]

And so, too, his image of a Hausa compound at Bamenda performed
as distinctly for him as it did for Basel Missionaries. Yet neither Voll-

behr nor the Basel Mission could reconcile the contradiction of thinking that diasporic Hausas were predominantly men constantly on the move while observing the more permanent arrangements of family life. Nor did Vollbehr use his observations and interactions with women, children, or a dancer to redefine Hausas as a category of African people only interested in long-distance trade. Vollbehr's contemporaries and many Hausas today have masculinized the narrative of Hausa dispersal and settlement so that it primarily reflects how men traveled and became successful in commerce, and how they fathered children, began lineages, and brought Islam to the Grassfields. In relegating the role of Hausa and non-Hausa women in this history, as well as men who did not participate in trade, this dominant narrative reinforces Hausas' local identity as self-interested strangers rather than a community of mixed cultural heritage whose past is not so easy to define.

Viewing this history through the imperfect lens that abakwa provides shows how men relied on relations with women to begin families, generate prestige, and signify belonging in local Grassfields contexts. For the many men engaged in commerce, unions with local women tied them into a regional political economy in which patriarchy, exogamous marriages, slavery, political power, and commercial success were intertwined. Even as these bonds separated people from familiar social and geographical spaces, they also facilitated connections between local economies and long-distance networks. With colonial intrusions, Hausa relations with Grassfielders took on new and diverse meanings that underwent consistent cycles of mutual transformation. Some palatine elites continued to welcome Hausas as clients and followers, but others viewed them as colonial auxiliaries who facilitated the usurping of their local power. Colonial directives during the war also meant that many Hausa diaspora men shared the violent experience of becoming soldiers only to be separated in conflict through the transposing of Europe's nationalist rivalries.

TWO

"People of the North"

LOCAL ORAL TRADITIONS WITHIN BAMENDA'S HAUSA COM-
munity are transmitted from elder to youth. Among the most popular
is the tale that is told about the desertion and reestablishment of their
community during the First World War. Listening to this story, the
children of Bamenda's Hausa quarter begin to understand why everyone in the city speaks of their neighborhood as Old Town, the original
center of a city that would come to grow around it like layers of wind-
ing ribbon. Grandparents and grandchildren alike know the history
of the former Hausa community at Up Station, how it began under
German rule, and why the Hausas living there had to leave—a story
that explains why the dancer and the family members of Vollbehr's
rendering would have abandoned their compounds, not knowing at the
time if they would ever return. When British forces invaded Bamenda
in the closing months of 1915, their predominantly Muslim troops from
Nigeria made a home for themselves at the station's barracks. But these
men found it difficult to eat the local cuisine—dishes like *achu* tasted
foreign in their mouths. When they complained to Grassfielders living
nearby—"natives" in the narrative—the soldiers were told that "their
brothers, the Hausas" were there before the war but had since left for
Fumban to escape hostilities.[1]

In this story, the Hausa soldiers drew a distinction between themselves and their surroundings through food. What they desired more than anything were the familiar tastes and textures produced by Hausa women like those in Vollbehr's paintings, women who pounded grains and spices with a mortar and pestle and prepared their meals and snacks in a cooking pot resting above the fire on a circlet of three stones. The soldiers' displeasure with the local diet led them into a dialogue with nearby inhabitants. The information revealed enabled the men to construct a historical connection to their new surroundings, for people who shared cultural affinities with them had once occupied that same space. The desire for the familiar was inspired by the pleasure of consuming what women of the Hausa diaspora produced. But the expressed discontent associated with the soldiers' inability to access this most basic of "diasporic resources" culminated in the acquisition of local knowledge connecting them not to a history of women and their labor but to a lost set of brothers.[2]

Like Vollbehr and Basel missionaries, oral traditions within Bamenda's Hausa community have had a tendency to simultaneously acknowledge yet relegate the participation of women in the diaspora. These inclinations reflect the gendered biases of abakwa, which emphasize patrilineality and the role of Hausa diaspora men as traders, brothers, fathers, and bearers of Islam. This reductive picture of diaspora life is only reinforced in British colonial records in which Hausa women, children, and men of lesser stature are unsurprisingly neglected. Dominant narratives among Hausas, Europeans, and Grassfielders, too, have all created a disproportionate focus on the activities of Hausa men, especially those who most clearly fulfilled the expected role of colonial auxiliary—the trader, soldier, and community leader. The diasporic brotherhood of Hausa men and the related erasure of women exist in each of these narratives to maintain varying forms of social order. Androcentric perceptions of history among Hausas project an idealized patriarchal order that supports male dominance in the present. This is compounded by the "ideal state of affairs" embedded in lafiya, which traditionalizes unequal status placement within the community and household. For the colonial state, the overarching focus on the economic, political, and militaristic roles some Hausa men occupied allowed its officials and even some Grassfielders to view them as a discrete, bounded group of perpetual strangers who lacked legitimate claims to land and belonging in the Grassfields.

These transformations eventually caused a reorientation in the local meaning of abakwa toward commerce, thereby masculinizing the experience of Hausa mobility and reinforcing the foreignness of the Hausa population. This occurred despite the cultural porosity that flowed through marketplace relations, friendships, and marriages between Hausas and Grassfielders throughout the colonial period. It also occurred despite the lack of precision British colonial officials displayed in their attempts to institutionalize Hausas' intermediary status as a group of "native foreigners," a category pregnant with contradictions and significant implications as an ambiguous form of belonging at best.

Over the course of the period under Britain's League of Nations mandate, which officially began in 1922, the state became increasingly involved in mediating relationships between Hausas and local Grassfields societies. Administrators viewed them as a category of people both foreign and native to the region—a wrench thrown into a colonial machinery that sought to rule through local "native" elites. By the early 1950s—and by the time Hadija entered the historical record—this mediation would have two linked, but conflicting effects on the ability of Hausas to achieve lafiya in the diaspora. Due to gradual changes in state policies, for many Hausas the economic realization of lafiya through the occupations that originally facilitated their entrance into the Grassfields became almost impossible to pursue. At the same time, the state unevenly enhanced the ability of Hausas to secure lafiya in homes and neighborhoods when, in 1947, it incorporated into its legal regime a form of Islamic law that institutionalized household patriarchy.

》》》•❙•《《《

On January 3, 1916, within three months of the soldiers' occupation of the Bamenda colonial station, the new colonial government's first political officer, George Sibbit Podevin, reached his new post.[3] Until his death during the influenza pandemic in 1918, Podevin kept a diary of his activities, including his first encounter with Grassfields Hausas just three days after his arrival. Podevin estimated their numbers at thirty men, ten women, and five children, all of whom were led by Dendelma, a *sarkin kasuwa* or chief of the market.[4] Dendelma and his followers had traveled from the Nigerian border and now sought Podevin's permission to start a Hausa market at Bafreng, a Grassfields chiefdom resting just a few kilometers below the Bamenda escarpment. Within the next four days, Podevin received two more Hausa delegations, both from Bamum. These groups were led by Sarki Mohamadu Balarabe and Sarkin Hausawa Galadima. They told Podevin they were the Hausas who had originally settled near the colonial station during German occupation. Balarabe even produced a book showing the original Hausa location, the one that had intrigued Vollbehr just four years earlier.

Given that the number of Hausas settling at the station would swell to roughly 250 people within just four months, it is plausible that the subjects of Vollbehr's watercolors—the dancer and the family—were among them, hoping to regain what had been lost: their homes and social connections, their contact with local markets, their acquired familiarity with the surrounding environment. Whatever the reasons or desires, Hausa oral traditions in Bamenda and Podevin's diary both reveal that these returning delegations wanted to resettle permanently, to advance their livelihoods, and to raise their families.

Podevin seemed just as eager for the settlement of Hausas near the station as Hausas themselves. One week after his initial encounter with Dendelma, Podevin expressed his hope for "a large settlement" of Hausas at Bamenda, complete with a daily market to service the needs of the colonial garrison and to stimulate regional trade.[5] He told Balarabe and Galadima that they would have to wait to settle until he could "start OBAKPA" for them.[6] Having been a temporary captain attached to a Nigeria regiment during the war, Podevin was likely familiar with Enugu's Abakwa Hausa quarter. In Bamenda, under his authority, he wished to control how and where it would come into existence. Without knowing it, Podevin wiped out all traces of women and family life from abakwa. Whether he learned and applied this one-dimensional understanding of abakwa from Hausas themselves or from his fellow colonial officers is unknown. Either way, when Pius Bejeng Soh conducted his research on the history of Bamenda in the early 1980s, it appears that Hausas had internalized this more recent definition. According to him,

Hausas called their settlement "Abakpa, meaning a square where there is a market."[7]

A primary reason Podevin endeavored to control this process stemmed from his concerns over the relationship between the settlement of strangers, claims to land, and local Grassfields politics. The British were under the assumption that most Grassfields chiefdoms were comprised of "natives" of a higher intellectual capability than groups found near the Atlantic coast. This meant that earning the trust of their leaders was a delicate task. They could, remarked Podevin, "form a very accurate idea of the true prospective of affairs." For these reasons the colonial administration could not "afford to play ducks and drakes with [its] promises."[8] Podevin thought he needed to balance the state's economic reliance on Hausas with the requirement to support indigenous authorities, fearing that such reliance appeared as a form of petty privilege for these African strangers. This thinking influenced even the most mundane activities. Just before making his way to Bamenda, Podevin decided to employ only Hausa men as porters on a tour in southern Nigeria, believing this display would "create [a] good impression if Hausas [are] seen carrying loads same as natives."[9]

Sarki Galadima acquiesced to Podevin's wishes to control the founding of abakwa at Bamenda, so he returned to Bamum to await the officer's orders. The other Hausa leader from Bamum, Sarki Balarabe, took a different course of action. He decided to squat at the station with his entourage of some twenty-five people, setting up camp near the buildings that housed the administrative headquarters.[10] Podevin was discernibly troubled by what he saw as their encroachment on government property. A week or two later, Sarki Balarabe was found in possession of Podevin's watch. Since Balarabe could not "satisfactorily account as to how he came by it," Podevin had the sarki detained in the guardroom. He then ordered him and his followers to vacate the premises and move to Bafreng where Dendelma was living. Roughly two months later, Balarabe requested to resettle at Bamenda, but Podevin refused.

Podevin clearly viewed Sarki Balarabe as a nuisance, as a man unfit to lead a Hausa community as a chief. According to his diary, Balarabe never officially settled at Bamenda, but local oral traditions tell a different story. They purport that Balarabe never sought resettlement at Bamenda but wished to remain in Bamum. This narrative takes the political power of resettlement out of colonial hands by giving Balarabe sole authority over the decision to return or to remain. Though he may have lived the rest of his days in Bamum, which the French would later take over, local Hausa oral tradition in Bamenda continues Balarabe's legacy as the true, original sarki of their community by the patrilineal transferal of that leadership to his son, a wealthy cleric and trader by the name of Malam Baba.

This leader, who Podevin soon came to understand as "the most influential" of Grassfields Hausas, traveled to Bamenda from Bamum in late January as part of Galadima's return entourage of more than fifty people. Malam Baba, Galadima, and Dendelma from Bafreng then convened with Podevin to discuss the nature of their resettlement. All parties agreed to recreate their village in the brickfields, the area below the high bluff from where soil had been extracted to build the colonial station above. Oral tradition again tells a slightly different, albeit complementary tale whereby Hausas established an encampment near the military barracks. But due to their loud drumming at night and women's pounding of corn in the early morning, they annoyed the British officers so thoroughly that the administration ordered the Hausa community to move down to the brickfields, referred to locally as poto-poto. The humorous nature of this Hausa story expresses an ironic joy in the fact that the work and rhythms of Hausa food preparation and music were both fundamental to everyday experience in the diaspora but also unintelligible to colonial officers who had the power to relocate their entire community. Podevin made no note of Hausas' disturbing his peace and quiet. The only aspect of Hausa life that seemed to perturb him in these early days of resettlement was Sarki Balarabe, the leader who likely set up that original, storied encampment.

Whatever the memory or recording, Hausa leaders agreed to establish abakwa down the bluff at poto-poto within the designated boundaries of Mankon territory. The Hausa leaders had to comply with a set of conditions if they were to secure this new location. They could only occupy the space if the chief of Mankon agreed, and once occupied, Hausas would have to pay an annual fixed rent on top of a colonial tax, keep the location sanitary, maintain order and discipline under the Sarkin

Hausawa Malam Baba, supply carriers to the administration when required, establish a "proper market," and provide "fresh meat . . . upon payment to all Europeans on the station."

Within two weeks of this meeting, poto-poto became home to more than two hundred Hausas, a number that would grow over the course of the year as more people—Hausas as well as some Grassfielders—made their way to Abakwa-Bamenda.[11] Hausa men, women, and children made the journey from the station down to poto-poto along the German-designed, African-built zigzag road that etched the side of escarpment, while others undoubtedly came through the Ndop Plain or from Nigeria by way of the Katsina Ala River and Kom. They would form part of a community that Podevin came to experience as law-abiding. They were, he wrote, "indispensable as far as the garrison [was] concerned," supplying provisions to the troops, who consumed one hundred pounds of meat on Sundays alone. Sarkin Hausawa Malam Baba was instrumental in purchasing the cloth needed to make uniforms for the administration's messengers. By providing cattle for the Navy and consignments to the Queen's ships docked at Victoria, Hausas "rendered great assistance" to the British administration and military.[12] Their meat markets in general were "well patronized by the natives," while the sale of live cattle was "also extensively carried on."[13] Their commercial activities helped Podevin introduce Nigerian subsidiary coinage to the region, similar to German officers' methods before him. Hausas' trade in rubber, collected from the northern and western boundaries of the Western Grassfields, also pleased the officer.[14] Moreover, the administration earned revenue through taxing these native foreigners at the high rate of 6 shillings per adult male, while "natives" were taxed between 1 and 4 shillings. Though Podevin paid no attention to Hausa women, their cottage industries and participation in local petty trade such as food items were likely central to the economic dynamism and daily well-being of everyone nearby.

British officers by and large considered the presence of Hausas as economically beneficial to their territory. One officer proclaimed, "The trader of the Cameroons is the Hausa, and without him the interior native would get anything [sic]. The Hausa . . . is in every town and centre, and where he is there is always a small stock of essentials and odds and ends."[15] While this is a gross underestimation of Grassfielders' trading activities, it is a fair representation of British opinions of Hausas during and immediately after the war. Some even thought participating in "the 'Haussah' trade" would be a good source of employment for "natives" as they struggled to overcome wartime disruptions.[16]

In the late 1910s, after the 1918 influenza pandemic killed roughly 1,500 people in the Grassfields, the Hausa population at Bamenda was set to move one last time to its present-day location. By 1921, this new site was firmly established, eventually becoming the heart, the Old Town, of Bamenda, one of Cameroon's largest urban centers. The population of Abakwa-Bamenda fluctuated throughout the years, as newcomers from throughout the Grassfields, Nigeria, and French territory migrated, and as smaller Hausa settlements developed in villages nearby, including Bamessi, Bamunka, and Bamessing.[17] By September 1923, Malam Baba's "Hausa Town" at Bamenda was home to 753 inhabitants.[18] Within roughly fifteen years, more than twenty other Hausa hamlets were established throughout the Western Grassfields.[19] The British administration did not let this process of settlement in the region go without intervention, despite many Hausas' attempts to do so autonomously. In the mid-1920s, the administration chose the Hausa location in Ntumbaw, while it appears that their community at Nsob had "sprung up" on their own accord.[20]

The colonial government was predominantly concerned with Hausas' commercial and cultural influence on local Grassfields leadership. For example, more than one hundred Hausas had established themselves in Kumbo, the center of the Nso chiefdom. Traders were particularly attracted to the town because of kola production and the central position of the market, which served as a meeting point between kola producers and long-distance routes northward out of the Grassfields. As in the nineteenth century, Hausa traders were the main engineers of the long-distance trade in kola nuts, transporting them using donkeys and human porterage. They would purchase kola in the northern Grassfields, at places like Kumbo and Kentu, as well as from kola producers in Bagam, Bamendjinda, and Bali. Nicodemus Fru Awasom states that the 1920s were the heyday of the kola trade in the Grassfields, as production of kola expanded to meet ever increasing demands in the north. In return, Grassfielders received salts from Benue and Bornu, as well as beads, spices, leather goods, household items, and textiles, including the fine, embroidered Hausa garments that Grassfielders increasingly coveted in the 1920s and 1930s. Local Grassfielders were avid participants in trading kola nuts, but Hausas monopolized the trade in garments.

Hausas also controlled the cattle trade, an accomplishment achieved relatively easily given their close relationship with Muslim Fulani graziers, or Mbororos, who began to enter the region in the late 1910s. The first Mbororos to arrive in the Grassfields came from Kano through Adamawa.[21] Their leader, Ardo Sabga, led his people to the Bamenda highlands where they settled in a community roughly twenty-five kilometers outside of Bamenda. Mbororos were attracted to the Grassfields because of their favorable ecological conditions for the raising of cattle, especially fertile pastures and salt springs.[22] A second great influx of Mbororos occurred around 1940; these groups also originally hailed from Kano but arrived in Cameroon by way of the Jos Plateau. Most of their members settled in the northern reaches of the Grassfields.[23] By this time, their numbers far surpassed that of the Hausa. Today, Hausas comprise just 1 percent of the Grassfields population, while Mbororos make up 15 percent.[24]

Mbororos were keen to focus on their pastoral activities and handed over to Hausas the business of herding cattle to the markets of urban centers like Victoria (Limbe), Douala, Enugu, and Calabar. Micaela Pelican's careful research on Hausa–Fulani relationships in the Grassfields notes that Hausa cattle traders "arranged a credit system with Mbororo graziers [enabling] them to engage fully in cattle trade, even in the absence of the required capital." Pelican also noted that though Mbororos believe they possess the best cattle-driving skills, they do not like to participate in a process that ends with the slaughtering of their cattle.[25] Hausas thus emphasized "their role as cultural brokers by accentuating socio-cultural and ethnic differences between Mbororo and Grassfields peoples." In so doing, they were able to exclude Grassfielders from participating in this trade in 1920s and 1930s.[26]

▶▶▶●◀◀◀

From the perspective of colonial and Grassfield observers alike, Fulani immigration had two opposing influences on diasporic Hausa

identity. The increased Fulani presence brought out the linguistic, cultural, and economic diversity in the condition of Muslim strangerhood,
but Fulani modes of dress and religious practices, including the ritual
slaughtering of cattle, fasting, and prayer, also united them with Hausas. Though specific distinctions between Hausas and Fulanis were
apparent, in the diaspora the common denominators that coupled them
together were strangerhood and practices associated with Islam. As a
result, these elements were foregrounded in the ways the British and local Grassfielders understood Hausa identity during the colonial period.

Both in discourse and in policy, the colonial state differentiated diasporic Hausas and Fulanis from "native" Grassfielders, even though
some of them, like the Chamba political leadership of Bali-Nyonga, arrived in the area at roughly the same time as Hausas in the nineteenth
century. The British classified both Hausas and Fulanis as "native foreigners."[27] Through the categories of *native* and *native foreigners,* the
British tried to make sense of African social and political life in their
mandated territory. According to Mahmood Mamdani, so-called indigenous groups were legally categorized as geographically fixed natives
and differentiated from each other by essentialized ethnic distinctions.
British colonial authorities organized these ethnic groups as tribes, and
each tribe would have its own set of customary laws. Conversely, non-
natives, including native foreigners, were differentiated hierarchically
from one another along racial lines: Europeans crowned this hierarchy and were followed by "subject races," which included "Coloureds,"
Asians, Arabs, and, at the bottom, African groups like diasporic Hausas
and Fulanis that were constructed as non-indigenous aliens but still
capable of having "a civilizing influence."[28]

However, over the course of the interwar period administrators did
not consistently concur on whether native foreigners should be defined
and governed as natives or as alien races.[29] For one, the British never
settled on what characteristics defined a native foreigner. In Nigeria, the
Interpretation Ordinance of 1914 stipulated that all aliens included non-
natives and native foreigners.[30] By 1939, however, an amended Interpretation Ordinance defined "the term 'native' as including a native of Nigeria
and a native foreigner, the latter phrase including 'any person (not being
a native of Nigeria) whose parents were members of a tribe or tribes

indigenous to some part of Africa and the descendants of such persons, and shall include any person one of whose parents was a member of such tribe.'"[31] Mamdani's model also does not fit British patterns of rule in the Grassfields. Paul Nchoji Nkwi and Jean-Pierre Warnier have shown how the Germans and the British tried to regroup chiefdoms by ranking them in a regional hierarchy. The authority of those chiefs deemed most powerful and helpful to the colonial enterprise was strengthened as colonial rulers enforced their regional paramountcy.[32]

Many of these colonial contradictions in defining Hausas as a group against Grassfielders emerged from officers' own documented experiences observing relations between these so-called natives and native foreigners. They saw "native" elite men dabbling in Hausa customs, especially clothing and adornment. Such cultural syncretism caused anxiety for officials as it undermined their project of ruling through distinct African populations, whether a race of Muslim strangers or tradition-bound tribes and chiefs. Podevin was no exception. In 1916, the king of Bagam presented himself to the officer as many other Grassfields leaders had done after the officer's arrival. Podevin remarked in his diary that the king wore a turban and Hausa clothes, speculating that the turban in particular crowned this African leader's head "in order to obviate [the] necessity of taking his hat off."[33] British colonial regulation required Africans to take off their headwear when meeting authorities in official settings, making an exception for Islamic rulers. Since the king of Bagam was not Muslim, Podevin believed he only sported Hausa dress to circumvent sartorial codes of deference to his authority.

On another occasion Podevin traveled to Bagam as the king had been exhibiting "great slackness" in carrying out governmental orders. Part of the problem, Podevin thought, was that the king was "far too much influenced by Hausas." He not only wore Hausa dress but he surrounded himself with Hausa followers. This was apparently too much for Podevin. To keep the king in line, he ordered him to relinquish his Hausa headdress in favor of "an ordinary chief's cap." He also barred the king from having Hausas in his retinue, preferring that principal headmen be the only persons to accompany him.[34] In the end, Podevin told all of the Bagam Hausa to pack up their things within four days and relocate to Bamenda. The king had no choice but to do Podevin's bidding,

thereby undercutting the long-established means of augmenting his local political power through the incorporation of useful strangers. The
chief of Bafanji was accused of similar tendencies. Podevin reprimanded
this leader by not only forbidding him to wear "Hausa headgear" but also
by ordering him to give up his love for Hausa drumming.

Evidence from colonial archives suggests just how resilient these
forms of African relationships were, however. Throughout the 1920s
and 1930s, officers noted that some chiefs continued to value Hausas as
clients, followers, and friends. In 1923, the chief of Nso at Kumbo was "on
the very best of terms with the [sarki] who has been allowed to establish
his compound adjoining that of the chief."[35] Fourteen years later, such
relations continued to obtain in Nso when another officer remarked
that the "acquisitive" Banso chief "generally feathers his nest from the
stranger within the gates."[36]

Colonial anxieties over modes of Hausas' integration into Grassfields
societies often materialized in a discourse centered on the imprecise
linkages between dress, religious identification, and cultural borrowing among African male leadership. In this discourse, cultural porosity
among Grassfields men indicated their weak and impressionable dis-
positions. In a 1939 report for the League of Nations, one administrator
wrote, "The young chief of Ndu is not a strong character. . . . In 'full
dress' he might pardonably be mistaken for a Hausa and a Mohammedan, but on one occasion when giving evidence in the Magistrate's
Court he had to unwind and remove his turban before taking the oath
on the Bible—he was an adherent of the Catholic Mission before he
became chief and found himself the heir to a number of women and expected to keep a similar number of wives himself."[37] Because the British
often identified style of dress as a marker of religious adherence, those
men who defied such simple categorization—especially leaders upon
whom the colonial system of Indirect Rule rested—were perceived as
being easily swayed by temptation and power, and therefore potentially
difficult to control.

Colonial authorities would have to contend with the fact that more
and more Grassfields men demonstrated their wealth and status through
conspicuous consumption of Hausa garments, with such trends inad-
equately representing changes in religious persuasions. In 1921, for ex-

ample, district officer W. E. Hunt noted in Bali that both men of chiefly status and men of economic means sought to showcase their wealth through wearing Hausa clothing. He noticed that many men of Bali wore "as many clothes as they [could] afford, imitating to some extent Mohammedan fashions, and adopting flowing robe and turban."[38] In marked contrast, he wrote that the women of Bali went "practically naked." Another officer noted similar clothing trends in his assessment report of the Bum area of Bamenda. "Woman's dress, as elsewhere in Bamenda," he wrote, "is conspicuous by its absence, a small piece of cloth, measuring about 1½ inches by 2 inches suffices the most fastidious; this garment is suspended from a girdle of beads or string and is worn in front of the body. A few women are seen wearing clothing similar to that found amongst the Hausa women of Northern Nigeria. When a woman is found fully covered with clothing in Bum, it may be safely assumed that she 'learns doctrine.'"[39] For British officers, adoption of Muslim dress among Grassfields men may or may not have indicated religious conversion, while the clothing of their female counterparts unequivocally symbolized adherence to Islam—or "learning doctrine."

Hausa modes of dress drifted onto the bodies of local Grassfielders in gendered ways that both signified and mystified possible transformations in religious orientation toward Islam and even in social identification as Hausa.[40] While the uneven appropriation of Hausa ways by Grassfields men, especially elites, often caused colonial authorities to become frustrated, they were much less concerned with the porousness of Hausa identification that allowed "native" Grassfields children, slaves, women, and even some poorer men to integrate themselves as clients, friends, wives, slaves, and potential converts in Hausa diaspora society. They too formed relationships through clothing but in ways that were not often apparent to outside observers. In the 1950s, for example, many Hausa or Hausa-ized women and girls wore mismatched patterns of cloth for their head wrappers, shirts, skirts, and body coverings. One woman named Aishatu Ibrahim explained that her friends, sisters, and sisters-in-law always interchanged their cloth when visiting one another. Giving cloth to another woman symbolized belonging through bonds of friendship and sisterhood, an act that reflects the Hausa concept of the 'kawa relation, bond-friendships between women that emphasize reciprocal obligations, mutual identification of partners, and exchange of gifts, like cloth, which increased "their value at each exchange."[41] Likewise, Aishatu noted that when one exchanged cloth with someone it meant "you love me, I love you."[42] The style of contrasting articles of cloth among Hausa Grassfields women thus displayed and was rooted in their affection for one another and the desire to create nonhierarchical ties within their own moral economy—a much more complex, intimate meaning than women simply appearing to "learn doctrine" (Figure 11).

▶▶▶●◀◀◀

Hausas' cultural influence in the Grassfields produced a spectrum of identifications and practices. Cultural shifts toward textile clothing undoubtedly worked in favor of those Hausas producing and selling cloth, such as weavers, dyers, tailors, and merchants.[43] But Hausas' position as privileged facilitators of the colonial economy, especially in the markets for kola and garments, was not to be had for long. For Malam Baba's Hausa community at Bamenda, the economic decline was rather rapid. In 1924, the troops that had been stationed at the garrison were transferred to Abakaliki, Nigeria. The daily Hausa market and the "native" weekly market on the bluff near the station suffered as a consequence. The departure of the garrison also signified a transformation in colonial governance, from a structure that required military backing to one that could do without. Though the British administration continued to recognize the important economic role Hausas played, most officers envisioned an imperial hierarchy that rested on the shoulders of the so-called authentic, indigenous African leader, the Grassfields chief or fon.

Economic struggles would continue for Hausas and Grassfielders alike as the effects of the Depression reached them in the 1930s. The prices for Cameroon's exported products to Europe and the United States dropped, while the related shortage of cash in the colony negatively affected long-distance and regional trade.[44] Adding insult to injury, from 1930 to 1934 a locust plague ravaged food crops and kola cultivation, dropping kola-nut production to roughly one-quarter of its rate in the 1920s. Hausa traders intensified their focus on cattle, a niche they could continue to exploit given their relationship with Fulani pastoralists. This trade saw many Hausas and Fulanis through difficult times. Eventually, the British administration grew worried that Grass-fielders were kept out of this lucrative business. Beginning in the 1940s, the colonial government began to challenge the Hausa monopoly in cattle trading, and by the early 1950s it had completely disintegrated.[45] Hausas became less and less important to the colonial economy, which was reflected in how they steadily faded away from the pages of colonial reports.

Broad political changes occurring throughout Africa during and after the Second World War also affected the position of Hausas in the colonial governance hierarchy. While Hausas' role in long-distance trade declined in the Grassfields, the British hastily put programs in place that would lead the British Cameroons on a path toward self-governance, a process that entailed allowing African representatives to sit on local governing bodies. Emergent nationalist ideologies that privileged in-digeneity over foreignness informed this process of increased African participation in the colonial state. Despite Hausas' economic decline at this time, and despite the disentanglement of occupational and collec-tive identity among Hausas, many Grassfielders continued to mark them as having gained petty privileges from colonial rule. Hausas' declining numbers in relation to the overall population growth of the communi-ties around them exacerbated this situation. In Bamenda, Hausas made up only 3–8 percent of all urban residents, their population remaining relatively constant at around 800 individuals, while Bamenda grew from roughly 1,600 in 1934 to more than 9,700 by 1953.

Acknowledging the marginal status that Hausa communities ac-quired by the late 1940s, the colonial administration at times sought to protect their political interests. In 1949, for example, the Bamenda divisional office envisaged that two "Hausa Stranger Members" from Abakwa-Bamenda and one from the Hausa settlement at Santa, a man known as Sarki Gudel, be appointed to the Ngemba Native Court Panel. In Santa, however, three Akum men, apparently on behalf of all "Santa Settlers," petitioned the nomination of the Hausa man. According to the petitioners, the Akum chief "wanted a Hausa headman who is very rich to represent us the natives." But the petitioners protested, arguing that

Gudel "does not understand our language and customs in the Ngemba Clan Council. What a curious thing." From their perspective, the Akum chief wanted to minimize the numbers of Akum men serving in government offices, which would allow them to check his customary authority. A Hausa sarki, by contrast, may have been potentially easier to control for the chief, given that his authority was required for Hausa settlement. In this instance, Gudel's position as an intermediary between the Akum chief and Akum plebeians converged with a history of petty privilege some Hausa men exploited as colonial auxiliaries who mediated relations between officials and "natives."

When the district officer came to Santa to settle the matter, the three petitioners laid out their argument a second time:

> We again told him ... why we do not want to hear the name Gudel is because (a) He does not understand our language and we do not understand his own too. (b) Since he is a Hausa or Fulani imigrant [sic] and not of Ngemba Clan, he cannot tell us what we want. (c) He is a trader who has merely settled here on account of trade and likely to return to his unknow [sic] home when he fails in trade. (d) His manners are not good. (e) We do not choose men because they are rich according to the [village head] Akum. (f) Another announcement about the D.O.'s nomination is that ... all Hausas [only] number 221 so that [we] cannot be represented by this Hausa headman Gudel whom the Hausas are not even in his favour.[46]

These Akum men emphasized the foreignness of Gudel and other Hausas in order to support their argument for "native" community representation. They projected his alienness through his unintelligible language, unknown place of origin, lack of local kinship affiliation, and overall cultural peculiarities. Trade and the material wealth derived from it were articulated as anathema to permanent settlement, community membership, and local political power. Just before closing their letter, they reminded the resident yet again, "Since this Hausa man from an unknown village has come here after us for trade not for rule, we do not want him to be our representative."[47] By this point in time, most Hausa men were employed in a number of different occupations. The figure of the traveling Hausa merchant who siphons wealth away from the colony was not much more than a stereotype.[48] Nonetheless, categorizing Gudel solely as a commercial agent and a traveler arriving "after" the

autochthonous Ngemba Clan substantiated the writers' claims that he
had no real ties to the surrounding community and therefore no right
to be its representative.

A year later, similar claims to indigeneity influenced colonial urban
planning in Bamenda.[49] Abakwa lay at the core of the population spread
in the area. According to the geographer and specialist in the urban history of the Grassfields, Christopher M. Awambeng, because Abakwa's
"legacy is . . . foreign," and because its population was marked by a high
degree of ethnic diversity from the beginning, there were greater in-
centives for 'strangers' and local inhabitants to immigrate there than
to "traditional settlements and centres."[50] Questions then arose for colonial administrators regarding how to bring organization to a rapidly
expanding urban space, which governing mechanisms should be put in
place to manage this community, and which people should be allowed
to serve on the town's governing bodies. Officials were desperate to do
"something . . . quickly, to stop the haphazard growth and ribbon development of the Stranger town below the escarpment at Bamenda."[51] As
debates ensued over the governance of this urban center, Fon Ndefru of
Mankon campaigned to envelop it under his authority. As with the case
in Santa, British officers concerned with the project of self-government
in Bamenda worked to ensure that Abakwa strangers were represented
on governing bodies. However, their superior, the Secretary of the Eastern Region in Enugu, took a very different stance. He believed that
only "the Native Authorities concerned . . . make provision for a Joint
Committee. . . ."[52]

With this new directive in mind, the Bamenda district officer held a
meeting with the Native Authorities of Mankon, Bafreng, and Bamenda-
Nkwe. They all had a stake in Bamenda's development even though, as
one officer indicated, "the three villages holding rights over the Abakpa
area are situated some miles from it."[53] There were also a few "stranger
residents" present at the meeting. According to an official report, "The
meeting was arranged by the so-called Mankon Abakpa Town Council, a body which, to use the senior district officer's words, 'really wants
to set up a little dictatorship with powers to rule the destinies of the
strangers.'"[54] Officials proposed that perhaps half of the town's governing
council be made up of "traditional" members, while the other half would

consist of "members to represent the Abakpa inhabitants"—for a total of twenty-two people. But the indigenous political elite insisted that they should comprise the majority of the council.

They wanted the community renamed "Mankon-Nkwen-Manda Town" and reorganized as a "Mankon Native Municipal Town with Fomankon as the President."[55] In 1951, Mankon elites claimed that only fifty Hausa men resided in Abakwa and that the majority of Abakwa inhabitants were "native" and not Hausa. They reasoned that since the British ruled Bamenda "over ten millions of miles from London," then surely the fon's residence ten miles away from Abakwa was a nonissue. Their desire to disempower a Hausa minority in part stemmed from a perception that Hausas continued to benefit from petty privileges acquired through British rule, even though Hausas' commercial opportunities had declined. Some Mankon elites believed that Hausas were conspiring with the British to control the entire province through the founding of an Islamic emirate: "The atmosphere of Mankon country [is] very gloomy . . . as the administration here is bent down to create a Hausa Emirate here with Mallam Sule Maman as a Sarki or Emir of the Province in the near future. . . ."[56] As in other colonial regimes, anticolonial hostility was often directed at foreigners like Hausas who were viewed as allies to the colonial administration.[57]

Even though the fon's demands annoyed British officers, new designs for urban planning fulfilled some of his wishes. First, Abakwa-Bamenda's cemetery was relocated with many of its dead displaced in the process. In the 1920s, a graveyard had emerged adjacent to the original settlement in an area that was worked as farmland for the Sarkin Hausawa.[58] Some of Abakwa's earliest settlers were buried there, including the settlement's first *sarkin pawa* (chief butcher).[59] With increasing settlement in the 1930s, the cemetery became congested. Not only were families lacking space in which to bury their dead, but colonial officials—influenced by public health concerns and a desire to develop the town center—prohibited burying the dead in the cemetery sometime in the late 1940s or early 1950s.[60] They also encouraged businesses and further immigration into the town center, which meant that buildings and compounds were either erected directly on top of intact graves or built with foundations that required the unearthing of the dead. This new area was named Sabon

Gari, "new town," while the original settlement became "Old Town," as
it is still known as today.[61] In the 1960s, Abner Cohen noted how changes
in the creation of a separate cemetery in Ibadan's Hausa Quarter, along
with a separate Friday mosque and Friday congregation, symbolized
the quarter's "new myth of distinctiveness" from Yoruba Muslims. Such
efforts "halted the disintegration of the bases of the exclusiveness and
identity in Sabo," whereas in Bamenda the removal of the Hausa cemetery can be viewed as an event that encouraged the quarter's incorporation into the broader community.[62] However, the paving of streets and
erection of structures on burial mounds in Bamenda's Sabon Gari also
had the effect of reinforcing the "oldness"—if not the "firstness"—of the
Hausa settlement.

The other change that had a most drastic effect on Hausas was the
transplanting of the daily market from Abakwa to the newly constructed
area of Azire on the other side of Ayaba Stream, an area clearly under
Mankon authority.[63] With the decline in cattle and kola trades and with
the removal of their market, diasporic Hausas—people who continue to
be regarded throughout West and Central Africa for their commercial
networks—were divested from the institution of the market that was
central to their community identity in Bamenda. One of the greatest
ironies for Bamenda's Hausa population is that the seminal feature at-
tracting the interest of Grassfields elites and colonizers, as well as the
settlement of strangers and locals alike, ultimately resulted in its removal
from their community.[64]

In response to these challenges, Hausa leadership in Bamenda organized as a branch of the *Jam'iyyar Mutanen Arewa* (Society of People
of the North) and brought their case to a United Nations Visiting Mission on tour in the region during the closing months of 1952, the same
time Hadija entered the Islamic courtroom. Bamenda's sarki, Mallam
Sulaimanu, along with three other leaders, implored the delegation to
help improve the conditions of their community. This is one of the only
pieces of evidence that documents collective complaint among Grassfields Hausas. Unlike other Hausa enclaves in West Africa, notably
Ibadan's Sabon Gari, Grassfields Hausa have generally not politicized
their ethnic identity but rather have worked within established political hierarchies.[65] These inclinations are present in the letter. The Hausa

leaders did not request assistance for Hausas specifically, but rather their settlement of Abakwa as a whole, which by this point included migrants from other regions of Cameroon and Nigeria, as well as Grassfielders. But, in professing membership to an organization that referred to itself as "people of the north," the leaders also reemphasized the foreignness of their origins and their ties to a homeland where communities similar to theirs, they argued, experienced a better quality of life: "We humbly beg the Administering Authority through the u.n.o. visiting Mission that we want the British Government to improve our Settlement to a better standard as those in Nigeria. We are directly under the control of the Administering Authority, and they are fully aware of the difficulty of our living here in this Country. We therefore appeal to the u.n.o. that our request be considered for improvement of our Settlement Abakpa Town by the Administering Authority."[66]

The in-betweenness at the heart of Hausas' "native foreigner" status is evident here. The leaders expressed alienation by living "in this Country," yet in seeking resources to benefit their community they were clearly committed to their permanence in Abakwa and hoped to maintain it for future generations.[67] As African incorporation into the colonial state increased, Hausas' practice of integrating themselves into established political hierarchies became more complicated. While there were individual exceptions to these patterns of economic decline in the 1940s and 1950s, it is not surprising that many Hausa leaders, who likely had memories—perhaps romanticized—of a more prosperous time, felt they had no other recourse but to reach beyond the colonial state to the United Nations, lying here at the perceived apex of the global governance hierarchy.

▶▶▶•◀◀◀

Members of Jamiyyar Mutanen Arewa expressed how their aspirations for communal lafiya were no longer being met. They could not count on trades in kola or cattle, nor could their neighborhood expect income that had once been earned through the Hausa market. But even as the state sanctioned Hausas' economic and political marginalization, it had managed to institutionalize patriarchal control on the home front. The signatories of the letter may not have perceived this as a tradeoff, but colonial authorities in many ways did. From the mid-1920s into the 1940s, Hausa patriarchs and their especially vocal Fulani counterparts launched repeated appeals to the government to establish an Islamic court in the region. According to an elderly inhabitant in Bamenda's Hausa quarter, adulterous liaisons involving married Fulani women were a primary factor driving African campaigns to found the court.[68]

Colonial officers who favored establishing an Islamic court maintained two arguments. Some officers feared that Muslims, most of whom were strangers, were in dire need of moral guidance. As late as 1944, Bamenda's divisional officer feared Fulanis' moral decline in particular: "Fulanis who have lived elsewhere say that the palavers went before an Alkali, and decry the absence of one here as being the case of the decline in the general moral standards. . . . A well-chosen Alkali . . . would have a stabilizing effect on a society showing signs of the need for it. It would check the tendency of the Ardos to become feudal barons by balancing against their power of wealth a detached judicial power."[69] The resident of the Cameroons extended these concerns to all Muslims in the division, suggesting, "A good Alkali . . . would have a most beneficial effect upon local Mohammedan manners and morals in addition to settling their disputes according to Islamic law."[70]

Other sympathetic observers were concerned about Muslim strangers' unprotected interests. Dr. M. D. W. Jeffreys was particularly adamant on this account. He argued that Fulani cattle owners had "no Native Authority, no Court," and with two exceptions, no representatives on Native courts. "Yet the Bororo pay one third of the total direct taxes," he wrote. Moreover, "Oppression by the agriculturalists takes the form of making farms either alongside or across cattle tracts or cattle traces to water and their claiming damages in the Native Court where, owing to lack of representation, exorbitant damages are awarded."[71] Other officers also considered their system of revenue through taxation. The state taxed Hausa strangers 6 shillings, and Fulanis were taxed through *jangali*, a cattle tax. These rates were higher than for "natives," who were taxed between 1 and 4 shillings. Due to increased Fulani immigration, Muslims came to number more than 7,000 by the early 1940s, and as their numbers grew so did revenue through the collection of jangali.[72] Requests for an alkali court in the Bamenda Division received greater consideration in 1943, in part due to officials' recognition that neither Fulanis nor Hausas saw any returns from taxes paid.[73]

By March 1945, the office of the secretary at Enugu approved the creation of the court. Only Muslims would be subject to its jurisdiction. The court would abide by the Maliki school of Islamic law, and the state gave it a C-grade warrant, which meant it was not allowed to try criminal cases.[74] The alkali was to adjudicate civil matters only, such as those pertaining to "debts, damages, inheritance, testamentary disposition, the administration of estates and Islamic matrimonial causes."[75] Finally in March 1947, two years after the initial approval, the court's doors opened at Ndop, a small town situated 30 kilometers east of Bamenda along the Ring Road, the main route connecting communities in the Western Grassfields that was constructed in the late 1940s and 1950s.

One of the primary policies framing the alkali's jurisdiction involved distinguishing which people and which kinds of cases could be heard at the court. The alkali could arbitrate cases only involving Muslims, whereas disputes concerning parties of multiple faiths would be mediated in native courts.[76] The alkali would not have the authority to try cases over the question of land titles either, as the lands Fulanis and Hausas occupied were not entitled to them because of their status as strangers.[77] Despite these policies, the creation of the court confused some officers in their attempt to rule people they understood as circumscribed by tribal tradition. In the early 1950s the agricultural district officer in Wum wrote to the resident to seek advice on a perplexing encounter in Bum. He had come across a dispute between a Fulani man and a Banso man, the latter of whom had converted to Islam. The officer felt that the matter would be best solved through a court. "But the question of which court arose," wrote the officer: "I said the Native court (as a matter of course) and the Fulani objected, saying that as the man has embraced Islam the case should go to the Alkali's Court. . . . The converted man has adopted an Arabic name, wears Hausa robes, lives in Hausa Abakpas and to all intents and purposes (probably as far as suits his convenience) has renounced his pagan background. Can he therefore sue and be sued in the Alkali's Court?" In reply, the resident simply stated: "As the man has embraced Islam he may as well go to the Alkali Court."[78]

What is perhaps more significant than the officer's confusion concerning which court would best serve this converted Grassfields man, is the manner in which he described the symbols of the convert's new religious and cultural affiliation. That he possessed an Arabic name, wore Hausa dress, resided in a Hausa settlement, and publicly practiced Islam all pointed toward his conversion. It is not irrelevant that two of the four factors listed hinged on Hausa cultural elements, given that many officials recognized African conversion to Islam through—in addition to Hausa dress, place of residence, and profession of the Muslim faith through prayer—adopting Hausa language and paying the increased Hausa tax.[79] The British thus both reinforced Muslim laws, practices, and behaviors as the fundamental elements of Hausa and Fulani identity, as well as emphasized Hausa dress and everyday living as the basic indicators of one's religious devotion.[80]

With the Islamic court's establishment, the politics of belonging in the Grassfields as a culturally porous group of Muslim native foreigners would converge with gendered contestations over ideal relations among individuals. Shamil Jeppie, Ebrahim Moosa, and Richard Roberts have argued that colonial authorities throughout Africa understood family stability in particular as a "cornerstone of the stability of the colony itself." In British colonies, officials changed the cultural meanings and applications of Islamic family law, namely by making the courts public and transparent through a new process of appeals, which itself required record keeping and codification of what was previously a flexible discourse of laws. These changes also required the professionalization of judges and scribes.[81] Such interventions reflect the broader tendency of European imperialists to govern the religious affairs of Muslims in multiple contexts, specifically by institutionalizing Islam and introducing "centralized religious bureaucracies."[82] These interventions in the legal realm depended on European ideas of African family life, sexuality, and gender roles.[83] Studies on late nineteenth-century British imperial ideology have also noted how colonial authorities paradoxically positioned Islamic institutions as backward while identifying with "the Muslim male and masculinist power structure." The idea of Muslim backwardness legitimated imperial hierarchies while the identification with masculinity highlighted the commonality of patriarchy, which justified extensive British involvement in areas like Islamic family law.[84]

Such dynamics are revealed in the alkali's very first case. On March 24, 1947, Malam Maman of Nsaw explained to the alkali that his wife had left him twelve years ago without returning even 1 shilling of his 50-pound brideprice. Back in 1935, Malam Maman had three wives. After a two-week journey, he returned home to be greeted by only two of them. The other wife remained in her room, refusing to cook for her husband—a significant rejection of her duties as a Muslim wife.[85] The woman's co-wives and female neighbors learned she was sick and began praying for her. This went on for a number of days until she left her husband to return to her mother's home. The husband asked the Sarkin Hausawa of Nsaw to intervene, hoping he would have the power to direct his wife back to his compound. But the wife's mother did not want her to leave. She told the sarki that Maman had flogged her daughter: "When she was sick, [Maman] could not allow her to sleep fine, he . . . always come and [flogged] her on the sick bed." But Maman tried to take his wife back anyway.

The Sarkin Hausawa was unable to settle the dispute, so he instructed the wife to live with her mother until the situation could be resolved. Defying the sarki's authority, Maman and a handful of other men went to his mother-in-law's compound to retrieve the wife a second time. The mother-in-law was praying outside when the men entered the yard. Maman found his wife and allegedly flogged her again. When the mother tried to help her daughter, Maman hit her, too, knocking her to the ground and wounding her left arm. The mother-in-law testified before the alkali that if her daughter wanted to go back with the husband, she would not stop her—but she could never "force her to him."

Though Maman admitted injuring his mother-in-law, the alkali ruled that "the wife in question [must] return to her husband," this a dozen years after she had left him. However, he pronounced that "the court would take away her marriage at the 2nd and 3rd time when one of the abuse laws is touched." The alkali listed out the "abuse laws" in a manner that not only articulated them as the uncontested laws of the land but also established his office as the ultimate authority governing Muslim marriages in the Grassfields:

1. If the husband will not feed his wife.
2. If the husband is not clothing his wife.
3. If the husband give wound on the body of his wife.
4. If the [husband] is not using his wife.[86]

The alkali's didacticism in delivering the verdict was meant to signal his authority over the Sarkin Hausawa of Nsaw, whose judgment to separate the wife from the husband was overturned. Though we do not know whether the wife abided by the alkali's ruling, the proceedings of this case provide an opening through which to discuss the connection between contending forms of patriarchy and ideal relations of belonging. The case demonstrates how legalistic and lived perceptions of male obligations in marriage could differ. The Sarkin Hausawa believed Maman's behavior was oppositional to community lafiya. Maman admitted as much when he offered his mother-in-law 10 shillings for hurting her, which she promptly refused. But the alkali did not deem Maman's actions heinous enough to prohibit him from reclaiming his wife, a decision that was supported both by his interpretation of Islamic law and by his position within the colonial hierarchy of power, trumping the authority of the Hausa sarki. In effect, he elevated Maman's entitlements as a husband over the sarki's role as community patriarch, the latter of which is not sanctioned by Islamic law but is an office borne out of a particular West African historical context. These conflicting realms of patriarchal authority in the diaspora emerged from Hausas' status as native foreigners. For both Hausas and Fulanis, this colonial category precluded them from being allocated culturally and linguistically bound customary courts merely informed by Islamic principles. Rather, Islamic beliefs, practices, and laws were to define these groups and ideal gender relations within them.

A few months after this first case, the alkali complained to the administration that his authority was jeopardized because he was not allowed to "exercise criminal power for at least [two] offences." These offenses were bigamy, defined as "marrying a woman before her divorce has been made absolute" by observing a period of waiting (also known as *idda*), and contempt of court, exemplified by "refusing to obey a lawful order from the Alkali, such as directing a woman to return to her husband with the object of effecting a reconciliation, or refusal to surrender or disclose details of an Estate for probate." The alkali even threatened to resign over the matter: "The Alkali pointed out that [bigamy] must be dealt with criminally under Mohammedan Law, and that unless he had powers to enforce his lawful orders, his authority and the dignity of the court would be destroyed. He felt so strongly on this point, that after the first 'test case' (when a girl of about 19 flatly refused to obey an Order of Court) he tendered his resignation on the grounds that under such conditions the Court would become a farce."[87]

About four months later, the colonial government endorsed the level of jurisdiction the alkali sought. From November 25, 1947 onward, the Northwest alkali's court could try cases of bigamy as criminal offenses, "provided that any sentence imposed shall not exceed six months' imprisonment with or without hard labour." In practice, such stipulations would apply to cases of adultery as well. For contempt of court, the alkali possessed the power to "inflict a fine not exceeding ten pounds or imprisonment with or without hard labour for a term not exceeding one month."[88] That the colonial government sanctioned the alkali's heightened power over women reflects British officers' complicity with local Hausa and Fulani patriarchs, as well as their own gender biases that understood the status and roles of women through women's dependent relationships to men. Indeed, British ideologies of gender, both at home and abroad, required that men define and control women's place in society and that female behavior be "compared against male behaviours."[89]

Reinforcing marriage as the ideal site of belonging for Muslim women therefore became the centerpiece to the alkali's moral and political authority in the Grassfields; transgressions relating to it, along with contempt of court, were the only criminal offenses this civil court could try. Government documents show that British officers in Cameroon did not regard this as a contradictory legal amalgam but rather as part of the logic of Maliki Sharia jurisprudence in which women's marital transgressions "must be dealt with criminally."[90] According to Philippa Levine, such legal transformations reflect the ways in which "colonial policy-making around sexuality derived from ideas of property," especially the "criminalization of a wide range of sexually connected practices." The "passing of property from fathers to husbands" was to be

ensured, in this case through a hybrid colonial and diasporic form of
Islamic law.[91]

$$\blacktriangleright\!\blacktriangleright\!\blacktriangleright\!\bullet\!\blacktriangleleft\!\blacktriangleleft\!\blacktriangleleft$$

Colonial categories and the institutions created to maintain them
arose from the entanglement of various African, Islamic, and colonial
concepts of social order that involved competing quests for belonging at
both community and household levels. Directives under Indirect Rule
resulted in policies that attempted to preserve Hausas' stake in local
communities by reserving them seats on emerging municipal councils,
but that also squeezed them out of the economic sectors from which
they had historically benefited. The different histories of Hausa integration—or lack thereof—in the Grassfields' many chiefdoms influenced
these political dynamics as well, from the chief in Santa who preferred
Hausa representation over educated and potentially rebellious young
men, to the fon of Mankon who sought to subsume Abakwa-Bamenda
under his authority. In response, some Grassfielders like the Akum men
in Santa called for a more democratic process based on majority rule
that would do little to ensure the representation of a minority group
they viewed as possessing distinct cultural boundaries—boundaries
that were enhanced through imperfect colonial categories.

This entanglement of competing claims for social order also involved
reducing the significance of women's roles in making Hausa diaspora
history even as African patriarchs' desires to control women became a
central component in building colonial governance structures. Despite
the power of these dominant narratives and institutions, individuals
did not uniformly share or abide by them, in part because Hausa diaspora communities were home to people of mixed cultural heritage with
varying degrees of allegiance to Islam and its prescriptions concerning
expected gendered behavior. The dispute involving Malam Maman, his
wife, mother-in-law, the Sarkin Hausawa of Nsaw, and the alkali is testament to this fact. Mutual transformation, set in motion through diaspora
and colonialism, generated projects like the alkali court, which institutionalized a particular vision of moral stability and protected, above all
else, men's control over women through marriage. While the case's outcome fulfilled Malam Maman's wishes, it did not negate the twelve years

his wife lived outside of his authority within the refuge offered by her mother and supported by the sarki. Fluid dynamics such as these paint a related, but highly altered, picture of everyday life for Hausas from the one Vollbehr portrayed forty years earlier. While the outcomes of alkali court cases are diverse in their impact on Hausa diaspora individuals, families, and gender relations, what is certain is that without such transformations there would have been no record of Hadija's journey or how she navigated Hausa society and its entanglements in the colonial Grassfields.

Part Two

Part Two

THREE

Slave or Daughter?

IN THE LATE 1940S OR EARLY 1950S, THE SOUTHERN KADUNA town of Lere became the site of social rupture, connection, and transformation in the relations of five individuals. The wealthy merchant Alhaji Gashin Baki, likely with his wife Talle, traveled there from Kano, spending much of his time with the chief of Lere, a Muslim like himself. For reasons contested in memory and in interpretation, the chief of Lere transferred to Gashin Baki his rights in two young women, one unnamed and the other soon to become Hadija. From Lere, Gashin Baki, Talle, Hadija, and the unknown woman traveled southward, descending from the Jos Plateau to cross the Benue River and then gradually ascend into the Grassfields, a distance totaling roughly 850 kilometers. Somewhere along the way, the unknown woman lost her tie to the group through either sale or death. Leaving her behind, Hadija, Talle, and Gashin Baki approached the Ring Road of the Grassfields, probably between We and Nkambe. They would have then headed toward Kom, eventually making their home within the Hausa diaspora enclave of Mme-Bafumen, a hinterland town just north of Fundong.[1]

Hadija and Talle maintained what appears to have been a childless compound, suggesting that neither woman had lived very long in the diaspora prior to their 1952 appearance in the historical record. They swept the grounds, pounded cornmeal, and washed clothes, while Gashin Baki managed his property, including 135 cattle, numerous bolts of cloth, cash, and household appurtenances totaling an estimated 2,180 pounds, a hefty sum for that era. Gashin Baki and Talle might have also been involved in instructing the newly converted Hadija in Islamic modes of prayer and expectations of her behavior in a Hausa household. By February 1952, Talle was pregnant. Gashin Baki would never meet this child, however, for he died of unknown causes not long thereafter, leaving both women to face an unprecedented situation in their lifetimes: they became widows in the diaspora with evidently no kin nearby on whom to rely. This predicament would become particularly acute for Hadija, as rumors of a possible slave status flowed around her, one factor among many that compelled her to take a very different course of action from that of her expectant co-wife following the death of their husband.

Both women were expected to undergo *takaba*, the established period of mourning for widows that lasts four months and ten days, or, in Talle's case, until the birth of her child. Described as "God punish on head" in alkali court documents, widows undergoing takaba must abstain from sexual relations. Takaba is thus similar to idda, though the latter prescribes periods of waiting for women whose marriages are dissolved by death, divorce, or annulment.[2] Completing takaba or idda enables previously married women (*zawarawa*) to contract new marriages. But Hadija apparently did not complete her mourning. Before the 130 days had run its course, she accepted a marriage proposal from an old man named Yusufu. She then requested her guardian and local Islamic teacher, Malam Audu Bakadijuya, to perform the ceremony. Malam Audu was happy to oblige: "then we all Bafumai People we joined at Hausa-chief's gate and we tied the marriage." But the Hausa chief himself, Malam Ibrahim Sarkin Hausawa, did not approve of this union, for he believed that Hadija, Yusufu, and Malam Audu had all gone "against Muhammadan law": he accused them of bigamy and brought his complaint to the alkali at Ndop. On October 8, 1952, the three individuals involved in the marriage traveled 80 kilometers from Mme-Bafumen to defend themselves.

With this series of transfers, losses, unions, and movements, new personal and corporate relations were formed, broken, and questioned—a dynamic combination of processes that flowed into and from the realities of Hausa diaspora life within and beyond the Grassfields. Like many women before her, Hadija had been a non-Muslim, non-Hausa woman before meeting Gashin Baki and Talle. Within the span of perhaps just a few years, she had become Hausa and was now subject to the social and spiritual doctrines embedded in Maliki Islamic law. The participants in this court case and in the history leading up to it were concerned not with Hadija as an isolated individual, but with the nature of her social relations—to the chief of Lere and her deceased husband, and to her co-wife, guardian, and groom.

These relationships and the gendered power inequalities embedded in them were vital to Hausa diaspora formation and everyday life. A close reading of the court case demonstrates, moreover, that contestations over how people should and did belong in the diaspora arose from these inequalities as well as from competing memories of the past. Hadija and those around her worked with and struggled against each other to negotiate the meanings of marriage, patronage, and political authority in decidedly paradoxical ways. On the one hand, the entanglement of Hausa social mores, Islamic law, local political structures, and colonial rule primarily determined the discourses of belonging articulated in this case. On the other hand, this very same entanglement produced ambiguities regarding acceptable forms of female dependency and patriarchal control. Court testimonies show, too, how distance and death could transform from factors that caused extreme social rupture and isolation into novel resources of power for people like Hadija who used their relative anonymity to make and remake history. Diaspora allows for such transformations, and it was through these transformations and the uncertainties they produced that Hadija defended her personal vision of belonging in the Grassfields.

⧯⧯⧯•⧯⧯⧯

When the courtroom drama began, the Sarkin Hausawa of Mme-Bafumen laid out his charge against Malam Audu Bakadijuya, Hadija, and Yusufu, a charge that centered on illicit sexual behavior between a widow and a man she was not divinely approved to marry. In tying the blasphemous marriage at his gate, the sarki believed the ceremony created disharmony within his community and, as a consequence, these three individuals directly challenged his authority. The accused pleaded guilty to the charges, admitting that the marriage did indeed occur before Hadija had completed takaba. Though they would not deny the objective truth of what had happened, they nonetheless marshaled defenses against a probable guilty verdict by professing ignorance. According to all three, none of them, not even Hadija, had been aware at the time that the marriage had interfered with her observance of takaba.[3]

Malam Audu was certain that Hadija was not "with the God punish" when he tied the marriage, and Hadija stated that she simply agreed to become Yusufu's wife after he proposed to her. Yusufu told the alkali he did not even know who Hadija was until some months beforehand when Malam Audu's sister encouraged him to consider marrying a widow who "will get out from God punish." Within a matter of days, Yusufu offered 40 shillings to a man named Baba Takum, presumably the head of household where Hadija had been living during her mourning period. With this offering, Yusufu declared his intention to marry Hadija even though he was about to leave Mme-Bafumen on business. Upon his return twenty-two days later, he met with Hadija, and to his chagrin she refused him. He left a second time. After fifteen days, he came back to propose again, but to no avail. Having given up, he decided to move on with his travels by planning a trip to Kurmi in Nigeria. The night before his journey, Yusufu was preparing his belongings when a woman arrived at his home. Hadija had sent her there as a messenger to request his presence. Yusufu went to Hadija at once, and, according to his testimony, "she said now she want me with marriage." To assure her of his promise, he gave her 5 shillings. The next morning he was off to Kurmi, leaving Hadija behind for an entire month. After this long separation, the two arranged for a Friday marriage within three days of his return to Mme-Bafumen. "Then," said Yusufu, "we sleep Saturday Sunday," intimating the consummation of their union.

In relaying this information to the court—a story in which travel marked the passage of time—Yusufu was asking the alkali to give him the benefit of the doubt. He knew Hadija had been widowed, and he knew she was observing takaba. But after such a drawn-out courtship lasting well over two months, he was certain that Hadija had finished her period of mourning and was therefore available for marriage and the related requirement of sexual intimacy. But then Yusufu informed the court that after their two nights together as husband and wife, the following Monday Hadija sent someone to him to say she did not like him after all. "Then I buy 100 kola-nuts," said Yusufu, "to make sacrifices for the sake this marriage divorced." Likewise, Hadija ended her initial testimony with this solemn admission: "Now the marriage was spoil, no marriage between us." The accused were thus on trial for an illicit marriage that had already run its course.

Up to this point, the court case exemplifies an unremarkable tale of a Hausa widow in search of a new husband, an old man looking for a younger wife, a courtship and brief marriage gone sour, and either an innocent misunderstanding or deliberate evasion of an Islamic tenet. Just as we find in Hausa society in Northern Nigeria at the time, divorce figured persistently and recurrently in the diaspora. Although Hausa social convention treats marriage as the normal condition of adulthood, its impermanence contradicts such precepts. It was estimated in the 1950s that Northern Nigerian Hausa women probably averaged three or four marriages before menopause.[4] Marital careers were thus highly individualistic and varied considerably. As such, the precise reasoning behind Hadija's desire to end her short-lived marriage to Yusufu remains difficult to deduce—at least beyond the apparent lack of fondness. Historically, Hausas have generally believed that women should not be forced to remain with their husbands if they genuinely oppose or reject them.[5] Though Hadija's final rejection of Yusufu may have been all that was needed to summon a divorce between the newlyweds, the motivations that guided her initial wish to remarry on the heels of her period of mourning are another matter entirely.

The stakes for abiding by the social norms of marriage and the tensions accompanying them were steepened when, seemingly out of nowhere, the court asked Malam Audu about the relationship between Hadija and her late husband, Alhaji Gashin Baki: "Is the woman is a slave [sic] or she is a daughter?" The malam replied in a decisive manner, "She is a slave, but she is not daughter." Hadija then retorted, disputing Malam Audu's knowledge of her status by asking him if he personally witnessed or possessed written proof of Gashin Baki's supposed purchase of her person: "I want Court to ask [Malam Audu] the time the late Alhaji bought is he present or where is the latter [sic] given to him by the late that he bought me, make he showed the latter [sic] to the Court."

Why the court had cause to inquire about Hadija's social status while tied to Gashin Baki is not apparent in the records of this case. The distinction between being "a slave" and "a daughter," however, is significant for reasons that are germane to this lawsuit and to our broader concern with the roles of women in Hausa diaspora migration and settlement. To express the question of female social status in terms of the oppositional dyad of slave or daughter, rather than slave or free person, is to indicate a highly contextualized and gendered conceptualization of slavery itself. A woman's status as a recognized member—a daughter—of her kin group, or as a slave beholden to that kin group had an important bearing on her rights and obligations both before and after she experienced a transfer from one guardian to another through marriage, commercial exchange, or inheritance. This is precisely what the court was attempting to determine, given particular imperatives governing women's responsibilities to husbands and owners under Maliki Islamic law. Yet, as this story unfolds in this and the following chapters, it will show that the relationship between female enslavement and marriage in many West African contexts was often less diametrically oppositional than it was conceptually ambiguous. The precepts of Islamic law, which were given great authority over the affairs of Muslim women under late colonial rule in the Grassfields, also contained discourses analogizing marriage to slavery.[6] Such relational significance between marriage and female enslavement not only affected legalistic outcomes but also provided opportunities for individuals to assert their status in new and contending ways in the diaspora. Hadija's mid-century travails also stress how slavery continued to shape long-distance networks, Hausa settlement patterns, and Hausa conceptions of wealth and masculinity, so much so that the idea of her being a servile concubine could serve as a powerful and widely understood trope.[7]

Theoretically, if the court were to prove Hadija's slave status, the case against the three defendants would be rendered moot, for the Maliki code of law stipulates that the length of takaba for a slave-concubine is equal to one period of menstruation or one month, a much shorter duration than the period of retreat for a free woman.[8] Had Hadija been

sanctioned to observe the briefer period of mourning that enslaved concubines typically practiced, her union with Yusufu would have been licit.
This logic explains why it might have been in Malam Audu's personal
interest to claim that Hadija was a slave. If he were to prove her unfree
status, then he could avoid a guilty verdict. In so doing, he could safeguard his local prestige as an Islamic scholar and teacher and retain his
guardianship over Hadija.

In response to these accusations, Hadija wielded what knowledge of
jurisprudence she had to take a stand for herself in a room full of men.
She stressed the importance of the eyewitness and the written record to
challenge the malam as he attempted to describe a past that she believed
was hers alone to author. While Gashin Baki's death left Hadija vulnerable to the whims of community patriarchs, her specific diasporic condition also armed her with new knowledge and a concealed biography that
she was willing and able to use in declaring her status as a free woman.
For its part, the court recognized the impasse it had reached, unable to
determine culpability for the parties accused, due to Hadija's contested
status. The alkali adjourned the case for three months, requesting the
presence of more witnesses, including Hadija's co-wife, whom he hoped
would provide an answer to the question at hand.

▶▶▶╏◦╏◀◀◀

When the court reconvened in January 1953, the plaintiff and three
defendants were joined by a number of people, all of whom made competing claims over Hadija's status.[9] The alkali began that day's proceedings by starting where he had left off, asking Malam Audu if he could
defend his assertion that Hadija was in fact Gashin Baki's slave rather
than his Muslim wife. His reply was at once direct and obscure: "I know
the chief of Lere received 10 bags from Alhaji Gashin Baki then give him
Hadija . . . and another woman."[10]

Hadija immediately denied Malam Audu's version of history:

> It is not so, about the 10 bags which [Malam Audu] is talking yes the chief of
> Lere has received 10 bags from the late Alhaji G. Baki my husband, but the
> 10 bags was paid to late before the chief of Lere take me and give to the late
> Alhaji for that good man who done to him. And the late have tied marriage
> with me before he put this Hadija (F) for me.[11]

In narrating her understanding of the past, Hadija attempted to project her word as a reliable source based on a first-hand account. Not only did she use the opportunity to once again stress her lawful claim on Gashin Baki as her husband, but she also refuted Malam Audu's assertion that the monetary transaction between the chief of Lere and Gashin Baki designated her lot as a slave-concubine. Malam Audu believed that Gashin Baki purchased Hadija and another woman as slaves with "10 bags," presumably ten bags of cowry shells, which were still used in parts of Nigeria as late as the 1940s, especially in transferring rights over women.[12] Hadija, however, insisted that no such purchase had taken place—that the chief's receipt of the ten bags concerned an entirely separate, unspecified matter. Rather, in an act independent of monetary exchange, the chief of Lere offered her as a bride to show his gratitude for benefits he derived from the presence of the "good" Hausa merchant.

This was not the end of Hadija's story, however. She deemed it important to tell the court that she had only become Hadija, a common namesake for Muslim women, on becoming Gashin Baki's wife. This renaming indicates that Hadija had not been Muslim before encountering Gashin Baki. Had she already practiced Islam, there would have been no reason for Gashin Baki to change her name.[13] In emphasizing the linkage between her renaming and her marriage, Hadija attempted to secure the alkali's confidence in her as a defendant, a knowledgeable witness, and a free Muslim woman. She wanted the court to understand, perhaps as she did, that her renaming unequivocally symbolized her conversion to Islam and status as a wife. For Hadija, marriage, religious conversion, and naming operated in tandem, and her husband was responsible for enacting all three. As he orchestrated her indoctrination into Hausa and Islamic ways, he likewise fashioned her status as a free Muslim woman of the diaspora. Her status, now enhanced because of her connection to the wealthy merchant, was intimately tied up with his intentions, and, to all who distrusted her, Hadija affirmed that she understood those intensions perfectly.

Hadija was unwavering in defending her status and her past. Nevertheless, the historical circumstances near the time of her birth and her later transfer to Gashin Baki present the possibility that she and Malam Audu could have both been right. While Chapter 4 will further examine the various distinctions between marriage and concubinage in Hausa and Grassfields societies, specific changes in recruiting girls for concubinage had already been underway in Northern Nigeria by the time Hadija was born. These fluid circumstances could mean that Hadija was theoretically both free and enslaved. According to Islamic law, free women could never become concubines. But when the British abolished slavery in Northern Nigeria for persons born after 1901, one consequence was that by the 1920s, men who desired concubines no longer had a pool of slaves from which to purchase girls, usually fourteen or fifteen years of age. Elite men then began to accept a new source of girls through legal innovation. According to Paul Lovejoy and Jan Hogendorn, "As the availability of slave women declined . . . masters [pressed] the free daughters of their slaves into concubinage. The servile status of the parents was considered inheritable as far as the eligibility of girls for concubinage was concerned, even though the girls were technically born free."[14] By 1924, this practice was so well established that the vast majority of girls headed for a life of concubinage were recruited from servile families. Moreover, the right of guardianship (*wali*) that masters wielded over their slaves aided this legal transformation, as masters extended it to their slaves' free daughters.[15]

Given the ubiquity and persistence of these dynamics into the 1940s in Hausaland, and given the role Hausas played as subcolonial district heads among non-Muslim peoples near Lere, it is altogether possible that Alhaji Gashin Baki and the Muslim chief of Lere put these transformations into practice to legitimate Hadija's exchange. Her parents could have been slaves or servants to the chief of Lere, thereby allowing the chief to operate as Hadija's guardian.[16] It is also possible that Hadija's non-Muslim parents deposited her as a pawn, a practice that revived amid the hardships experienced during the Depression and perhaps the Second World War.[17] Given the nature of Lere's political hierarchy in the 1940s, Hadija could have been directly enslaved as well. In the nineteenth century, Hausa-Fulani emirate forces obtained many slaves from the region around Lere by military means and through "discretionary slave removal." Though such actions were officially outlawed under colonial rule, the British authorized Hausa-Fulani Muslim chiefs to politically and socially oppress Lere's non-Muslim inhabitants, a structure that would have afforded chiefs many opportunities to capitalize on their positions of power.[18]

However he acquired her, the chief of Lere intended to transform his power and control over this young female into a tool of patronage and economic gain by transferring her as a concubine to his allies and clients. These circumstances do not preclude the possibility that Gashin Baki manumitted Hadija first before marrying her.[19] In any case, it is very likely that this context accounts in some way for what happened to Hadija before she headed toward the Grassfields. But, if the court records are accurate, Hadija chose not to divulge anything about her life prior to joining Gashin Baki. Rather, she constructed a personal narrative of the more immediate past as evidence supporting her insistence that she had once been someone's daughter who later became a Hausa man's wife.

After she spoke, both her supporters and naysayers in the court that day shared oral accounts based on their earlier interactions with Gashin Baki, divulging what he had told them about Hadija and what she had meant to him as a companion. In this vein, Malam Audu tried to reinforce his position by relaying a conversation he had with Gashin Baki concerning the inheritance of his property: "I know one thing that [Hadija] is a slave, because I was told by the late Alhaji Gashin Baki that if he died [Hadija] will not going succeed him except £50." With this information, Malam Audu was able to introduce critical elements from a separate court case regarding the inheritance of Gashin Baki's estate. Undoubtedly because Gashin Baki was wealthy, the case drew the attention of an inquisitive British colonial official. In a letter addressed to the senior district officer in Bamenda, the Wum district officer wrote about Hadija in particular, designating her a "slave wife" in the colonial record. He was distressed that the alkali had incorrectly allocated the "slave wife" the same amount in the estate distribution as Gashin Baki's senior wife, Talle, a total of just over 122 pounds.[20] Consequently, the officer ordered a "suspension of the judgment." Citing the district officer of Kano, whom he believed possessed greater knowledge than the alkali regarding Islamic jurisprudence, the Grassfields officer reiterated that "no slave can inherit his or her master's property on the latter's death." Muslim widows could indeed inherit a share of their husbands' property as well as own land. Such entitlements were unavailable to female slaves—concubines or otherwise—at least without consent from their masters.

Because Gashin Baki apparently wanted to bequeath Hadija only 50 pounds, less than half of what she would have been legally entitled to as a wife, Malam Audu believed this was the proof needed to substantiate her enslavement. In so doing, Malam Audu hoped not only to challenge the reliability of Hadija's testimony, but also to cement her status as a slave in the minds of community members and in the pages of the written legal record. A clear advocate of the perceived status quo, the Wum district officer was determined to do likewise in a move so characteristic of the contradictions embedded in colonial governance. Even though the British had formally abolished slavery in Northern Nigeria by 1936, a full sixteen years before Hadija's trial, they were disinclined to meddle with domestic enslavement, largely for the purpose of keeping African patriarchal structures intact. Ibrahim Jumare, Paul Lovejoy, and Jan Hogendorn have all noted that the colonial regime in Northern Nigeria was particularly reluctant to condemn concubinage in order to maintain the loyalty of the aristocracy.[21] Such a stance echoes the many British officers of Cameroon who stood by the administration's decision to allow the alkali court to try civil matters only, with significant exceptions for the criminal acts of bigamy and contempt of court.[22]

Despite Malam Audu's entreaties, the alkali remained unconvinced that Hadija's relationship to Gashin Baki was one of unequivocal bondage. The court decided to continue its examination of witnesses. A man named Sa'idu unhelpfully remarked that "Hadija was given to Alhaji Gashin Baki by the Chief of Lere." Malam Ibrahim, the sarki of Mme-Bafumen and plaintiff in the case, contradicted the statements of Malam Audu by affirming that Hadija was indeed "Alhaji Gashin Baki's wife not his slave as they are talking." And yet another individual merely stated that he saw Hadija and Gashin Baki together but had no knowledge of Hadija's status.

The court then turned to two new witnesses, H. Adama and Gashin Baki's wife, Talle. The outcome of their testimonies was as equally contentious as those above. H. Adama's recollections added specificity to the transaction that placed Hadija under Gashin Baki's authority, while Talle's statements brought greater insight into the more intimate details

of how the two women related to each other and to Gashin Baki. First it
was H. Adama who made his declaration: "I was told by the late since he
is in life that he was given Hadija as wife by the Chief of Lere ... during
the time he went there he borrow the chief of Lere money. When he was
short for tax money, the chief of Lere give him Hadija as wife not slave."
Through H. Adama's testimony, the litigants and alkali learned that the
chief of Lere desperately needed tax money to pay the British administration. Because he was a wealthy trader and, according to Hadija, a
"good man," Gashin Baki decided to lend money to the chief in his time
of need, and in return the chief was happy to offer the young Hadija as
his new bride.[23] Unfortunately, the details of taxes, debt, and lending in
Lere could still not prove or disprove that Hadija was a slave who was
gifted or traded as a form of payment. What is clear, however, is that colonial demands for taxes, collected by chiefs and African district heads,
coalesced with pre-colonial gendered patterns of exchange between local
rulers and long-distance merchants to occasion the obscure transfer of
this young woman from one man to another.[24]

H. Adama clearly desired to see Hadija incorporated as a free woman
in Mme-Bafumen. Talle, on the other hand, was determined to relegate
Hadija to a history of slavery while protecting her own social standing
in the diaspora:

> Yes I do hear [Malam Audu's and Hadija's] talks both of them, but Hadija
> is a slave of the late Alhaji Gashin Baki. He didn't married her as daughter,
> because I will cook twice and the Hadija once.... Our knights [sic] they same
> because my own is two times and Hadija once.... I got no witness and I can't
> swear but if the Hadija knows that she is not a slave make she swear.

In providing the court with such a detailed, intimate account of her
life with Hadija, Talle attempted to secure her own supremacy in the
hierarchy of women once belonging to Gashin Baki's compound. She
emphasized this when she brought up the matter of "cooking," an erotic
euphemism implying a woman's provision of both domestic and sexual
services. To say that she "cooked" for the late Gashin Baki two times
to Hadija's one implies that Talle had more "nocturnal access" to her
husband.[25]

If the colonial officer in Wum had been concerned about this aspect of
the case, he likely would have turned to F. H. Ruxton's colonial handbook

for Maliki law, a summary of French translations of the fourteenth-century text, the *Mukhtaṣar*. In reading Ruxton's text, the officer would have noted a contradiction between the law and Talle's testimony. According to Ruxton, "every husband shall . . . spend an equal number of nights with each of his wives. He need not, however, have an equal amount of sexual intercourse with each, but may follow his own desires." Moreover, "each wife, whether slave, Muhammadan, Christian or Jewess, has equal claims on the husband's time."[26] If Ruxton was correct, Talle's experience as the wife with greater access to her husband had historical antecedents that lay beyond Malikite norms, indicating a highly syncretic understanding of Islam in Hausa diaspora society. In her analysis of marriage and slavery in early Islamic legal writings, legal and religious studies scholar, Kecia Ali states that most schools of Islamic jurisprudence did accept that a man who was "married to both a free woman and an enslaved woman owed two nights to the free woman for every night spent with the slave." Malik, however, was an exception. In his *Mudawwana* he "consistently differentiated less between enslaved and free people than his counterparts. He seems to have held that both free and slave wives were to receive the same number of nights." One area where the *Mudawwana* differs from colonial interpretations of the *Mukhtaṣar* is the idea that wives or concubines could make claims on their husbands' time: "At stake, rather, was the husband's freedom to spend his time as he chose as opposed to the wife's right to a portion of his time."[27]

According to Lovejoy's research on female enslavement in Northern Nigeria, despite the inconsistencies of these Malikite tenets, or perhaps because of them, "men did not always follow . . . norms"; however, "women from respectable families could expect husbands to do so."[28] In the public forum of the alkali court, Talle at once endeavored to establish her respectability and position as the free and privileged wife while insinuating that Hadija embodied the ultimate antithesis of these qualities. Whether Hadija was her husband's slave-concubine or her junior wife, Talle likely believed, as many women in mid-century Hausaland did, that mothers-in-law and senior wives could treat any new woman of the household—free or unfree—as subordinate.

Part of the explanation behind this household hierarchy in Hausa-speaking communities may be found in the ambiguity that could cloud the division of women into categories of wife and slave-concubine. For instance, men of limited means who could not afford a substantial bride-wealth could take slaves as wives. In other situations, kinship groups have appended outsiders by incorporating slave women and their off-spring as the wives and children of the owner.[29] More specific to the time period considered here, historian Barbara Cooper has shown that with the gradual abolition of slavery in French-occupied Maradi, Niger, a process beginning in 1901, master–slave relations were "remapped" onto interactions between senior women and junior wives within Hausa households. One manifestation of this change, which occurred primarily between c. 1920 and 1945, was that the labor of junior wives replaced slave labor. Cooper also indicates that as "colonial rule continued and access to slaves from elsewhere declined . . . issues surrounding the control of women became more acute, and were expressed in terms of differences between 'legitimate' wives and concubines, and between 'Muslim' and non-Muslim women." Moreover, the "ranking of wives could mask the friction generated by an unequal division of labor as rivalry between women, seen throughout Hausaland as inherently contentious, deceit-ful, and 'jealous.'"[30]

Indeed, it is quite evident that Talle intentionally belittled Hadija's role in Gashin Baki's household by denying her the status of a legitimate *kishiya*, or co-wife. Though the root word for *kishiya* is *kishi*, or jealousy, it is a characterization that belies the fact that co-wives have often provided one another important practical and emotional support.[31] In refusing to claim Hadija as her own kishiya, however, perhaps Talle was trying to mark her as someone socially and sexually insignificant in their house-hold, someone who was not worthy of inciting feelings of jealousy—es-pecially given that she had recently given birth to a daughter, a likely product of the greater access to her husband she enjoyed. Then again, whereas a man's first marriage was often a political contract between his family and that of his wife, it was common for a man to choose a junior wife or concubine out of love and desire. A Muslim Fulani woman of the Grassfields, now widow of a once prominent leader, remembered how much she had loved her husband. The love went unrequited, however, for even though she gave birth to four children, including the heir to his title, she always felt that he loved his slave-concubines more than he ever loved her.[32]

With the formal, though by no means actual, end of slavery in Northern Nigeria in 1936, Talle, as a newly widowed woman, probably felt she had a particular social position and reputation to carve out in the diaspora. Hadija's potentially low social ranking as a slave and her allegedly illicit behavior in marrying Yusufu together provided Talle with an opportunity to claim that respectability. Of course, Talle's assertions could have also been motivated by a desire of a more materialistic kind—to place into her hands and out of Hadija's a greater proportion of her deceased's husband estate.

Whatever Talle's motivations, Gashin Baki made it clear to the men around him that Hadija should inherit some portion of his wealth, be it because of moral obligations, affections, or both. According to Malam Audu, in one of their last moments together, Gashin Baki told him that "if he died make they hold Hadija fine"—make sure someone takes care of her. Similarly, Gashin Baki's adult son Sanda, who with his brother Wada traveled to the Grassfields from Kano to be at their father's side, tried to explain with greater clarity how his father, with his death in sight, had envisioned Hadija's place within the family: "I know when I came from Kano the late called me inside his room and called Hadiza then he asked me who is this, I replied for him is my mother. Then the late although he died Hadiza is owing him £50 make we pay her and after that hold her fine as our mother." Whether or not Sanda knew Hadija before his journey to the Grassfields is unknown. It is apparent, however, that Gashin Baki was determined to ensure Hadija's well-being after his death, so much so that he sought confirmation from his grown son that he might look upon Hadija in the same manner as he would his own mother.

Despite the sincerity of Sanda's recollections, Hadija's status remained unclear. On the one hand, Gashin Baki's children might care for Hadija as their mother, suggesting but certainly not proving her status as a free woman. On the other hand, the 50-pound allotment was, again, lower than her share had she been a legitimate wife. Moreover, Gashin Baki's insistence on securing money and support for Hadija in his oral will, communicated to confidants, points to her potential vulnerability as an enslaved woman: why else would Gashin Baki mandate setting aside money for her if she were a legitimate wife whose inheritance was guaranteed through Islamic legal processes?

After much debate consisting exclusively of conflicting testimonies, the court turned to its last and frequently used resort, the Qur'an. Responding to Talle's provocation, the court asked Hadija, "Are you going to swear on Muhammadan Kuran that the late have married you, you are not a slave for him?" In asking her this question, the court did not present the Qur'an as a legal text but as a talisman, indicating that the trial would be decided by ordeal and not by law. This is the ordeal of *mubahala*, which requires an individual to swear on a statement as both "a conditional curse" and "a purifying oath" in order to strengthen his or her assertion. A liar who swears an oath of mubahala will suffer a great misfortune within the coming year, possibly death. While Talle could have undergone mubahala herself in order to strengthen her testimony against Hadija, doing so might have endangered her or her infant daughter. Moreover, as people usually regard "the call to the ordeal [as] more important than the execution," Talle derived a measure of social and spiritual power from instigating mubahala and exposing Hadija to Allah's curse while protecting herself and her child.[33]

Despite the risks involved, Hadija confidently replied to the court, "Yes I am going to swear on Muhammadan Kuran that the late have married me, I am not his slave." After receiving approval from the male litigants that she might swear on the Qur'an, Hadija did so. Those present in the courtroom no longer contested her word, whether they believed her or not. It was now up to Allah to decide her punishment if she had lied. But the alkali was left perplexed by Hadija's sinful actions during her period of mourning: "You know that you are not a slave then why [when] you make Takaba . . . you didn't make as God said?" Hadija offered a telling admission, a sign of her incomplete inculcation into Muslim Hausa ways: "I never know, and they didn't informed me the months I will make Takaba."

The court could now determine culpability. Hadija and Malam Audu were to blame for the sacrilegious and short-lived marriage between Hadija and Yusufu. The court found Yusufu not guilty, however, because he too swore on the Qur'an, stating he was unaware that Hadija had been observing takaba when they consummated their marriage. The court mufuti thus wrote the following verdict:

> What was in Muhammadan law book since the Hadija have swear Kuran that she was married by the late Alhaji there fore [sic] she is a wife to the late and she go against Muhammadan law for having no make (Takaba) for four months and ten days there fore she for the wife will pay £10 fine, and [Malam Audu] who is the guardian will pay £5 fine, but [Yusufu] have take oath on Muhammadan Kuran that he didn't know that Hadija is a wife and he didn't heard that Hadija have succeed the late.
>
> Charge: Finding [Malam Audu] the guardian £5 fine and [Hadija] the bridal with £10 fine and 10/- costs.[34]

There is no certainty that the people of Mme-Bafumen ceased questioning Hadija's social status or servile origins. But about eight months after the trial, the Bamenda senior district officer put the worries of the Wum officer to rest on the matter: "In the case of Hadeji's status as a full wife. This point has been further confirmed in court as the result of a subsequent criminal action taken against her for not observing the law regarding Tenabu."[35] Considering that Hadija resolved her own trial by undergoing the ordeal of mubahala, it appears that a reserve of spiritual power was available to women, including perhaps a female slave, in asserting and proving her personal claims of belonging to an Islamic court and through it to the colonial state.[36]

▶▶▶•◀◀◀

In this story, Hausa diaspora individuals related to each other through marriage, bondage, friendship, community authority, and filial devotion. The establishment of the alkali court in the Grassfields ensured that these participants not only expressed themselves through the form of testimony but also spoke for the dead. Everything they uttered about their own experiences and social positions stood in relation to some other person, whether that person was alive or deceased. As much as kinship obligations, fondness, or economic interests shaped these relations of belonging, they were just as equally defined by tensions, even animosity, borne out of the power asymmetries that made some people much more vulnerable than others in this small corner of the Hausa diaspora world.

This trial illuminates social inequalities based on gender difference and status, and it reveals how these unequal relations of power changed in meaning as people traveled into and negotiated the diaspora—a context at once framed by Hausa social norms, Islamic law, colonial rule, and local Grassfields societies. To create a sense of social order amidst a growing population of Muslim "native foreigners" in the Grassfields, especially Fulanis and Hausas, the British institutionalized the patriarchal rights and obligations associated with a hybrid form of Maliki Islamic law. In bringing a charge of bigamy against Hadija, Yusufu, and Malam Audu, Malam Ibrahim Sarkin Hausawa utilized these laws to exercise and reaffirm his moral authority as Hausa chief of Mme-Bafumen, a position he inhabited through transformations in Hausa titles on becoming permanent strangers to local Grassfields hosts. For their part, Hadija and Yusufu attempted to follow Islamic norms governing the termination and commencement of marital unions, but they also drew from non-Hausa or pre-Islamic Hausa ideas that permit women to leave undesirable marriages without having to prove abuse or neglect on the part of the husband.

Patriarchal authority in Hausa diaspora households and communities thus emanated from multiple sources of knowledge and power. The debates in this court case indicate that such entanglements provided opportunities for individuals to use their dominant social positions to bar marginalized individuals from belonging to the community in the ways that they sought. But the entanglements also opened possibilities for even the most vulnerable to wield state-sanctioned and divinely ordered patriarchy to work in their favor. When coupling this paradoxical dynamic with the fact that death and distance could cause both painful rupture and empowerment through the severing of social ties, it is clear that these diasporic transformations formed a double-edged sword thrust between profound structural inequalities and human agency.

Questions over the nature of Hadija's relationship with Gashin Baki brought many individuals together to effectively assess problems of status, knowledge, and authority within a community that straddled both local and distant contexts. For Hadija, it may appear that her union with Gashin Baki was one that existed in memory only. However, Gashin Baki's ties to her and to Talle outlived his death, shaping their lives as widows of one kind or another, influencing their actions and their words as they both attempted to craft a place for themselves in local society. This duality of death differentially affected Gashin Baki's male and female survivors, just as it did Talle and Hadija, whose potentially distinct social rankings were never questioned while Gashin Baki was still alive. These were questioned only after he died, a point in time when Hadija lost her direct, visible linkage to Hausa diaspora society, and with it Gashin Baki's personal articulation of what he intended Hadija's social standing to be. As a consequence, she was both more vulnerable to the conflicting memories and interests of those who would come to surround her and yet more free to forge the kind of ties she desired.

Gashin Baki's death and this court trial each represent peripeteia, a turning point, in Hadija's life where her fortunes were ambiguously reversed. When she lost Gashin Baki, she lost her immediate relation to Hausa society in the Grassfields. Entering takaba gave her time to mourn Gashin Baki and to contemplate the options she had in refashioning her ties to the community. Because she and those around her possessed different forms of knowledge, memory, and social power, her mourning and subsequent decision to integrate herself as Yusufu's Hausa wife caused the alarm and contestation so clearly described in the alkali court documents. Yet the trial, its verdict, and the records produced revealed another turning point so central to Hadija's experiences and to the Hausa world more broadly: the role of marriage and female enslavement in the making of diasporic space. Through marriage or concubinage, Gashin Baki acquired a new companion and heightened prestige as Hadija took her first steps into the diaspora. While their story is remarkable in the manner of its archival inscription, the following chapter shows that it was not a unique point of reversal in the lives of Grassfields Hausas but was in fact foundational to them.

Figure 1. "Military station in Bamenda with a Hausa village in the foreground," Ernst Vollbehr, watercolor, c. 1912. Used with permission of the Basel Mission Archives / Basel Mission Holdings.

Figure 2. This image has two different captions in the archive. As a photograph, it was described as "Haussas on trek with donkeys." On becoming a postcard, the scene became, "A Hausa caravan in the Grassfields in Cameroon (West-Africa)." Wilhelm Zürcher, photograph, 1932–1939. Used with permission of the Basel Mission Archives / Basel Mission Holdings.

Figure 3. King Fonyonga II of Bali-Nyonga, "wearing a hausa [*sic*] robe." Gottleib Friedrich Spellenberg, photograph, Bali, 1902–1903. Used with permission of the Basel Mission Archives / Basel Mission Holdings.

Figure 4. "Hausa Chief and his attendants at the Sowing Festival." Anna Wuhrmann, photograph, Fumban, 1915. Used with permission of the Basel Mission Archives / Basel Mission Holdings.

Figure 5. "Hausa butchers on the market in Fumban." Martin Göhring, photograph, 1905–1912. Note the line of musicians on the right. Used with permission of the Basel Mission Archives / Basel Mission Holdings.

Figure 6. "A Hausa musician outside the mission house in Fumban." Anna Wuhrmann, photograph, 1911–1915. Used with permission of the Basel Mission Archives / Basel Mission Holdings.

Figure 7. One of King Njoya's wives using the Hausa treadle loom, a significant innovation given that weaving had previously been the sole province of men. "Untitled," Anna Wuhrmann, photograph, 1911–1915. Used with permission of the Basel Mission Archives / Basel Mission Holdings.

Figure 8. Hausa malams fabricated amulets (*laya*) by writing Qur'anic verses on small pieces of paper, which were then sewn into leather pouches and usually tied about the neck as a form of medicine to ward off evil. This watercolor depicts a young, elite Bamum woman wearing Hausa amulets at the nape of her neck. Ernst Vollbehr, watercolor, c. 1912. Used with permission of the Basel Mission Archives / Basel Mission Holdings.

Figure 9. "Nzinzie, the Hausa wife of King Ndjoya," Anna Wuhrmann, photograph, Bamum, 1911–1915. Used with permission of the Basel Mission Archives / Basel Mission Holdings.

Figure 10. "Haussatänzerin (Bamenda)," Ernst Vollbehr, gouache on paper, c.1911. Used with permission of the Leibniz-Institute for Regional Geography, Archive for Geography.

Figure 11. In the 1950s, Aishatu Ibrahim traveled with her daughter, Rahila, and a friend to visit another friend, Niera, who lived in Enugu, Nigeria. The style of contrasting articles of cloth signified Hausa women's affection for one another and the desire to create nonhierarchical, sisterly ties (*'kawa*). Clockwise from the upper left: Aishatu Ibrahim, Niera, the daughter of the Sarkin Hausawa of Mme-Bafumai, and Rahila. Photograph taken in Enugu, c. 1955. Courtesy of Aishatu Ibrahim.

Figure 12. Mairam "Mairo" Suleman was born in Kano. She traveled to the
Grassfields near the turn of the twentieth century and was a member of a
Hausa delegation that came to Bamenda from Fumban during the First
World War. She was the senior wife (*uwar gida*) of Bamenda's first limam,
stepmother of Limam Alhaji Baba Malam Shuaibu, and mother-in-law
of Aishatu Ibrahim. Photographer and date are unknown. Courtesy of
Aishatu Ibrahim.

FOUR

First Reversal
Marriage and Enslavement

HADIJA'S PREDICAMENT, SO PUBLICLY DEBATED AND SCRUTI-nized, points to the complexities of diaspora life that emerged from the layers of legal, moral, and cultural knowledge that accompanied Hausas and others who joined them as they settled in the Grassfields. Social status, gender roles, and the lawfulness of sexual intimacy loomed large for community patriarchs, commoners, and colonial officials. The question of Hadija's social status set in relation to Alhaji Gashin Baki's ambiguous intentions reveals debates on Islamic and Hausa practices of slavery and marriage that did not merely float along with individuals migrating into the diaspora. These institutions were central to ramifying Hausa diaspora networks and establishing settlements, and in turn they shaped people's experiences of travel, strangerhood, and living at a distance. In effect, marriage was recalibrated through the "necessary mathematics of distance."[1] For immigrant women in particular, distance and dislocation from consanguine relations or other cultural resources placed even greater importance on marital bonds as a form of belonging, as the fall into kinlessness in severing those ties could form a gendered space of diasporic liminality, just as it did for Hadija and even for Talle. As noted in Chapter 1, men, too, relied on their unions with women to strengthen corporate networks, to enhance their wealth and prestige in acquiring

dependents, and to signify their mark on the landscape through establishing a family compound. In short, the conceptual linkages between
marriage and female enslavement were a precondition of the diaspora
and formed the terrain upon which women and men contested ideal
forms of relation.

Discussing female enslavement in tandem with marriage may seem
a controversial point of departure for a study of gender and diaspora.
But the fact that Hadija's court case critically brings these institutions
together indicates that the connection between them was important
enough for historical actors in the Grassfields to investigate and, hence,
important enough to analyze as a central aspect of Hausa diaspora life
as late as the 1950s. The relationship between marriage and enslavement
must be explored in light of the multiple historical influences at play for
Muslim Hausas in the Cameroon highlands. Meanings and practices of
female enslavement and marriage in and around the Grassfields, from
the Hausa world of Northern Nigeria, and within Maliki Islamic jurisprudence all require examination. First, however, this chapter builds
from Hadija's first reversal connecting her to Gashin Baki. Bringing
her story together with oral histories of elderly Hausas living in the
Grassfields will demonstrate that a range of unions between men and
women were not only a fact of the Hausa diaspora but made its existence
possible.

▶▶▶┃•┃◀◀◀

When Malam Baba came to Bamenda from Fumban in late January 1916, he arrived as part of Galadima's entourage of more than fifty
people. He was a cleric and a trader, and district officer George Sibbit
Podevin soon understood that this wealthy man had come to lead the
reestablishment of the Hausa community at Bamenda. Malam Baba had
lived and worked in and around the Grassfields for nearly two decades
before settling in Bamenda. According to his son Alhaji Zakari Mama,
Malam Baba was born in Kano State in the latter half of the nineteenth
century, and he came to the Grassfields to trade in slaves, a fact Zakari
Mama supported by displaying the shackles his father had used to control his human property so long ago. But Malam Baba did not come to
the Grassfields unaccompanied. Like a number of men, he brought two

Hausa wives with him. And later, as he traveled throughout the region to advance his slave dealing, he married two more women—one from Bafia and the other of Tikar origins, two areas that lie just to the east of the Grassfields. Zakari Mama claims that these women became Muslim upon marrying Malam Baba and joined his household as junior wives. Four women, two from Hausaland and two from Cameroon, came together in expanding the Hausa diaspora through space and through their productive and reproductive capacities as wives and mothers.

Though the maternal heritage of Malam Baba's children was diverse, Zakari Mama declared that all of his brothers and sisters were raised as Hausa and in the literal image of their father. Those individuals who claim patrilineal descent from Malam Baba bear the mark of that heritage on their tattooed faces: nine vertical markings—two at each temple, two on each cheek, and one between the eyebrows—signify their cultural tie to Hausaland.[2] For Zakari Mama and many others of the diaspora, patrilineality is central to being Hausa, as it allows them to trace their heritage to Hausaland through lines of Hausa fathers. Zakari Mama did not reflect on the meaning of abakwa. But his father's story and the way in which he grafted the women from Bafia and Tikar societies onto it reflect the dynamics that lay at the heart of the original abakwa narrative created in the Benue River Valley.

Such stories of travel, marriage, and settlement are not only central to Hausa diaspora histories in Cameroon but in numerous locales throughout Western Africa. In the 1960s, historian Nehemia Levtzion collected oral histories and traditions from Ghana's Middle Volta Basin in order to examine relations between Muslim strangers and local chiefs during the pre-colonial period. Like the history of Islam in the Grassfields, Levtzion's area of study underwent a process of Islamization that had never been revolutionized by jihad, so the face of Islam had been "represented by peaceful traders and Mallams."[3]

Hausas began traveling to the Basin during the late fifteenth century to acquire kola nuts by exchanging a variety of products from Hausaland, including textiles, leather goods, jewelry, livestock, dried onion leaves, and natron. Their presence increased considerably in the nineteenth century. It was said that at least one malam accompanied every caravan in order to keep records, provide advice on which days were opportune for travel, and offer "prayers for the success of the adventurous trip."[4] A recurring theme in the oral traditions suggests that these malams were the most instrumental in leaving traces of their religion along trade routes, sometimes leaving the caravan at the request of a local chief in order to offer religious services. The chief would then give the malam a wife, often his own daughter—an act that represented the cementing of new local ties and the birth of a Muslim community.

Malams were not the only Muslim men to make such inroads into local populations. Levtzion's sources revealed that chiefs in Dagomba State often gave their daughters in marriage to immigrant Muslims of various professions. Offering one's daughter was regarded as a "generous gift," but one that was accompanied by a chiefly motivation to "bind a Muslim" to his court. Descendants of these marriages were most commonly raised as Muslim.[5] This is particularly true for the chief butcher in many communities. In Yendi society, oral traditions state that the first butcher trading in meat was a pagan named Na Dimani, but at some point during the eighteenth or nineteenth century, "a Hausa Muslim, nicknamed Baba, came to Yendi. He helped the 'royal' butchers in their trade and married into the chiefly family. Subsequently, the office of the chief-butcher was given to his descendants."[6]

Abakwa was not a defining concept for Hausa diaspora identity in regions to the west of Hausaland since the term emerged from Hausa experiences in the Benue River Valley and was then carried southward. Nevertheless, marital practices between migrant Hausas and chiefs in the Middle Volta Basin were similar to those in the Grassfields. Exogamous marriage practices among Grassfields societies, together with lineage heads' power to control marital arrangements and slave dealing, facilitated the settlement and economic networks of male Hausa strangers. Through marital alliance, Grassfields notables acquired prestige and wealth in accessing luxury goods and new followers, while Hausa men gained access to local markets, slaves, goods, knowledge, and new social relations. When Hausa men and women reflected on their local maternal heritage, these gender dynamics often became a focal point in their narrations of the past.

Alhaji Zakari Mama's wife, Hajiya Sa'adatu, was particularly outspoken on this aspect of her family history. According to her, around 1930 the chief of Kom at Laikom asked Malam Baba to bring Hausa people to "his country." In response, Malam Baba sent his friend and Hajiya Sa'adatu's grandfather, Mohamadu Maikyaungida, with a group of Hausa followers to trade and perhaps settle in the chief's village. Maikyaungida traded salt and cattle with the people of Laikom. For Hajiya, however, this history forms the backdrop to a story of greater significance to her own life. In our interview, she imagined the conversation that Maikyaungida had with the chief, the latter asking what the Hausa man wanted from his compound in return for the trade he brought to the area:

> Maikyaungida . . . he carry salt at Kom. He meet Laikom chief. The Laikom chief. He give the Laikom chief the salt. Then the Laikom chief, he asked, "Now Maikyaungida, what do you like from my compound?" He said, "You want say I give you money?" He say, "No, I no like money, I like some small woman." He said he like some small woman. Chief say, "No, baby girl that not be . . . only small small girl." He say, "No I like 'em so." Then they give him my grand-mère.

His wish granted, Maikyaungida took the girl from Laikom and kept her at Bamenda, which was some distance away: "She stay there till she be woman until time she married him. They change her name to Hadiza. As they change the name for Hadiza, they born my mother."[7]

In Sa'adatu's tale, the child-bride, later to become Hadiza, had been a ward of the Laikom chief. Her guardian gave her to the Hausa merchant, Maikyaungida, as a gift of thanks or as payment for the trade he brought to his chiefdom. She was only a child when this transfer of her person occurred, too young to marry but young enough to be acculturated into Hausa ways and to learn the Hausa language. Maikyaungida brought his child-bride back to a compound in Abakwa-Bamenda, where she lived and worked until she came of age to marry: "The girl stayed in a compound in abakwa and grew to woman. They made her Muslim; they washed her and named her Hadiza. Then she get married [and] go to husband's house." She then gave birth to her first child, Fatu, who later became the mother of Hajiya Sa'adatu herself. This tale shows that over a period of a few years, an extreme transformation took place in the life of one girl, from being a young daughter, ward, or perhaps a slave, of a chiefly household in one Grassfields community to becoming a Muslim wife and integral member of the Hausa diaspora in another. Through ritual cleansing and naming, through language acquisition, cultural adaptation, and religious conversion, through marriage, pregnancy, and motherhood, this Laikom-born girl would come to participate in the creation of a Hausa diaspora family.[8] Her story also shows how common it was for Hausa men to take local, non-Muslim women and girls as wives or concubines with the intention of moving them to other areas of settlement. These marital alliances were therefore not only about geographically binding Hausa men to a particular chiefdom as Levtzion suggested. As the stories of Maikyaungida, Malam Baba, and Gashin Baki show, they could also solidify patron–client relations in one locale while augmenting a traveling man's status as he entered another.

In its multiple permutations, abakwa implicitly incorporates the participation of local, non-Muslim women in expanding the diaspora. Yet it fails to encompass the history of every woman belonging to Malam Baba's household, particularly his two Hausa wives who journeyed to the Grassfields at the turn of the twentieth century. It also fails to acknowledge the travel and work of Mairam Suleman, known affectionately as Mairo (Figure 12). Born in Kano, she traveled to the Grassfields near the turn of the twentieth century and was a member of a Hausa delegation that came to Bamenda from Fumban during the First World War. The patrilineal chronicle of abakwa erases any representation of Hausa women like Mairam and Malam Baba's Hausa wives—women who trekked long distances alongside their male counterparts. In ignoring the roles of a particular segment of women in this history, abakwa conflates "the politics of travel and actual travel" and informs who in Hausa diaspora society could claim memories of "staying, going, and returning"—and who could claim ideal forms of belonging.[9]

It is true that the majority of Hausas traveling outside of Hausaland during the nineteenth and twentieth centuries were men, but many of Hausaland's women took up these arduous journeys as well, and did so in multiple ways. The Canadian missionary A. W. Banfield wrote in 1905 that the Hausa trader in the Gold Coast "lives like a gypsy, and one often sees a Hausa man with his children and wives, each carrying a load, going from their country down to the coast to buy English goods."[10] Other sources show that Hausa men migrating from Northern Nigeria to Ibadan and Accra took women and children with them.[11] And let us not forget Ernst Vollbehr's keen eye in creating lasting images of Hausa women and family life near the German colonial station at Bamenda.

Even if men did not intend to settle in the diaspora, they often desired the company and labor of one or two wives. Many women looked forward to these trips. A woman named Aishatu Ibrahim living in Bamenda's Old Town remarked how her mother and father enjoyed traveling together in and outside of the Grassfields during the middle part of the twentieth century, selling cattle and craft items in exchange for cloth.[12] Traveling with one's husband also meant that a wife within a polygynous household might have sole access to her husband for a finite period of time.

Travelers' marriages also facilitated travel among Hausas. According to J. Spencer Trimingham, writing in 1959, "If a trader already has four wives but does not wish to take any one of them with him on his travels for fear of inciting jealousy or because they are strictly kulle (secluded), he will arrange a temporary marriage with a fifth." This is called *auren jin da'di*, a "marriage for pleasure." The man "informs a cleric that none of his wives can travel with him and he wishes to take a temporary wife. He arranges for the cleric to be in the zaure or entrance hut of his compound at the time he leaves it to commence his journey and is married for the period of the journey. The clerics connive at the practice for, they say, 'he has renounced his wives for that period,' interpreting liberally [an] ambiguous Qur'anic passage." When the man returns home and hands the temporary wife "the previously stipulated mut'a (consolatory gift)" at the zaure, "divorce is automatic."[13]

For wives who remained behind in Hausaland, it was generally expected that their migrating husbands would someday return—whether or not they left with another woman. Many male migrants chose not to settle in the diaspora or to settle only temporarily, working toward the goal of eventually returning home to their families. Linkages between Hausaland and the diaspora were thus maintained through communication, repeated travel, and the prospect of a final return. These expectations did not preclude traveling husbands from entering into unions with local women, however, as the cultural availability of polygyny made it possible for them to sustain their ideal forms of masculinity, their wealth, and their networks both at home and in the diaspora.

In fact, many itinerant merchants and other traveling men deployed their bonds with women in a geographically dispersed polygyny where a man's wives would reside both at home and in diaspora settlements.[14] In some instances this form of separation eventually led to complete spousal abandonment. In other cases the men and women involved managed to maintain this lifestyle, the men relying heavily upon their wives' ability to support themselves and their children during their husbands' prolonged absences.[15] This was likely an extension of the Hausa form of marriage known as *auren takalmi*, marriage of sandals, usually practiced by older men and women. In these marriages, a man had wives in separate towns, which he visited on regular travels associated with *yawon kasuwanci*, the walk of marketing.[16] One Grassfields Hausa man, Alhaji Gambo, had maintained wives in the Grassfields and in Nigeria, visiting them depending on the nature and timing of his business ventures. In his old age he brought his wives together to live near him in his Grassfields compound in Sabga.[17] On the other end of the spectrum, a Hausa woman named Mariam Muhamed discussed how her father—a malam, healer, and trader who came from Lafiya, Nigeria—abandoned his first wife when he traveled to Bamenda, where he decided to settle upon marrying Mariam's mother.[18] The cultural precedent of auren takalmi clearly facilitated trade, male travel involving greater distances, as well as settlement in the diaspora.

In his research on Ibadan's Hausa community in southern Nigeria, Abner Cohen recorded a number of instances where men left their wives in the North indefinitely, only to marry a second wife in the South. This factor, along with high divorce rates, led Cohen to characterize Hausa diaspora marriages as "highly unstable."[19] But spousal abandonment and divorce should not be conflated. "According to Islam," Limam Alhaji Baba Malam Shuaibu stated in one interview, "if a man has his wife and he leaves for about one year, two year, three year, four year, five year, and he doesn't see the wife, and she comes to me or the alkali, in Islamic law, I will give her four years . . . to go and find the man. . . . If she really looks for him, truly, for four years and she doesn't see him, then she should come back to me. Then we will tell the woman to do . . . idda, four months, ten days. . . . If she finds a [new] man she can get married to him."[20] With such stipulations set in law and enacted by community patriarchs, traveling husbands were theoretically assured of their household control over wives remaining at home for up to four years. Women, of course, did not always abide by these customs, and some of them may have also enjoyed their greater independence.

▶▶▶•◀•◀◀◀

Multiple forms of marriage enabled the expansion of Hausa networks and ideal forms of masculinity anchored in the accumulation of dependents, clients, and property. Hausa itinerant traders, Qur'anic teachers, butchers, and other men making their livelihoods in the Cameroon Grassfields traveled side-by-side with women originating from Hausaland and sojourns along the way, and through polygyny they often formed relations with women from places of settlement as well. In most cases the geographical space separating newly settled women of the Grassfields from their points of origin was incredibly vast. Whether a woman was of Hausa birth or not, as Hadija's predicament shows, marital bonds were vital to the process of establishing her social ties and status in the diaspora.

In mid-century Hausaland, the importance placed on marriage as the normal condition of adulthood trumped the significance of a woman's ties to her consanguine relations, even though status placement among women was often independent of the male status order.[21] This included matters of socioeconomic status, as it was common for household wealth to be distributed unevenly between husbands and wives, with women often occupying a lower class position than their husbands.[22] Women also depended greatly on their husbands to have access to paradise in the afterlife, since women had less spiritual worth than did men in local conceptions of Islam. Using insights from the work of Guy Nicolas, Barbara Cooper explains that Hausas in Maradi believed that women must have a marital tie before death, "a literal thread to a man who has the 'pull' to get them into heaven through prayer."[23]

In the diaspora, marriage ties may have taken on greater significance in how the status of immigrant or newly incorporated women was reckoned within Hausa settlements. Upon her transfer from Laikom to Bamenda, Hajiya Sa'adatu's grandmother, Hadiza, was recognized in the Grassfields, first and foremost, through her marriage to

Mohamadu Maikyaundgida. While her identity and social status may have changed over her lifetime, it is undeniable that the original and primary link to her adoptive society was fashioned through her nuptial bonds. Moreover, some of the safety nets on which many divorced or widowed women in Hausaland could rely—whether these women were of Hausa or other ethnic origin—were simply not present for a good number of wives in the diaspora. For example, in Hausaland, after the termination of a marriage women would generally return to their fathers' compounds before remarrying.[24] In the diaspora, if a husband's death, abandonment, or pronouncement of divorce left a woman without the form of belonging that marriage entailed, the distance separating her from her consanguine relations was sometimes insurmountable and she could end up without members of her kin close by. In the diaspora, distance and patrilineality could come together to form a gendered space of liminality characterized by temporary kinlessness and geographical isolation.

Exploring the relationship between marriage and social status in Hausa society as a function of the nature of relations between men and women cannot take for granted the free status of the individuals involved. In Hadija's case, proving the existence of her marriage itself became absolutely essential for her to establish a social status as a free woman. Her trial also shows how both men and women could take advantage of the ambiguity between marriage and slavery.[25] In the Hausa cultural lexicon, the ambiguity between female enslavement and wifehood is expressed in a variety of ways. For example, the term *baiwa* refers equally to a gift or the act of giving, to a betrothal of a woman to a male suitor, and to a female slave. Barbara Cooper has also shown that the Hausa metaphor of a rope "tying the knot" of marriage is related to the language of slavery. If a marriage ended, the bride's family would have to return the bridewealth payment to the groom, known as the *igiyar aure* or "the rope of marriage." Similarly, it is said that a slave woman could "cut the rope of her slavery" to earn freedom by "bearing her master a child or by paying him a redemption fee."[26]

Though everyone I interviewed admitted that slavery and slave trading were integral to the history of the Hausa diaspora in Cameroon—including how this trade shaped the regional political economy and Hausa

activity within it—few of them preferred to acknowledge the continuation of slavery beyond the points of European-initiated abolition, especially if their own mothers had been slaves. Given what we know from
the alkali documents on the persistence of domestic slavery and concubinage into the twentieth century, however, a large number of the women
participating in the expansion and reproduction of the Hausa diaspora
lived day to day in varying degrees of unfreedom.

Historical research on Hausa society in Northern Nigeria has shown
that the ambiguity involved in distinguishing a wife from an enslaved
concubine was in part responsible for British colonial ambivalence on
the entire matter of domestic slavery. The British system of Indirect Rule
rested squarely on the shoulders of the Sokoto Caliphate's aristocratic
and mercantile classes, a patriarchal society heavily interested in con-
solidating its power over women—free and unfree. Paul Lovejoy attests
that concubines were indeed slaves even though the British wanted to
believe that there was no fundamental difference between concubinage
and marriage. Lord Frederick Lugard, the architect of Indirect Rule in
Africa, declared that concubinage was "a question of marriage rather
than slavery."[27]

As noted in Chapter 3, though free Muslim women could never become concubines, British antislavery policies pressed Hausa men to in-
novate new means of obtaining concubines from the ranks of free girls
born to non-Muslim, servile families. These practices led to blurring the
meaning of *sadaki*, payment given by a groom to the bride through her
guardian (wali) to legally bind the marriage. According to Lovejoy and
Hogendorn, an advisory council on concubinage and dowry was established in 1931 "to investigate ... the extent to which *sadaki* was being used
to purchase girls of servile origin for purposes of concubinage." Some
administrators believed that no amount of legislation would eliminate
concubinage in the colony, "especially the recruitment of freeborn girls
of servile origin," a practice that continued well into the 1980s, as Ibrahim Jumare has documented.[28]

Like Hausa communities in Northern Nigeria, Grassfields societies
also preferred female slaves to males, a cultural and economic inclination
that was grounded in conceptual linkages between the labor or use of
female slaves and that of wives—the primary distinction between them

being that a slave was an acquired outsider.[29] Denis Fomin suggests that the gender preference for females was a change that occurred over the course of the nineteenth century. By the 1820s, the transatlantic demand for Grassfields slaves declined, and one of the primary ways that adult men came to showcase their wealth was by building a large following "through marriage, especially acquiring slave wives."[30] As a result, "female slaves became increasingly important in the centralized states of the Grassfields."[31] Even though female slaves performed various social services in courts and in palaces, "their main role was that of wives" such that women were always absorbed in this manner and, unlike Hausa society, never as concubines.[32] Ritual integration in marriage was the only means by which a female slave—a vulnerable outsider—could be assimilated into her new society.

Accepted gender norms in the Grassfields meant that women held value as farmers, wives, and potential mothers. Robert Brain has noted that in Bangwa society along the western slopes of the Bamileke plateau female slaves were "kept in the compounds of traders and chiefs for distribution to loyal subjects, impecunious retainers and sons and successful warriors," with the purpose of solidifying royal relationships.[33] Though the situation that obtained in Bangwa society was not ubiquitous, Warnier states that it was not entirely dissimilar from societies on the Bamenda plateau. Nkwi has also noted that many chiefs and rich notables in the Western Grassfields placed a high value on female slaves who, along with freeborn girls, were used "in cementing diplomatic ties and promoting trade friendship."[34] In general, the line distinguishing a wife from a female slave or slave-wife was not drawn very starkly in the nineteenth-century Grassfields nor was it during the colonial period. The research of Brain, Fomin, Nkwi, and Warnier points to changing dynamics in the nineteenth century that muddied the waters between marrying a female outsider by offering bridewealth and enslaving a female outsider through purchase with the later prospect of social integration through marriage. In the 1920s, Raymond Buell observed that "many old men . . . buy girl babies from native parents at a low price, and then sell them when they come to maturity at a large profit. While technically, the native law as to dowry has been followed, the system is really a kind of slave traffic."[35]

Prior to the nineteenth century in the large matrilineal chiefdom of Kom, the very same chiefdom from which Maikyaungida acquired Hadiza, "a female slave could cost as much as fifty goats. Later they were sold for . . . cowries, iron bars and guns. Good looking young women who could easily be taken as wives fetched the highest price."[36] In his interviews with middle-aged residents of Oku, Nicolas Argenti noted that many of them "are aware of grandmothers of theirs having been bought as slaves for a sum of cowries from the neighboring chiefdom of Kom and married—probably in the late nineteenth or early twentieth century."[37] Kom notables may have acquired some of these disposable children through raids or during periods of food shortage when it was commonplace for a father to sell one of his children—a member of his wife's lineage—in order to obtain food for his family. Given that a number of Hausas living today in Bamenda recognize maternal heritage from Kom, including Hajiya Sa'adatu and the limam, transformations in Grassfields slave-dealing in the nineteenth and early twentieth centuries may have served to meet the demand for wives and concubines among Hausa diaspora men.[38] Importantly, not all Grassfields societies were so equivocal in their distinctions between female enslavement and marriage. Bamileke peoples to the east regarded selling someone as a kind of betrayal whereas giving a woman in marriage was a form of alliance.[39] Nonetheless, the examples given here show that Grassfielders did not uniformly abide by this principle across time and space.

For its part, the Maliki code of law practiced in the Muslim courts of West Africa is also far from clear on distinguishing the status and identity of Muslim wives from female slaves and concubines. Through her careful reading of Maliki, Hanafi, and Shafi'i texts, Kecia Ali has argued that early Islamic jurists' use of analogical reasoning consistently paired marriage and enslavement, employing one to sharpen understanding of the other. Analogy, according to Ali, "requires an essential similarity that allows for comparison, but it also requires difference." Much of the relationship between female enslavement and marriage stems from understanding slaves and females as legally disabled: both were "legally inferior persons constructed against one another and in relation to one another." Ali also states that these legal disabilities merged "in the person of the female slave," who could exercise no "sexual or marital self-determination."[40]

At the heart of the relationship between marriage and slavery was the concept of *milk*, "a form of authority or dominion" over wives and female slaves that was an exclusively male privilege. There were two different kinds of milk in relation to wives and female slaves: the former established with the payment of a dower and the latter with purchase. Milk through either marriage (*milk al-nikah*) or enslavement (*milk al-yamin*) was required in order for sex to be licit. Hence, lawful sex was dependent on legalized male control. There has been much debate over whether dower and the purchase price of a female slave should be compared, but it is clear that both exchanges provided one man with "exclusive access to and control over a particular woman's sexual capacity."[41] Likewise, a man could unilaterally relinquish control at any time of his choosing, effectively pronouncing divorce or manumission through what Islamic legal scholar Norman Calder has termed "performative utterances."[42] Historian Yossef Rapoport further suggests that "repudiating a wife and freeing a slave rests on . . . their capacity to destabilize a basic unit of social organization." Thus both divorce and manumission "were an extreme manifestation of patriarchal authority, as well as its symbols, precisely because they severed the ties that held a household together"—a valuable reminder that slaves were often essential household members even though they were not usually kin.[43]

Though enslavement and marriage have shared theoretical and practical similarities in the lives of Muslim African women throughout history, individuals have perceived differences between the two institutions and how they limited or broadened the scope of options they could use to improve their daily lives. Concubines and female slaves were not allowed to marry but were bound to their masters without recourse should their masters prove abusive. Wives, on the other hand, could seek divorce in such cases.[44] A wife could never be her husband's legal slave, and she was due certain marital entitlements pertaining to matters of companionship, maintenance, and inheritance, as well as her right to manage her own property. A female slave, whether a concubine or not, could not expect to benefit from any of these rights, at least legally. Despite the norms associated with Islamic jurisprudence, Ali makes the point than any of the hierarchies central to Islamic households could be "tempered to a greater or lesser degree by affection." Moreover, as pointed out above,

Malik "consistently differentiated less between enslaved and free people" than did Hanafi, Shafi'i or Hanbal, a position that was partly shaped by his owning a reported—and probably exaggerated—three hundred concubines.[45]

Ali's analysis focuses on early jurists whose doctrines obviously did not apply directly to the lives of Muslims in twentieth-century Cameroon, but they were undoubtedly influential in both theory and in daily practice. Ali and historian Judith Tucker submit that gender issues are especially subject to approaches embedded in these early texts. Ali in particular argues that "core ideas about maleness, femaleness, sexuality, and power that structured marriage in the early jurists' thinking survive in myriad ways."[46] Hadija's case tells us no differently.

>>>I•I<<<

The various relationships Alhaji Gashin Baki contracted with the women of his household are representative of the many unions that facilitated Hausa diaspora ramification. With his death, he left behind two women in the Grassfields, a wife with child and the other of unknown status. Yet these were not the only women over whom Gashin Baki had once exercised patriarchal control. The arrival of his two elder sons, Sanda and Wada, from Kano suggests that Gashin Baki had been married to at least one other woman before departing Kano, participating in the geographically dispersed polygyny characterized above. Furthermore, after he died, the community's solution to Hadija's temporary kinlessness was to place her under the guardianship of one of his acquaintances, Malam Audu. Taking this vulnerable social position into account, we can understand why Hadija found it necessary to establish marital ties hastily to another man of her choice, Yusufu, attempting to create through him a distinctive linkage between herself and her adoptive society.

If Hadija was in fact a free woman and legitimate wife of Gashin Baki, and given the importance of marriage in the local identity formation of immigrant women in the diaspora, it becomes clearer why Hadija made particular choices after the death of her husband. Just as the importance of establishing a protective kinship alliance and link to Allah may have led her into a hasty marriage with Yusufu, her awareness of the heightened degree of vulnerability that a concubine could experience at the hands of her master—as opposed to the expected rights of a wife—spurred her to assert her free status despite the penalty that accompanied this admission.

However, these very same reasons could have prompted an unfree Hadija into outright dishonesty, taking advantage of that very same ambiguity before the authority of the alkali to claim a status as a free woman. If Hadija had been Gashin Baki's slave concubine, it is possible to view her situation in the diaspora and the decisions she made after her owner's death in a slightly different light than had she been a free woman. She had no alternative methods by which to establish herself as free but to obstinately argue for it in the court of the alkali. None of the witnesses in the case mentioned anything about a possible "death-bed manumission" on the part of the deceased husband, a common practice among Muslim slave owners. Hadija never gave birth to a child, which in accordance with Islamic law could have theoretically secured her freedom upon Gashin Baki's death, regardless of whether he promised manumission. Perhaps his use of the kinship idiom of motherhood ("hold her fine as our mother") was an indirect extension of an Islamic principle that an impregnated slave shall receive the name "mother of offspring" upon the birth of her master's child and be manumitted owing to that newfound motherhood.[47] But Sanda's testimony suggests that the family would maintain Hadija even after receiving the 50 pounds Gashin Baki set aside for her. Was "hold her fine" a euphemism for inheriting her as a slave? Though it is clear that Gashin Baki incorporated Hadija into his notion of family by instructing his children to care for her, he did not unequivocally view Hadija as a wife either, stating she should receive an inheritance that was much less than Talle's.

Though claiming an identity based on free wifehood and adherence to Islam came with an admission to sinful behavior and acceptance of criminal punishment, for an enslaved Hadija this risk outweighed the alternative, which was to resign herself to further enslavement. By exploiting the conceptual and legal relationship between wifehood and concubinage, Hadija was able to elevate her social status in the public forum offered by the alkali's court, an institution of diasporic and colonial origins to which she had access as a woman ambiguously incorporated into Grassfields Hausa society. Paying the fine and court fees associated with the guilty verdict can thus be viewed as an act symbolizing self-redemption. Through this redemption Hadija could also claim a share of Gashin Baki's estate, a total of just over 122 pounds. Hadija's choice to confess her transgressions through the ordeal of mubahala ultimately resulted in her elevating and securing her status as a free woman, establishing herself as an incorporated member of the Muslim Hausa diaspora, and claiming a fair portion of her former owner's wealth.

It is also entirely possible that Hadija was misled on what Gashin Baki's intentions were as he brought her from Lere to a new and distant location. He could have exploited the conceptual ambiguity separating marriage from slavery to claim access to Hadija's domestic and sexual services without recourse. Symbolizing her incorporation into the diaspora by naming her Hadija could have indicated a clear intention to marry her as a free woman or masked the social reality of her slave status. He could have also renamed her to mask her alienness to Hausa society as they entered the Grassfields.[48]

Hadija took advantage of this opportunity to claim a public identity as a free Hausa woman, but the identity and social status of many other women in the diaspora were defined, negotiated, and remembered in more intimate settings. Hajiya Hajera, an elderly Hausa woman born in the Grassfields village of Bamessing, told a story of how her father had at one time traded in slaves but then abandoned these activities to become a butcher, a decision he allegedly made after slave dealing became illegal in Northern Nigeria. He and his three wives traveled from Northern Nigeria to Bamessing where they raised their family. Two of these wives had always been free, while one had been his former slave. He had had a number of slaves in Nigeria, but upon freeing them he chose to take one woman as his third wife, naming her Yakamata to symbolize both his motivation for freeing and marrying her, as well as the expectations behind this woman's new role in Hausa society. *Ya kamata* means that someone must do a certain act. In this case Yakamata's owner felt compelled to manumit her, a deed that was required before the two could contract a legal marriage.

In explaining the significance that ya kamata had in naming this woman, Hajiya Hajera's grandson recited the proverb, *Ya kamata shi yake yi 'kari hatsin Hausawa*: "He must increase the grain of the Hausa people." Pamela Schmoll has noted that food is often a metaphor for children among Hausas, and as such, offspring "appear to be both a concrete manifestation and a symbol" of "collective 'prosperity.'"[49] The name thus reflects the ways in which patriarchy and patrilineality left their imprint on family life and identity. In this proverb, the subject is male: it is a man who "must increase the grain"—the population and wealth—"of the Hausa people."[50] And it was the control or milk that Hajiya Hajera's father exercised over Yakamata that made his sexual advances licit and that obliged her to consent. Within the context of this family history, the father's act of naming his new wife Yakamata tied her fate directly and intimately with his. If abakwa situates patrilineality as the normative means by which Hausa identity is recognized in the diaspora, the proverb analyzed here similarly locates men as the historical agents promoting the ramification of prosperous Hausa communities. First-generation men of the Hausa diaspora, like Hajiya Hajera's father, Malam Baba, and Mohamadu Maikyaungida, brought with them particular notions of what elements heightened their prestige in both immediate and distant locales. In the narrative Hajiya Hajera constructed, her father was a good man who committed an honorable act in freeing and marrying his former slave.

Similar to her own father, Hajiya Hajera's father-in-law and former chief butcher of Bamenda, Sarkin Pawa Audu Tunku, came to the Grassfields from Northern Nigeria with two free Hausa wives, Shetu and Hadiza, and two enslaved concubines. One of the concubines originated from Bafia, just east of the Grassfields, and was bestowed the name Zamad da Sarki, or "caused to reside with the chief." Audu Tunku purchased the other concubine in the Adamawa region and named her Ruwan Jira, literally "water waited for," an epithet Hausa women have used to refer to younger females, be they friends, servants, or junior wives. It is derived from the saying *Ruwan jira, mai ha'kuri ka sha shi*, which implies that the younger woman must exhibit patience in times of adversity.[51] Audu Tunku's son, Alhaji Adamu, claimed that these women were given these names because they were neither Muslim nor Hausa.[52]

Though it may be tempting to correlate the naming of the wives and slave-concubines revealed in this chapter to the precise gender roles these women undertook at the behest of their husbands and owners, the many inconsistencies that exist preclude the creation of a hard-and-fast rule. Yakamata, Zauna da Sarki, and Ruwan Jira all experienced enslavement. Yet the names Zamad da Sarki and Ruwan Jira signified a lifetime of enslavement, while Yakamata's name apparently symbolized the moment and expectations of her freedom and acculturation into Hausa ways—though it is possible that Yakamata's manumission is a product not of her owner's actions but of how Hajiya Hajera imagined her father. Unlike the Muslim names Hadija and Hadiza, the Hausa names Yakamata, Zauna da Sarki, and Ruwan Jira do not imply that these three women underwent any form of religious conversion. This conjecture does not mean, however, that Hadija of Lere and Hadiza of Laikom experienced a complete Islamic education even though the men to whom they belonged perhaps intended this to be the case. Hadija's admission in court regarding her lack of knowledge on how many months constituted takaba provides evidence to the contrary.

Limam Alhaji Baba Malam Shuaibu stated that non-Hausa women incorporated into the diaspora learned how to work and prepare food from their co-wives. This may have been the case with the women of his own family. His mother Hawa'u (born in Fumban) and stepmother Mairam (born in Kano) likely taught their Hausa ways to a girl from Kom who would become their co-wife in Bamenda (Figure 12). "As for the prayers," he said, "the men taught them when they were still young before they ever got married to them."[53] Given the various ambiguities involved in correlating the naming and statuses of the women mentioned here, it was not uncommon to find immigrant women of the Grassfields Hausa diaspora lacking adequate knowledge of Qur'anic principles. At best, this may indicate that Hausa husbands and owners possessed insufficient knowledge themselves or were unenthusiastic about educating the women of their compounds due to a rather "relaxed attitude toward marriage and what constitutes a 'good' Muslim household." According to Barbara Cooper, in Maradi, "When non-Muslim women [were] brought into a household [through marriage or concubinage]," it was culturally expected that they would "be exposed to their husband's superior understanding of God and . . . gradually learn proper religious practice" from the women of his family. "A young Muslim man need face no impediment to marriage, therefore, for his own grasp of Islam and his mastery of the women of the household was understood to be sufficient to render the entire family Islamic."[54] At worst, women's lack of education could also mean that men deliberately prevented their wives and slaves from learning the Qur'an in order to keep them unsettled and uninformed of their duties and rights in these new and sometimes isolated diaspora settlements. Deborah Pellow noted similar tendencies in Accra's Sabon Zongo. One of the men she interviewed "recalled that in those early days of his youth, girls did not go to *makaranta* (Qur'anic school) because 'girls were considered grown earlier than boys.'" Another man told her that even though many husbands do teach their wives at home, "the elders felt that when the woman knows more than the husband, she will try to overcome him."[55]

▶▶▶┃•┃◀◀◀

For Hausas in the Grassfields, the meaning of abakwa proposes that the patrilineal tie to the past overrides all others. As the diaspora grew and extended itself by incorporating diverse groups of people, patrilineality was to be the proof of its wholeness. Many people's historical claims to Hausaland reflected its meaning. This was particularly true for Alhaji Zakari Mama, the son of Malam Baba, and for Limam Alhaji Baba Malam Shuaibu, who understood the "the production of diasporic space" as a process wherein a man's success in trade led to settlement, fatherhood, and the spread of Islam.[56]

Many Hausas I interviewed did not know what abakwa meant, nor did they know the history that brought it into their language. This did not stop the elderly sarkin pawa, the chief butcher of Bamenda, from creating a definition based on abakwa's relevance to his own life. He thought that abakwa was a contracted form of *a ba kowa*, which signified to him that Hausa settlements are places to "give to everyone," to share with all people.[57] This personal ideology about Hausa settlement is more akin to the idea that Hausa settlements are places of flexible, inclusive assemblages of diverse people with shared affinities or needs—a far cry from creating distinct and bounded Hausaness through solely recognizing the genealogies of men. The sarkin pawa's inclination to imbue abakwa with this meaning is also reflective of the variety of ways other individuals spoke about the past. Though some were more inclined to trace their family's history though the ostensibly unbroken lineage of their fathers, others spoke at length about the lives of their mothers, their memories of childhood play with maternal grandparents, and the rupture of immediate connections to parents, spouses, and children through distance, divorce, illness, death, and miscarriage. One of the sarkin pawa's grandchildren, Umaru, was so excited to learn more about his Kom heritage that he asked to accompany me on my trip to Laikom, where he could directly engage with the chief on matters of family history. These people's memories and interpretations of historical events embody the mixed references of diasporas, decentering the patrilineal link to Hausaland as the quintessential quality of being Hausa in the diaspora.[58]

Perhaps the most powerful challenge to the narrative of abakwa came from Limam Alhaji Baba Malam Shuaibu's own household. Where the limam equated settlement with increased wealth in people and possessions, one of his wives, Adama, argued that migrant men settled in the diaspora because of failure. Men left Hausaland to seek economic advancement, but they failed and were too ashamed to return home, even if that meant abandoning a wife or wives and their children. What Adama emphatically stated was no less than a profound indictment of men's power to define ideal forms of Hausa masculinity grounded in male control over women and children, to put that definition in the service of geographical and economic expansion, and to construct the narrative of her community's history:

> We just grow up and heard from our grandfathers. That one would just leave, like Nigeria, and leave behind his wife, two children, three or four or five, and comes and looks for money. And he doesn't have the money, so he settles here, forgets about his family and gets married here again. Many did this. As you came to look for it [money] and you didn't succeed, so they are shameful to go back. My great-grandfathers, it was shame that made them stay here and not to go back to Nigeria, because they didn't get what they came for. So they will marry here and leave the others there. There are many of them here.[59]

In the next interview Hadijah Sali and I conducted with her, Adama reemphasized her argument:

ASL: That is why when they leave their people there and come here they don't
    agree to go back again. That they came to come and look for money, they
    don't get the money. It is shame. They will stay here until soon they will
    get married, have children. Soon you will see children coming to look for
    their father. They don't see the father. Even if they see their father, he will
    not agree to go.

HS: Go. Shame.

ASL: Or he will say, you people should go, I'm coming. It's shame! You have
    come and looked for money and you don't have. So you don't want to go
    back because of shame.

HO: Shame?

ASL: And that shame, too, is also foolishness, because if I don't have I will go
    back.

HS: I will not be ashamed.

ASL: I will not be ashamed. But some people are ashamed that they won't
    go back because they don't have anything. They will leave the compound
    with women, children, and come here because they want to look for
    money. To go back, no! Eh-eh! You come and stay here, after you die here.
    That's careless. It's not fine.

HS: While your family hasn't seen you.

ASL: While your family is thinking that you have gone to look for money.
    They will only put eye thinking that you are there when you're not there.[60]

Adama's indictment emerges from the empathy she has for her past and
present counterparts in Hausaland, women like Gashin Baki's older wife
or wives who did not know when and if they could expect their husband
to return. In Adama's narrative, traveling men who failed in their business dealings experienced a kind of shame that obstructed their aspirations to obtain wealth and caused paralysis in their movement.[61] Adama
calls the entire framework of commercial diasporas into question by
simply placing the feelings of abandoned families and chagrined men at
the center, a sentiment that resonates with the Hausa proverb *Hang-yé
(harara) ba shi kawo wonda ke da nisa*, "Gazing at a man who is a long way
off will not bring him to you."[62]

Adama also connects the experience of abandonment that travel creates with abandonment brought about by death. This entails women ne-
gotiating their day-to-day lives while waiting for husbands to return, but
it also encompasses women's lack of knowledge about their husbands'
well-being—whether they are alive or dead. Gashin Baki's wife in Kano
may have been concerned with these unknowns until she learned her

husband had died. Or perhaps he had divorced her, for there was no inheritance for her to collect from the alkali. Gashin Baki was no failure in business, but to Adama his decision to leave his family only to die in the diaspora was a careless one. The narrative of abakwa might mean that local unions with women and the attainment of ideal masculinity created the diaspora, but this process also involved failure and the dishonorable act of forgetting. The diaspora's contested tales of belonging thus occur at the level of community and household gender relations, as well as the manner in which those relations are defined.

FIVE

Second Reversal
Death and Survival

IN NOVEMBER 1951, A YEAR BEFORE HADIJA'S TRIAL BEGAN, AN infant boy died in the village of Pashi. When the child's body had been prepared for burial, a man named Ibrahim came to carry him away. On his way to the burial site, three men approached him. One of them, Aliyu, was the child's father. He had heard that his son was near death and rushed to be with him before he died. The shrouded body in Ibrahim's arms told him he was too late. "I went and took the child. I hold [him]," remembered Aliyu. "When they finished digging buried ground they said make I bring the child. Then I said to [my father-in-law] to wait my family to come and see the child. Then [Ibrahim] come and hold the child by force and he is the first to beat." Ibrahim did not deny what had happened, only he believed Aliyu had instigated the fighting.

The conflict that erupted on this sad day reflected Aliyu's anguish over his sudden loss and his anger toward Ibrahim for intruding into his most intimate affairs. Ibrahim interfered with Aliyu's ability to share his son's burial and his mourning with his kin, and this created an immediate conflict that thrust painful, unsettled domestic disputes into the light. Not only was Ibrahim the man who sought to orchestrate his son's funeral, but he was also the man who had committed adultery with his wife—the mother of the child. Her name was Maryama, and two months earlier she had left Aliyu to live with Ibrahim, taking their baby with her.[1]

The deaths of the infant boy and Alhaji Gashin Baki transpired less than a year apart. One was a helpless child who depended on the care of others, the other a wealthy man on whom others depended. Yet both of their deaths prompted intense social reckoning for those who survived them. Death is a transitional process. As the souls of the dead move into the afterlife, the living experience social disintegration that re-quires repair through bereavement and ritual.[2] Arnold van Gennep and his contemporary Robert Hertz theorized that mourning in particular represented a state of social liminality as survivors live temporarily be-tween the world of the living and that of the dead. Hertz went so far as to say that mourners could not be full-fledged members of their society, for they do not "follow the ways . . . which are proper to individuals who are socially normal and which are the sign of this community to which (for a time) they no longer belong."[3] The social group mediates the manner in which mourners emerge from this liminality: community or family leaders conduct funerals, ensure observance of mourning rituals, and distribute inheritance to facilitate survivors' reincorporation into soci-ety and to reinforce the values of the community as a whole.

But the experiences of those who survived the infant boy and Gashin Baki demonstrate that the transitional processes death inspires are not so neat and tidy. Aliyu's anguish over the loss of his son reminds us that while mourning does occur in ritual settings, such settings never encap-sulate the emotional totality of bereavement.[4] Gendered conceptions of power and belonging also shaped how Hausas encountered death and its social repercussions, producing crucial turning points in how women like Talle and Hadija asserted their status in the diaspora upon ending a period of mourning that men are not sanctioned to observe. Death and its associated rites have furthermore been occasions for the "elaboration of differences" within communities and families, as well as the negotia-tion of culture and social relations.[5] The disputes over Hadija's marital tie to Gashin Baki, whether she appropriately observed takaba, and the exact amount of her inheritance were part of the contentious, transi-tional process brought about by Gashin Baki's death. Like the fighting over the body of Aliyu's and Maryama's son, it was through these and similar disputes that people challenged and reinforced the Islamic values of the Hausa diaspora community, especially ideal relations between men and women. When the alkali heard what had happened in Pashi, he asked all of the adults involved, "Are you in Muhammadan law or you are not in Muhammadan law?" He then reprimanded Ibrahim for his illicit relationship with Maryama, saying, "If you took a woman [and] you keep her for your house without tying marriage and kept her like adultry [sic], [you] will be punished."

Death presents survivors with a social paradox. While the dead continue to "shape the society they left behind," those left behind use the silence of the dead to reaffirm hierarchies or to contest them.[6] Death in the context of diaspora also inspires questions about how rituals reconstitute the beliefs and morals of a community when that community is culturally porous, as well as divided and stretched across hundreds of kilometers. Within the Hausa diaspora, the relationship between death, gender, and distance highlights how inheritance in particular was based on kinship networks that were widely dispersed but connected by patrilineal ties. Death stimulated further movement to, from, and within the diaspora as heirs, usually male, sought to collect inheritances and as widows searched for old and new relations upon completing takaba. Death thus brought about peripeteia—movement that collapsed diasporic space and highlighted gender differences in access to wealth and relationship to place. Death could also signal the cultural porosity at work in Hausa settlements, as both migrants and Grassfielders searched for new relations upon the deaths of others. Hausas were flexible in their incorporation of local inhabitants, some of whom became Hausa while others did not. This history indicates that while death may reconstitute the values of a community, it does not reflect concrete boundaries in identity formation or belonging.[7]

▶▶▶╏•╏◀◀◀

When Alhaji Gashin Baki died, the lives of his female dependents, two distant sons, Malam Audu, and Sarkin Hausawa Malam Ibrahim all changed course. As Talle and Hadija contemplated the death of their ill husband or owner, his sons Sanda and Wada began their journey from Kano to the Grassfields. After Gashin Baki died, Malam Audu and the

Sarkin Hausawa kept watch over Hadija and Talle, and they worked with the alkali to ensure the transfer of his wealth to his inheritors.

Likely because Gashin Baki had been a wealthy man, the Wum district officer was interested in every aspect of his inheritance and determined that the alkali follow the law with utmost precision—so much so that he was bent on codifying Hadija's status as a slave. The officer also questioned the identity of Gashin Baki's eldest sons and the sex of Talle's unborn child. In a letter to his superior at Bamenda, the officer feared that Sanda and Wada "might not be sons" after all, even though the alkali in the Grassfields had received a letter from the chief judge (Alkalin Alkalai) of Kano confirming that they were. "There is no conclusive proof that they are the sons of the deceased gentleman," he wrote. "To accept a letter from the Alkalin Alkalan [sic] of Kano, is not, in my opinion, sufficient proof." Moreover, the officer was suspicious of Sarkin Hausawa Malam Ibrahim, who became the estate's trustee. The Sarkin Hausawa oversaw the inheritance allotted to Gashin Baki's children, including Talle's unborn child. The officer did not trust that he was an honest man, having "[heard] news that he was somewhat of a humbug." The officer even approached the Sarkin Hausawa and demanded to see the money, and in a response clearly meant to evade the officer's intrusions, the sarki said "it was safely buried away and there was no need to disturb the hiding place." The officer was further concerned that the alkali prematurely assigned proportions of the estate's distribution among Gashin Baki's children, for the amount Talle's unborn child inherited depended on whether it was a boy or a girl. The alkali "treated Talle's child as though it were a male issue" set to receive the same amount as Sanda and Wada—572 pounds each.

The Wum district officer's proclivity for actively intruding into the alkali's deliberations and African families' affairs was tempered by his senior officer's assurance that "short of the most exhaustive and exhausting investigation no better solution than that pronounced by the alkali will be discovered and I am satisfied that on the evidence adduced the alkali's judgement is just, except in one small respect." This exception concerned Talle's child, who turned out to be a girl. The alkali admitted the error, and all parties agreed that her inheritance be decreased accordingly. The Bamenda district officer also offered his opinion that "no court of law does more than the Alkali did and that the responsibility for any breach of the court's order or for fraudulent winding-up of the estate lies solely with the trustee," Mallam Ibrahim.[8] With that statement, the district officer removed his office from further involvement with Gashin Baki's legacy.

Gashin Baki's death and gender differences in Hausa society brought about different kinds of turning points in the lives of people who survived him. Like many other women in the diaspora, Hadija and Talle observed a transitional period of mourning that was supposed to ritualize their reentry into Hausa society as respectable women to be married again. But confusion over the duration of time Hadija observed takaba resulted in a major investigation that questioned whether the two widows shared the same social status and therefore the same amount of inheritance. Contestations over the rightful distribution of Gashin Baki's legacy also point to crucial questions over the relationship between material transfer, gendered identities, distance, and generational networks that operated throughout the Hausa diaspora world. Examining the manner in which alkalis, Hausa sarkis, and colonial officers treated the inheritance of itinerant and settled Hausas illuminates how individuals in the Grassfields coped with legacy allocations in a geographically dispersed context. Inheritance cases also demonstrate how people formed and contested ideal social relations in competing claims over the dead and related transfers of wealth.[9] Lastly, survivors responded to the deaths of Gashin Baki and so many others by seeking out new forms of belonging that could both reassert and challenge dominant social relations in the diaspora.

》》》•|•《《《

The graves of most Muslims in the Grassfields go unmarked. However, in Bamenda's Muslim cemetery those families with more money than most sometimes request the construction of a rectangular cement molding to enclose the dead. Before the cement dries, someone etches the name and dates of birth and death of the deceased. One of the moldings was particularly descriptive. The epitaph, written in Hausa and Arabic, tells the grave's visitors that the woman buried there is Hajja Fatimatu Inna Miya, the wife of Mallam Mohammadu Dalailou. She was born on December 30, 1930, and on October 5, 2006 "she returned to see Allah" (*ta koma ga Allah*).

Hajja Fatimatu's uncommonly detailed epitaph memorialized her first and foremost as Mallam Mohammadu Dalailou's wife. We do not know how many children she had or which siblings survived her. Her marriage was her primary relationship at the time of her death. The previous chapter examined marital relations and the cultural necessity for women to create or continue ties to Hausa communities through marriage. Hajja Fatimatu's marital tie was secure at the time of her death. But for many Hausa diaspora women who outlived husbands, those ties could be temporarily or indefinitely severed. The death of a husband caused discontinuity in the ties between his wife or wives and society, as well as the tie between women and paradise, depending on one's interpretations of the Qur'an. Observing takaba is part of the process a widow undertakes to become reincorporated into her community as a respectable woman.

Van Gennep and Hertz agreed that the duration of mourning depended on the "closeness" of the relationship between the deceased and his or her survivors: "Widowers and widows should belong to this special world for the longest time."[10] But the different ways Hausa men and women have ritually responded to death indicate that this transition is a gendered process. Only widows must observe takaba before their reintegration into society. There is no male equivalent following the death of a wife. The gender of the deceased and the survivors is central to understanding the ways death and the rituals surrounding it reassert ideal relations among men and women.[11] Hertz recognized a similar difference in his research on Indonesian societies. From his perspective, a deceased husband "retains all his rights over his wife.... The widow is literally the wife of a person in which death is present and continuous."[12]

Becoming a widow is a ritual phase for Hausa women. It is a temporary condition that another marriage can remedy unless the widow has reached menopause, in which case a son might invite her to reside in his home. Baba of Karo remembered her period of mourning in distinctive detail:

> When you are in mourning you boil water every Friday morning, you make it very hot, and you go behind your hut and wash your body; you come in and massage your body with oil. Every day you do your ordinary ablutions

before you say your prayers, you wash your face, your feet. . . . The cloth and blouse and kerchief that you wore at the beginning of your mourning are not changed until the end of it. You cannot cut your hair. You cannot go to feasts or naming-feasts or any ceremonies. . . . When your husband dies, you must wail; if you loved him, then you are sad at heart also, he isn't there. If you didn't particularly like him, you wail because of compassion, you had got used to him and now he isn't here.[13]

While enduring this period of social and spiritual inbetweenness, Hausa widows can usually expect to receive support from fathers and brothers. They are obligated to provide for daughters and sisters whose marriages have ended through death, divorce, or annulment. However, these male kin often pressure their kinswomen to remarry if they are young or middle-aged. Neither Talle nor Hadija had male kin living nearby, so they had to rely on local community and religious patriarchs. For immigrant women in the diaspora, the distance separating them from consanguine relations compounded the social liminality that the deaths of husbands and owners produced. Gender influenced the power one could wield to take some measure of control over the direction of his or her life course following death and the effect it had on social relations. Widows, whose phase of discontinuity between themselves and their communities is culturally sanctioned and ritualized, were more constrained than men in their capacity to refashion a sense of belonging on their own terms. This is not to say that some of them did not succeed.

For these widows and others, surviving death brought about a new search for belonging. Part of this search entailed the transfer of wealth from one generation to the next—be it the passing of material possessions, money, animals, people, land, or a home. Parker Shipton has shown that the passing of such property communicates the relative worth of the articles themselves and indicates the relative worth of people and the relational bonds between them. It also illustrates "disparities in the way the sexes and ages are trusted and treated."[14] Patrilineal descent patterns among Hausas, reinforced by Maliki law, stipulated that widows like Hadija and Talle share between them one-eighth of their deceased husband's estate, while widowers could take twice as much.[15]

The gendered processes of social disintegration and reintegration that death causes influenced the varying ways Hausa men and women dealt with hierarchies of power and authority. This is especially evident in inheritance matters, as these cases formed the context in which most Hausa widows appear in the historical record. They also point to a particular colonial intervention into Muslim life that was shaped by monetary concerns: the Native Affairs Treasury could claim one-tenth the total value of inherited properties—no matter how large or small—in each case brought before the alkali.[16] These were called *ushira* fees. It was in the treasury's best interest and the alkali's (for it was the treasury who paid him) to bring as many inheritance cases to court as possible. Hausa chiefs also benefited as they received a reward (*la'ada*) from the alkali court—taken from the value of the deceased's properties—if they oversaw the transport of properties to the court.

Polly Hill noted in her 1972 study in Katsina that rural Hausas of Batagarawa considered inheritance to be a family matter, with only a few cases referred to the alkali's court in Katsina.[17] There were likely many inheritance matters that did not reach the alkali's courtroom in Ndop, especially for the distribution of properties owned by deceased women. But given that many people died in the Grassfields with families spread throughout the diaspora and Northern Nigeria, the intervention of Hausa and Muslim leaders, especially Hausa chiefs and the alkali, was often necessary.

The relationship between death and diasporic space more broadly is also a significant factor in continuing social linkages among diasporic Hausas in various locales as well as in Northern Nigeria. The situation of those who survived the death of kin in the diaspora and the limitations or choices they had regarding their own mobility were inflected greatly by gender, though other factors such as age and location of residence were also important. Some of the stories below explore why some widows sought to return to Hausaland upon the death of their husbands, while others chose to remain in the Grassfields. For these women, a host of contingencies informed their options, the most significant being whether a woman had children, especially sons, and whether she was past childbearing age.[18] Cases involving widows with young sons show that these women possessed great tenacity in ensuring the proper inheritance and well-being of their sons. Save for husbands like Gashin Baki who were especially wealthy, most Hausa widows inherited rather small amounts of wealth. They could not rely on that inheritance as substantial income, nor could they claim direct ownership rights of their husband's houses. Having a son—and a son who earned at least a moderate income to support the mother—was the surest path a woman had to maintain herself in the future.[19]

In the midst of the dry season, on December 1, 1947, a Hausa man residing in the village of Bamungo died and left behind a wife and a sister. His only known possessions were eight cows, whose value the alkali estimated at 45 pounds. After collecting a tenth of these funds for the court, the alkali distributed the remainder. The widow received the value of two cows, while the deceased's sister was allotted the balance. The sister, however, resided in Kano State with her family. Perhaps because she had no natal kin in the diaspora or saw no personal advantage to remaining in the Grassfields, the widow agreed to bring her sister-in-law the money she inherited. The alkali explained, "I gave the money to the hand of the late wife, because she said that she will go back to their country, [a] village in Kano."[20] The court scribe then wrote on the widow's behalf, "I receive the sum of £20 [and 5 shillings] for the [sister] . . . named Shatu," a statement she verified by her fingerprint.[21]

While this widow from Kano state saw no reason to remain in the diaspora, the two court cases to follow show how two other widows, Diddi and Garuwa, struggled to maintain their families in the Grassfields by securing wealth for their sons. Both women were raising young sons when their husbands died. Diddi's husband, the former Sarkin Hausawa of Ntumbo, died within two years leading up to the court date in 1959, her son still in his youth. Garuwa's husband had died a number of years prior to her appearance before the alkali, and her sons had since entered manhood. The issue in these cases was one of contested inheritance; both widows were fighting for their sons' claims to the properties of their deceased husbands.[22]

Part of the motivation behind these women's efforts may have derived from a mother's desire to ensure the well-being of her children. Yet another part was likely grounded in the cultural necessity for Hausa widows to guarantee their own care and comfort in the march to old age. Widows with young children have an incentive not to remarry, for another marriage could result in a woman's separation from her children.

Hausa male in-laws from the deceased husband's family often claim children at the time of weaning.[23] Mapping this dilemma onto diaspora networks, having children heavily influenced immigrant widows' decision to remain in the Grassfields. There were modifications to these practices, which usually relied on the nature of the deceased husband's assets and the availability of caretakers. If the deceased husband owned a home, the widow had the option of staying there with her children, but she would likely have to earn an income on her own. In Enid Schildkrout's study of widows in Kano in the late 1970s and early 1980s, nearly two-thirds of the widows interviewed who had children were either living in their late husbands' houses with their children or living with their children elsewhere. Most women had a clear preference to stay with their children, even if it meant greater economic hardship. Widows, however, were not required to observe kulle, and as such they had the opportunity to earn more income than married women.[24] Outside the parameters of marriage, motherhood was paramount in encouraging women to continue their residence in the diaspora—even those women without consanguine relations nearby.

In October 1959, the widow of the deceased Hausa chief of Ntumbo, Diddi, accused her husband's successor of stealing the forty-three head of cattle that her son Adamu had inherited two years prior to the court date.[25] As her son was too young to manage the herd himself, Ntumbo's new Hausa chief—evidently the son of Diddi's co-wife—was entrusted to maintain the herd until Diddi's son could take over this responsibility. Diddi, however, was suspicious of the chief's scruples and told him she would hire a cowboy to look after the cattle instead. With two of the chief's proxies, she went to Mbaw one morning where the cattle were kept. On arrival, Diddi counted only thirty-five head. The cowboy looking after the cattle informed her that the Hausa chief sought to prevent Diddi from taking any cattle with her. She stormed back to Ntumbo and confronted the Hausa chief directly: "I asked him why he lie for me." Receiving an inadequate response, Diddi implored the alkali to "take over for my [son's] cows." After deliberating over apparent inconsistencies with the father's will and how the estate had been distributed, the Ntumbo Hausa chief agreed to hand over thirty-seven head of cattle plus the value of another four cattle in cash.[26]

Because the new Hausa chief was also the son of Diddi's deceased husband, there may have been confusion over how many cattle he and Diddi's young son were to inherit. Diddi's actions in this court case suggest that though her widowhood may have prompted her to stop at nothing to secure her future and that of her son, it also allowed her to manage her daily life beyond the confines of kulle. The case also illustrates the trumping power of the alkali over the Hausa chief and his desire for wealth. In a similar case below, we find that Bamenda's limam acted on his brotherly duties to assist his widowed sister in her predicament to secure a place of residence for her and her two sons.

In June 1960, Malam Ahmadu Limam of Bamenda brought a man named Kuku Makeri to the alkali's court.[27] The limam contended that Kuku Makeri unlawfully dispossessed his sister, Garuwa, and her two sons from their compound after the death of his sister's husband, Magaji Aska. Kuku Makeri defended himself by stating that Magaji Aska, while on his deathbed, submitted documents to him that transferred the ownership of the compound to him. He also said there was a second letter concerning the legacy of his farm, but this was given to his wife's father. Inquiring further, the alkali asked Kuku Makeri if Garuwa told him whether her husband gave him the compound "as [a] present" or if he was to "look [after] the compound till his sons grew?" Kuku Makeri replied that Garuwa had remained silent on these matters as she handed over her husband's papers. For her part, Garuwa confirmed,

> Yes, my husband is not servant for [Kuku Makeri] and he get no relation with him but they are friends. So when he fall sick he near to die he move all the documents of the compound.... If he died, make [Kuku Makeri] looked after the compound when his son's [sic] grew they enter the compound.... So when the late died his son reached the maximum of man, his uncle [Malam Ahmadu Limam] want to fixed [sic] the compound in order [for the late Magaji Aska's] son stay inside. Then [Kuku Makeri] prevent [this].

Like Diddi, Garuwa was determined to secure her sons' material well-being and through them her own. Unlike Diddi, however, Garuwa had the added task of proving that her deceased husband had indeed owned the property at stake and was neither a tenant nor servant of Kuku Makeri's. Though Kuku Makeri initially denied Garuwa's claims, after hearing from her two grown sons he capitulated, agreeing that the compound was indeed owned by the late Magaji Aska and that he had been charged to look after (Arabic: *kalife*; Hausa: *kalifu*) the property until the sons were ready to occupy the space themselves.[28]

Parker Shipton has suggested that "convey[ing] an entrustment from forebears to heirs, is to bind past to future, securing one's own place in a sequence and a process. It is to enter a flow."[29] What of Diddi, Garuwa, and the widow who returned to Kano? Can we say that widows like them entered such a "flow," given that they lived in a world of patriarchy and patrilineality in matters of entrusting wealth and heritage in the diaspora? Neither Diddi nor Garuwa could claim for themselves the late Ntumbo chief's forty-odd cattle or Magaji Aska's compound. They were neither the forebears nor the primary heirs. Through their maternal bonds to their sons and their need to secure a place for themselves in their old age, they were instrumental in binding their husbands' material pasts with their sons' futures. Likewise, the widow from Kano State promised to transfer the better part of her husband's legacy to his sister, apparently the only remaining survivor in his family. In so doing, she effectively overcame the distance separating her from Hausaland to extend her husband's legacy through time and space.

These women were facilitators in Hausa patrilineal inheritance patterns, passing property from one generation to another for a family in which their belonging was ambivalent. Neither legalities nor religious imperatives framed their relations with these patrilineages, but their experiences and affections through diasporic motherhood and widowhood ensured a lasting social tie. For Diddi and Garuwa, their dependence on the lines of men they helped to create was important enough to struggle for. These two women may not have directly given inherited wealth to their sons, but they exercised their "own place" in that sequential process to the fullest extent possible. Each woman was a caretaker and beneficiary of a particular flow that reestablished her presence in the diaspora and the continuation of the diaspora itself.

▶▶▶•◀◀◀

Death in the diaspora also stimulated travel into and within the diaspora. In such instances, the travelers were almost exclusively men like Sanda and Wada, male heirs of itinerant or settled Hausa men who had died in the Grassfields. The Ndop alkali communicated regularly with Islamic judges in Northern Nigeria. Through the diaspora's networks, inheritance distribution amongst family members stretched across distances connecting Hausaland to the Grassfields could be administered rather straightforwardly.[30] Distributing inheritance of itinerants and settlers to family members in Hausaland may be viewed as a way for the dead to be symbolically or posthumously reincorporated into their communities of origin. But distance could be an obstacle in more ways than one. Like the Wum district officer's suspicions that Sanda and Wada were not actually the sons of Gashin Baki, conflicts did arise over the identity of successors. People traveling to collect a family inheritance could become untrustworthy strangers in the eyes of locals, while in other cases travelers died as strangers, leaving community leaders with no clues on how to go about passing inheritance to distant survivors. People thus overcame distance to claim the dead while others became obscure through it.

When male descendants like Sanda and Wada traveled to claim legacies of the dead, they themselves entered a temporary existence as diasporic Hausas. They appeared to have stayed in the Grassfields for at least a year or more, and perhaps permanently. The amount of wealth they inherited was substantial. However, that most sons and family members did not obtain such vast amounts of wealth suggests that material considerations were not the only factors compelling them into temporary mobility. Identifying oneself as an heir was part of the process of honoring the dead, and it was an important pathway for people throughout the diaspora and Hausaland to witness the expansiveness and diversity of Hausa lived experience.

Whether a deceased man was a settler or an itinerant, if someone in the Grassfields knew who his relations were and where they lived, the alkali was able to manage the man's legacy. Garba Na Kirki appeared in the court records as an itinerant Hausa traveling without his kin. In April 1955, he left his home in Enugu for the Grassfields, and then went on to a town called Gude in the Adamawa region, where he died shortly thereafter. The alkali at Ndop administered Garba's estate, which amounted mainly to clothes and cooking utensils. After his death, their value of just over 86 pounds, less court fees and a debt of 14 pounds to associates in

Pinyi, belonged to his son Abani who traveled from his home in Goram, a town located near Kano in Nigeria, in order to claim his inheritance.[31]

When the settler Musa Lamin died in 1953, he was survived by family members in Garoua and by his wife Dudu in the Grassfields. He had left Garoua to settle in the Grassfields village of Binka with his wife. The records attest that Musa Lamin traveled regionally a good deal, for he had contacts indebted to him—and he to them—in Konanne, Bali Nyonga, and Kumba, the latter of which lies south of the Grassfields and was the location of his death. Community leaders in Kumba had his big gown, jumpers, and trousers sold on the market. The district officer of Kumba and the Sarkin Hausawa of Konanne ensured that the money from these sales and the cash he left in their respective towns were brought to the alkali. The amount collected was over 94 pounds. Debts were paid, money returned to friends, and more than 12 pounds were given to the deceased's brother and a messenger for the pains (*wahala*) they undertook to travel between Garoua and the Grassfields. The alkali doled out the remainder of the estate to Dudu, and to Musa Lamin's mother, sister, and brother in Garoua.[32]

Inheritance distribution in the above cases was administered with relative ease, even though it involved the hardship of travel for male heirs. In other instances, however, distance produced mistrust as people, including district officers, negotiated the claiming of the dead. In August 1956, Mallam Jibiril Dan Koli, "a Hausa man," died at Sabga Babanke in the Grassfields. Apparently from the town of Kibiya, south of Kano city, Mallam Jibiril carried with him a number of items, some rather atypical. Along with his horse, some cash, two turbans and black gowns, he also owned seventeen caps, paper, and a "Masanga casting." Perhaps Mallam Jibiril earned money on his journeys by selling caps or making charms from the Qur'anic verses he wrote on pieces of paper. Perhaps he sold glass bangles and beads produced by the Masaga guild in Bida, Nigeria. Though the historical record offers so little information, the things he left behind tell us he was likely a modest man with more than a few talents and interests. He was also a father, and his son and daughter, Usumanu and Diddi, were to inherit what their father owned upon his death. On August 28, the alkali deposited 81 pounds in favor of Usumanu and Diddi, both of whom were unable to attend the court hearing. Usumanu was imprisoned in Bamenda at the time, while Diddi lived in Mayo Ndaga in British Cameroon's Adamawa Division, more than 200 kilometers from Ndop.[33]

Without the alkali's knowledge, Abubakar Sarkin Hausawa of Bamenda wrote to the sarki of Mallam Jibiril's hometown in Nigeria to inform him of the latter's death. The Kibiya chief apparently wrote a letter in reply, testifying that the primary heir to Mallam Jibiril would have been his brother Yusufu. Because Yusufu was dead, however, Yusufu's son, Malam Ibrahim, should have received a share of the estate. Therefore, Malam Ibrahim was sent to Ndop about six months later in March 1957 with letter in hand in order to "claim the properties of the late Mallam Jibiril."[34] The alkali was skeptical of the letter's message and its messenger, for there was no official stamp on the letter, which would have verified Malam Ibrahim's claims. He then told Malam Ibrahim that he must return to Kano to ascertain a stamped letter from the alkali of Kibiya, the chief judge of Kano, or the emir of Kano that restated his rights to Mallam Jibiril's inheritance.[35] Perhaps because the cost of yet another trip to the Grassfields was too great, Malam Ibrahim never returned.

After waiting nine months without a sign of Malam Ibrahim's return, the alkali wrote a detailed letter to the Bamenda's district officer, explaining the story in full and requesting his approval to distribute the inheritance to Usumanu and Diddi as originally planned.[36] The alkali reasoned that Malam Ibrahim "did not come with the letter from the Alkali of Kibiya or from the chief Alkali of Kano, that shows . . . he is not the man who is going to succeed the late Mallam Jibiril." Below the alkali's closing ("I have the honour to be, sir, your obedient servant") and signature, the district officer inscribed his handwritten response, "Alkali, As I see it, the decision of the court, unsatisfactory as it is, is binding and Usumanu cannot now be prevented from lifting the deposit made in his favour." Though the alkali repeatedly referred to Usumanu and Diddi in tandem as Mallam Jibiril's survivors, both entitled to shares of their father's estate, the district officer imagined the issue of inheritance among Hausas as one that flowed through men only. Though daughters were and are entitled to inherit property from their fathers, the district officer's limits of knowledge regarding Hausa inheritance practices would have effectively erased Diddi's role in connecting her family's past to its future—had he distributed the estate himself.

Though not all of the deceased men above were as wealthy as Alhaji Gashin Baki, most carried with them some measure of wealth or form of property. There were exceptions, however. When a man named Tijani died in Banso in 1955, he had just over six pounds' worth of belongings.[37] He left his hometown of Bauchi for unknown reasons. While in the Grassfields, he incurred debts to two malams and seemed to have gained little in return. The alkali dispersed monies to the Native Affairs Treasury as ushira fees, to the Hausa chief of Nso as la'ada for taking care of the deceased's property, and to the malams to whom Tijani was indebted. No survivors were identified in the court records, indicating that most people in the Grassfields knew very little about this man or his family. We will never know why Tijani decided to leave his home or why no one in his family came to the Grassfields to claim him. Perhaps he is what Hausas in the homeland call a 'dan dandi, one who, for a variety of reasons, wanders out into the world seeking to avoid social or economic constraints in his home community or perhaps just to learn about the world, performing odd jobs along the way.[38] Or perhaps he is the archetype of Adama Shuaibu Limam's critique of the Hausa diaspora as commercial diaspora—a man who abandoned his family to seek a fortune, only to fail and leave them with unanswered questions.[39]

>>>•|•<<<

Inheriting wealth was a form of social reincorporation as people survived the deaths of others, and this reincorporation in Grassfields Hausa communities was greatly influenced by the factors of gender difference, distance, and kinship networks. Death in the diaspora also inspired questions about how values were reinforced in settlements where the pursuit of lafiya rested on local relations with a diverse assemblage of Grassfields peoples. As noted, death brought about a search for new forms of relation for survivors, and it was not uncommon for people to search for belonging in ways that accentuated the porousness of Hausa society.

Many Hausa men in the Grassfields were concerned with the continuation of their patrilineages through sons and leaving a legacy in the diaspora. If a Hausa man had no sons through which to extend his patrilineage—and sometimes even if he did—he could turn to child fostering or adoption, which are widely practiced among Hausas. According to Abner Cohen, fostering (*yaye*) in particular was "one of the most important institutions of Hausa migration, in the building up of the network of Hausa communities, because of its role in the rapid demographic adjustments required by the economy of these communities." Fostered sons, whose legal parents were usually still living, viewed their foster fathers as fathers. Because foster sons could only inherit from original parents, foster fathers frequently considered them to be better business clients than their own sons. A foster father might even develop more sentimental ties to the foster son precisely because the management of wealth did not play a fundamental role in their relationship.[40]

Though foster sons could be part of the foster father's extended family, Hausa men and women have also been known to incorporate children of various ancestries into their families through adoption. Adoption, however, is different from fostering, as it is usually associated with raising an orphaned child.[41] Indeed, the death of kin not only affected those who traveled to or were married into Hausa diaspora society, but the life experiences and identities of Grassfielders living in or near Hausa settlements were influenced as well. Hausa neighbors could become adoptive parents to Grassfields orphans, especially if they were living a fair distance away from their parents' extended kin.

Through adoption into a Hausa family, orphaned children could acquire new forms of belonging while the Hausa family increased its wealth in people, a circumstance reflecting how death could bring about mutual transformations in the lives of both migrants and indigenous Grassfielders. These children unevenly adopted Hausa knowledge and practices, a process that was influenced by gender difference. What follows is the story of a pair of Grassfields siblings who became orphaned in the 1940s. It illuminates how gender dynamics as well as one's place of residence worked in tandem to shape the siblings' options and strategies during their experiences as adopted Hausa children. For the boy in particular, his friendships, Qur'anic education, and experiences of itinerancy and trade with an adoptive father had a profound effect on his identity formation, in large part because these elements were central to male Hausaness in the diaspora during much of the colonial period.

In the 1920s, a Kom man named Bobo moved his family from Bafunge to settle in Abakwa-Bamenda.[42] Some people say the family came to the Hausa settlement because of its economic opportunities. Bobo was a petty trader and farmer who grew plantains and coco yam. Others, including his son, Ali Bobo, believe Bobo was accused of witchcraft in Bafunge. He and his family then escaped by going to Abakwa-Bamenda, which "was just like a free town. So people come from different places to settle . . . because there was no problem." When Bobo arrived, Sarkin Hausawa Malam Baba gave him some land on which to farm and build a home. Not long afterward, Bobo's wife gave birth to a girl but the mother died from complications. Some people in Abakwa-Bamenda recalled that Bobo brought his newborn daughter to neighboring Hausa women who were nursing. People in the community came to call her Mommy Nono—*nono* being a Hausa word that refers to the breast, udder, or the milk they produce. Not everyone thinks this story is true, however. One person who knew Mommy Nono well suggested that she received this name not because she had Hausa wet nurses but because she had loved drinking cow's milk as a young girl.[43]

By 1935, Bobo had a second wife, and she gave birth to Ali. He would be the second youngest of Bobo's nine children. Roughly ten years later, this second wife also died, and not long afterward Bobo died, too. Some believe he was bitten by a poisonous snake while fishing in the stream that flows through the Hausa quarter. Regardless of the cause, at that moment all of Bobo's children were orphaned. We do not know what happened to all of them, but the stories of Mommy Nono and Ali demonstrate how death became a diasporic turning point in the lives of these Grassfields children, primarily because of their young ages and location at the time their father died.

Abakwa-Bamenda resident Aishatu Ibrahim told me it was her aunt who raised Mommy Nono. While everyone in the quarter came to know the girl by that name, Aishatu's aunt gave her adopted daughter a Muslim name, Hajera, and sometimes she also called her *tallafi*—an orphan, "a child received for bringing up."[44] Mommy Nono became fluent in the Hausa language ("*Ta magana Hausa sosai!*"), and as she got older she earned an income through petty trading, producing and selling fried corn and groundnuts much like the urban Hausa women surrounding her. Though her adopted family called her Hajera, she never converted to Islam. Unlike the Hausa woman who raised her, Mommy Nono engaged in farm work on her father's plot, which one of her brothers inherited. Perhaps because of social influences from other Kom people who had by that point settled in an Abakwa-Bamenda neighborhood called the Bun Quarter, Mommy Nono turned to Catholicism and attended services at Our Lady of Lourdes.[45] She married a Bamiléké man for a time and moved out of the Hausa quarter. But the marriage dissolved, and Mommy Nono moved back to her father's plot in Abakwa where she lived with her brother Lucas until she died around 2002. Though people did not portray Mommy Nono as a particularly independent woman, the fact that she never remarried after her brief marriage indicates that perhaps she was. Living with her brother likely helped to normalize her single womanhood in the quarter, given Hausa conceptualizations of women being dependent on their kinsmen after terminating a marriage. One woman simply stated that "she was not a problem woman."[46]

Ali Bobo's path to adulthood through his relations with Hausas in Abakwa-Bamenda was markedly different in character and experience from that of his sister. Our knowledge of his life history is more detailed because I interviewed him directly; it was not based on what others remembered. As a child Ali spent much of his time playing with age-mates in the Hausa quarter. Most of them were Muslim. He began to dress like them and followed them along to makaranta, immersing himself in Qur'anic teachings. He started to become "used to" Islam. The community was also "used to" him. The limam of Bamenda started calling him Ali, similar to the way Mommy Nono's caretaker endearingly named her Hajera. About a year after Bobo's death, Ali attached himself to a Hausa cattle trader from Ndu named Garba Shungar. Ali explained their relationship: "You know when you are orphan, you get some Pa. . . . If you are humble, submissive to the person, they just decide to take you along." Ali traveled with Garba Shungar for three years, apparently never returning to Bamenda during that time. He carried and washed Garba Shungar's clothes and was responsible for making him tea. Traveling from market to market, they slept on the roadside, but once in a while they sought out nicer accommodations in the homes of strangers. Garba Shungar would offer the customary gift of money to the wives of the compound as a token of appreciation for their food and hospitality. Garba and Ali were not alone on their journeys. The trader had four wives of his own, and he commonly brought along two of them who took turns cooking for him.

Most accounts of Hausa diasporic trading networks suggest that Islam provided a unifying ideology, helping merchants to easily establish bonds of trust across vast stretches of land. What is striking about Ali's narrative is that itinerancy itself reinforced his identity formation as a Muslim. According to Ali, "A Muslim cannot move with someone who is a Christian . . . because Muslims do not eat everything," and "Muslims usually move with Muslims, because they can pray together and they can eat the same type of food." On their journeys, people knew Ali was Muslim, as he carried his "prayer things," including his mat, his kettle, and his sandals. Though he knew Hausa, he mainly spoke Pidgin English. If questions arose regarding his identity or origins, Ali would tell them he was an adopted Hausa child. In his storytelling, Ali seemed to imply that being recognized as Muslim far surpassed any wish he may have had in his youth to be viewed as Hausa—even if such a desire ever surfaced.

For reasons unexplained Ali decided to leave Garba Shungar after three years of traveling. Ali suggests that he wanted to start his own life, but he also seemed to regret his decision to part ways. Because he left Garba Shungar before he was old enough to marry, and because he was an orphan, Ali had no father to "[find] him a wife to marry," as is "Muslim tradition." It therefore took him a much longer time to save enough funds to ready himself for marriage. After leaving Garba Shungar, Ali resided in the town of Mamfe for roughly five years, eventually finding employment at the high court as a "night-watch" and custodian. He was then transferred back to Bamenda in his early twenties, where he continued the same work.

Neither Mommy Nono nor her half-brother Ali were born Hausa or claimed a Hausa identity in their adulthood. Yet their relationships with and proximity to Hausas deeply affected their life paths and identities, though in markedly different ways. Some of these differences may be attributed to the siblings' gender difference and their respective ages at the time of their father's death. Mommy Nono was a nubile girl when her father died, a *bururwa*. Whereas men like the limam and Garba Shungar viewed Ali as a son adopted into the Hausa community, Mommy Nono's age and lack of a male guardianship likely positioned her as a potential wife or concubine in the eyes of many Hausa men rather than a daughter to be raised. Had Mommy Nono entrusted herself to an itinerant merchant as Ali had done, for instance, this likely would have been her fate.

Ali's identity formation as a Muslim was deeply entrenched through his boyhood friendships, Qur'anic education, and temporary adoption with Garba Shungar. His travels and the way in which he presented himself strongly reinforced his sense of belonging to a distinct community of people who held religious beliefs and practices in common.[47] Mommy Nono, on the other hand, was more influenced by her relationships with Hausa women, and her more sedentary lifestyle among those who knew her since infancy did not require her to emphasize her difference or sameness either way. Everyone knew who her family was and how she was raised. Though another woman in her position may have just as easily become Muslim as she did Christian, it was not uncommon for the women of one family to opt for Christian monogamy while the men chose Islam and its concomitant polygynous marital practices that more closely resembled those of their natal societies. Again, Hausas' desires to rename the children Hajera and Ali, two Muslim names, did not equally correlate to religious conversion. Like Hadija, their renaming symbolized their uneven incorporation into a domestic unit, be it a permanent or mobile one.

>>>•<<<

Gendered power dynamics in Hausa society influenced the divergent manners in which people coped with grief and contestations over their means of social reintegration after the deaths of others. The colonial edifice of power that incorporated Islamic patriarchal norms into its administration often intervened to assert its authority and to challenge the ways Hausas worked through social issues related to death—be it the death of Aliyu and Maryama's son and the related tensions among those who cared for him, or questions over the identities of Gashin Baki's survivors and the sums of money they were to inherit. The certainty of death consistently produced social instability as people transformed from wives to widows, husbands to widowers, and from sons and daughters to heirs or orphans. Beyond these intimate ruptures, death also caused tensions to surface as survivors like Hadija negotiated their new identities and how they claimed relations to the dead. In these moments, the dead influenced the lives of the living from beyond the grave. At the same time, the dead were also silent observers as survivors reasserted or contested dominant social relations.

The gender and location of survivors and the dead themselves shaped the strategies people could implement in forging new relations or reaffirming old ones. In particular, contested claims over the wealth of the deceased were grounded in real and fictive kinship relations built on dispersed patrilineal descent networks that were affected by distance and cultural porosity. When mapped across the vast spaces connecting Hausaland to the Grassfields, gender and location had a significant bearing on how people managed the shifting sites of belonging that death set in motion. The confluence of these factors prompted continued mobility throughout the diaspora, fostering in travelers and settlers an awareness of the broader Hausa world. It also obscured the identity of potential survivors—patrilineal or otherwise. As much as the methods of reintegrating liminal figures could reinforce the values of a widespread community, especially for widows and male heirs, it could also be the platform for integrating new people like Ali and Mommy Nono, whose search for belonging worked through local relations and highlights the fluidity of Hausa identification.

SIX

Third Reversal
Conflict and Judgment

HADIJA'S CONNECTION TO ALHAJI GASHIN BAKI BROUGHT ABOUT her movement into the diaspora. This event irrevocably changed her social and geographical orientation, a transformation in context and in identification that constitutes the very fabric of Hausa diaspora history. When Gashin Baki died, like all survivors of the dead Hadija found herself in a new position of relation to her surroundings: her tie to local society had become unclear. These points of reversal were ambiguous in their meaning. Was she a woman married into the diaspora, and then a widow who could claim Gashin Baki as a former husband? Could she really be the beneficiary of wealth obtained through long-distance trading, considering that she might have once been a human item in that very same trade? Though Hadija lived through these uncertainties from the moment of her exchange in Lere, they only surfaced in the historical record because of a third moment of peripeteia that was inextricably tied to its predecessors. Hadija negotiated a new, albeit ephemeral form of belonging in marrying Yusufu, but the Sarkin Hausawa of Mme-Bafumen intervened and transformed this brief union into a conflict by claiming the couple had disobeyed divine law.

The sarki's criminal charges against them and Malam Audu prompted these individuals and their witnesses to travel again, this time to Ndop where they voiced contested tales of the past. These tales, mediated and recorded in the form of testimony, reflected how some people's search for belonging converged with and overrode similar desires in other people. Status hierarchies partnered with gendered inequalities to influence the rationale for defining and judging such conflicts, but they did not always determine discourses or outcomes. Hadija, Yusufu, the sarki, and many others like them entered the alkali's courtroom with different kinds of knowledge and from different social positions. Yet the very factors that could have condemned Hadija to enslavement were the very same factors she was able to manipulate to establish her freedom. Multiple patriarchies converged with the distance and anonymity that travel created to influence Hausa diaspora life in the Grassfields, setting in motion points of reversal in how people established and disputed ideal forms of relation.

Women were not the only individuals voicing their struggles in the courtroom. Though Hadija's actions and status were the primary focus of her trial, conflicts over acceptable forms of masculine behavior, the means by which men acquired new wives, and men's knowledge of Islamic principles were at issue as well. Yusufu, Malam Audu, the Sarkin Hausawa, and the alkali debated over Hadija's past relations from different positions of interest and frames of cultural rationale. Yusufu wanted to marry a new young wife out of personal desire and to enhance his sense of belonging in augmenting his wealth in people. Malam Audu was Hadija's guardian and believed he had the divine right to label her social status as a slave and to control whom she married and when. The Sarkin Hausawa of Mme-Bafumen and the alkali touted the importance of Islamic principles in terminating and forging marriages, especially since marriage was the primary way to control women's sexuality and reinforce community patriarchy in the Grassfields.

In her work on gender and legal discourses in Muslim Swahili communities, Susan Hirsch noted that Islamic law and Swahili cultural norms construct the "legal and social positions" of married men and women as "pronouncing husbands" and "persevering wives [who] are expected to endure marital hardships without complaint." Law produces a particular institutional discourse that shapes people's social lives. However, it is through disputes in Islamic courts that "gender is made, remade, and transformed in fundamental ways," as people negotiate "through and against gendered subject positions." Like Hadija, litigants in court cases could often transform others' "assumptions about their status," producing a context in which dominant gender relations are reproduced but also undermined.[1] In the Grassfields, Hausas similarly policed and negotiated ideal forms of relation and competing spheres of patriarchy, but they did so with the added element of distance, which separated diaspora settlements both from Hausaland and from each other within the Grassfields.

The previous chapter explored how the survival of death was recalibrated through distance and gender. This chapter demonstrates that conflicts involving relations among men and women often arose out of similar circumstances. The distances examined here are much shorter than those that detached Hadija from Lere or Gashin Baki and his sons from Kano. Rather, these distances separated established Hausa diaspora communities within the Grassfields region as people traveled between places such as Nwa, Lassin, Ndop, and Dumbo in order to establish beneficial relations or to escape unsatisfactory ones. Given that the alkali court in Ndop was the only location in the Grassfields where disputes among Hausas were officially recorded until 1957, its archive allows an examination of relations beyond one single settlement.[2]

▶▶▶•❘•❘◀◀◀

During the very same months that Hadija fought to secure her social status, a Hausa couple in the town of Binka had their own battle to wage when they became the targets of neighborhood derision for reasons distinct from, yet ultimately related to Hadija's dilemma. The conflict erupted over the healing of an ailing young boy, the son of a prominent Hausa compound head, a *maigida* named Aliyu. In his delirium, Aliyu's son cried out the names of Magajiya Dibino and her husband Salimu, identifying the couple as the sources of his illness as well as the very healers who could cure him. Aliyu implored the couple to help his son. They then instructed Aliyu to bring them water, which they "put in [their mouths] three times." Aliyu's son drank the water, after which the couple "jumped" over the boy—again, three times. Salimu instructed someone to retrieve from his home "Hausa medicine called (Gadal)," which,

according to one Bamenda Old Town resident, has spiritual and aphro-
disiacal qualities, and is also used by women to assist them in childbirth
and to enhance the flow of breast milk.[3] Once Salimu obtained the gadal,
he ground it, mixed it with water, and told the boy to drink. Though
the couple's treatment healed the boy, it also confirmed in Aliyu's mind
that Magajiya Dibino and Salimu were witches who threatened the well-
being of his family and community. After the couple had treated his son,
Aliyu and two women began to beat Magajiya Dibino. They tied her up
with rope, smashed hot peppers into her eyes, and called her a witch.[4]
Then another group tied up and beat Salimu, making it clear that he too
was a witch deserving of punishment. Though both husband and wife
survived this attack, Salimu's wounds appear to have been less severe
than Magajiya Dibino's, as she alone was advised to seek medical care at
the local hospital to alleviate her suffering.[5]

After bringing their case to the Ndop alkali court where they found
justice for the crimes committed against them, Magajiya Dibino and Salimu tried to continue on with their lives in Binka. But just two months
after their initial ordeal they were once again made aware of how fragile
their sense of belonging was. On a January day, Salimu had gone out
to "the bush" to work. When he returned he found an empty home, his
wife nowhere to be found. A neighbor told him she had been called to
Maigida Aliyu's compound where a crowd was starting to form. Upon
entering Aliyu's home, Salimu saw his wife restrained by ropes. He tried
to free her, but a man held onto her cloth while others began to slap and
beat Salimu. Aliyu and others involved then called "all Binka boys" to
assist them in the fray, confirming that many in the village viewed Salimu and Magajiya Dibino as undesirables. Ultimately the couple lived
through this second round of fear and violence, one that somehow did
not seem to diminish their desire to belong, even as neighbors beat them
and broke their teeth.[6]

Witchcraft—known as *maita* in Hausa and more appropriately translated as "soul-eating"—is an actual substance within the belly of the
witch whose sources of nourishment are the souls of other people.[7] In
Hausa thought, humans are comprised of a body (*jiki*) and a soul (*kurwa*).
According to Pamela Schmoll, "The soul seems to have both life (*rai*)
and be life."[8] Victims of soul-eating, like Aliyu's son, may experience

a number of symptoms, from a slow wasting away, to headaches and pain in the neck and back, to displays of madness. Schmoll writes, "The affliction seems to speak of the total dehumanization of the individual as life is drained out of him. At one level he becomes deprived of those functions which help make him human." The victim is transformed from a human who consumes to one who is consumed. The treatment for soul-eating is difficult as it rests upon the ability of the victim to identify the soul-eater. In the case of infants, small children, and adults too debilitated to speak, the attackers are rarely found. In the cases Schmoll observed in the Hausa-speaking regions of South Central Niger in the mid-1980s, soul-eaters that victims managed to identify were simultaneously punished as they performed their cure. Once they were sought out, they were then "stripped naked, and made to jump over the victim three times without touching him," releasing the soul back into the victim's body. This release was characterized in Binka as "vomiting the son," an intense, forceful bodily ejection of the soul. And similar to what happened in Binka, Hausa soul-eaters in Niger "would then perhaps be beaten and exiled from the village."[9]

But there is more to this story than possible soul-eating attacks and communal retribution. Little is known about the couple or their assailants, what they did for a living, or whether they were born in the diaspora. But the Hausa titles of *maigida* and *magajiya*, which preceded the names of Aliyu and Dibino, respectively, point to other factors lying at the root of these violent outbreaks. Maigida identifies a man who is a household or compound head and usually a known patron in the community. In a gross simplification of the history behind the latter title, magajiya, over the course of the twentieth century it became associated with women who organized *karuwai*, previously married women working as prostitutes or courtesans. These women have also been known to perform *bori* spiritual practices, which pre-date the spread of Islam among Hausas and involve the worship and possession of spirits (*iskoki*). Prior to the 1804 jihad in Hausaland, the title magajiya was held by the most important female of royal descent who served as a valued adviser to the sarki. With the formation of the Sokoto Caliphate, however, women in general ceased to hold state titles: the office of magajiya was stripped of its political influence to the point where all that remained was its authority over karuwai. Though various Hausa individuals, including married women, have either practiced or supported bori worship, and though not all karuwai are bori mediums, karuwai and the magajiya are sometimes socially perceived as bori practitioners even though they are not exclusively so.[10]

The persecution in Binka occurred within several frames of historical reference, even though the individuals involved likely held many aspects of Hausa cultural heritage in common. Nothing illustrates this more pointedly than the witness testimony of Buba Huseine, likely a Fulani man. Believing that, as a Muslim, he was not to acknowledge the existence of witchcraft, he admitted the following in court: "But myself I know perfectly [Salimu] is a witch although it is not in Muhammadan book." His adherence to Islam masked as contradiction the cultural syncretism involving Islamic and other forms of African belief. Similarly, while the position of the magajiya was once venerated within Hausa society, the ordeal in Binka unambiguously shows that the title on its own did not ensure a particular site of belonging for women in the diaspora. That Magajiya Dibino and Salimu did not have any allies defending them indicates the extent to which the title of magajiya had lost its currency in 1950s Binka.

While many Hausas in the Grassfields note a clear distinction between bori mediums and witches, some grossly conflated the two or used the idiom of witchcraft to demonize the pre-Islamism and associated lack of patriarchal control over female reproductive power that bori signifies. Some inhabitants of Bamenda's Old Town believe this happened to that community's magajiya and her husband around the same period of time. Everyone remembered her as the leader of bori practitioners in Bamenda—a woman who played an important role in celebrating marriages. Some people say the magajiya and her husband—a childless couple—left Bamenda on their own accord, but others believed they were accused of witchcraft and exiled, having to make a new home for themselves in Sabga.[11] But Limam Alhaji Baba Malam Shuaibu challenged these opinions: "People are telling lies. To say such a thing is not good." She did not practice witchcraft, rather, "She gives treatment for witch."[12] The magajiya of Binka, on the other hand, was much stronger in her powers than the woman in Bamenda. "That one saw very far. If she entered here right now, she would see everything that is in this house. That one she charged a lot of money, but this one here [in Bamenda] you just bring fowl, like five fowl, to make sadaka. That one for Binka, wai wai wai!"[13]

The idiom of witchcraft itself is highly gendered in Africa. Ralph Austen has noted that female witches are "totally stigmatized," while males may be "recognized as both witches and legitimate figures of political and ritual authority."[14] Women who are accused of witchcraft are frequently active in the public sphere and therefore signify the escape of female reproductive power from domestic space. Female sexuality, as expressed in the language of witchcraft, is thus often viewed as a "force liberated from reproductive imperatives."[15] That Bamenda's magajiya had no children of her own was not lost on her neighbors. This characterization of witches echoes the ways in which Hausas have come to describe karuwai, namely as deviants from the Islamic adulthood norm of marriage.

There is no certainty that Magajiya Dibino was engaged in spirit possession or in organizing prostitutes, nor is there certainty regarding the couple's denial in court over their use of witchcraft. Given that soul-eating capabilities are usually congenital, Magajiya Dibino defended herself by stating, "Since my mother born me I never eat witch." Still, their neighbors' accusations of witchcraft, the nature of the violence, and the title magajiya together suggest that the couple's stigmatization was grounded in gendered conceptions of power and fear. Although Salimu was victimized alongside his wife, the extent of Magajiya Dibino's injuries and the fact that she was the initial target of violence in both episodes indicate that Maigida Aliyu sought to reassert an ideal patriarchal order through female disempowerment. In so doing, the Binka vigilantes also established Salimu as a husband who did not possess the power to control or protect his own wife. Indeed, views of liberated women causing communal harm had important consequences for the men who married them. Salimu and the Bamenda magajiya's husband, a butcher named 'Dan Dumbu, were both subject to persecution and derision for their nonconforming masculinity, including their lack of wealth in children.[16]

But as with Hadija, the spiritual beliefs interwoven in the Islamic court's practices paradoxically worked in the couple's favor. Hadija utilized the ordeal of mubahala to affirm her freedom and inheritance. Witchcraft was and remains a false accusation in Ndop's Islamic court and has therefore provided a legal shield for alleged witches, including Magajiya Dibino and Salimu.[17] Every Grassfields Muslim accused of soul-eating in the court denied the charges by turning the tables on his or her accusers: suspected witches came forward as plaintiffs who formally sued defendants for libel.[18] The alkali found Maigida Aliyu and his co-defendants guilty. They were fined for their criminal offense and additionally charged 1 pound for Magajiya Dibino's blood, 3 pounds for Salimu's blood, and 2 pounds for Salimu's tooth. Here the blood spilled from the magajiya's body was worth less than the blood and teeth of her husband.

For Hadija and Yusufu, and for Magajiya Dibino and Salimu, fortunes were reversed as community patriarchs criminalized their actions for upsetting the moral underpinnings of community peace—or lafiya. Though one conflict dealt with illicit marriage and the other with witchcraft, both involved policing women's sexuality and emphasizing adulthood norms of marriage as primary ways to signify male authority and its role in controlling female sexual desire and reproductive power.[19] This does not mean, however, that women have never acted to reinforce established patriarchies. Talle and the women who beat Magajiya Dibino are testament to this. Maintaining community hierarchies has served the interests of many women like them, including postmenopausal women, female kin of prominent men, senior wives, and female slave owners. Deniz Kandiyoti developed the concept of the "patriarchal bargain" to indicate which rules or scripts regulate gender relations "to which both genders accommodate and acquiesce," even though individuals often act to contest and negotiate those norms. This concept aids in assessing the ways in which women support, implement, or strategize within patriarchal systems while they themselves are subjugated by them. Very often, men in turn provide certain rewards, protections, or benefits to those women who aid in the control of other women.[20]

As Chapter 4 demonstrated, marriage among Hausas in the Grassfields took on added meaning since the patrilineal logic of abakwa reinforced its significance as a site of belonging for women, especially those women who were not Hausa by birth or women like Hadija who traveled to the Grassfields. Whereas men forged different kinds of relationships through which to gain social capital—patron–client relations, friendship, or religious conversion, for example—Hausa or Hausa-ized women had fewer avenues. These considerations run the risk of reinforcing male perceptions of female honor in Hausa society. But in the writing of Nana Asma'u, the poet, scholar, and daughter of Usuman dan Fodio, there is evidence that elite Fulani and Hausa women "set a high value on a respectable married life in accordance with the norms of their society. In particular, they valued fertility, modesty, piety, neighborliness, an active contribution to household economy, and the care of children."[21] Regulating marriage was also the central element legitimating the authority of the Grassfields alkali within the colonial hierarchy of power. The creation of the alkali court institutionalized Islamic norms governing relations between men and women, elevating their significance over competing views developed from the diaspora's mixed historical references, including those such as the office of the magajiya that predate the entrenchment of Islam in Hausa society.

Islamic sexual ethics have heavily influenced the cultural import and role of marriage among Hausas over the course of the last two centuries. Whereas most modern Muslim authors and Hausas alike amplify the significance of women's domestic and maternal roles within marriage, Kecia Ali notes that "premodern Muslim legal writings presented a model of spousal relations in which parental relations were peripheral and children were secondary. . . . Although in the practice of the courts other family duties might get a hearing, in the jurists' treatises, a wife's main duties to her husband were to obey him and be sexually available. In exchange, he fed, clothed, and housed her."[22] This pattern is reflected in the alkali court records in which no court cases dealt explicitly with women shirking their duties as mothers or caretakers. On the contrary, the vast majority of cases involving men and women dealt with conflicts related to marriage, namely divorce, bigamy, and adultery.

Given the significance of marriage in establishing one's local identity in the diaspora, it is no surprise why so many cases involved men and women arguing over it. The brief union between Hadija and Yusufu shows that as socially obligatory as marriage was, it was also an unstable site of belonging. In many ways, the founding of the alkali's court institutionalized that instability.[23] Marriage's uneven social significance combined with multiple patriarchies and distances separating diaspora settlements to produce contexts that could jeopardize a woman's search for belonging in one location but empower another woman somewhere else. As Hadija's case also shows, husbands, wives, and lovers were not the only people who navigated these factors. Parents, siblings, and community patriarchs also intervened to manage marital relations on behalf of their kin, neighbors, and sometimes themselves.

)))•I•(((

Many men took advantage of both married and single women who were made differently vulnerable due to distances separating them from consanguine relations, their mobility between Hausa settlements, and the ever-present ambiguity that glossed over distinctions between marriage and female enslavement. One could argue that Malam Audu tried to manipulate public knowledge about Hadija's little-known past to secure her status as a slave, which only would have benefited him as her guardian and as a defendant before the alkali. But Hadija's appearance in court, though singular in the extent of the investigation into her past, was nonetheless foreshadowed by circumstances involving other young women, their husbands or owners, and their families.

About five years before Hadija's hearing, Alkali Malam Ahmadu Yola mediated a dispute involving a woman from Ndop named Shatu, her daughter, and three men from Lassin: the defendant, Musa; his brother; and the Sarkin Hausawa. According to Shatu, her daughter "was stolen by the certain man about 7 years ago. After 3 years I heard she was at Lasin [sic] and she married the [defendant]." At that point, Shatu said she sent a message to Musa to request that he let her daughter travel back to Ndop to visit her. Musa refused, apparently harboring no sense of obligation to his wife or mother-in-law. He explained his rationale straightforwardly and unapologetically to the court: "I will [not] send her to her mother because I bought with my money." Since a purchase marked the tie between himself and Shatu's daughter, Musa believed her natal kin had lost all claims on her and that his control over the young woman was paramount. Even when the alkali ordered him to let the woman leave Lassin, he remained obstinate. On the grounds that Musa stood in contempt of court, the alkali sentenced him to the prison yard. The court then sent an emissary to Lassin to retrieve Shatu's daughter, but "the older brother of Musa ... prevent her and said no body can took this girl, they have bought the girl with their money. He and [Sarkin] Hausawa Lasin they began to contempt the court."[24]

In the year following this case, the daughter of Mbem's Sarkin Bambadawa found herself in a similar predicament. Her father had married her off to Ibrahim, a male slave belonging to Mallam Tukur, also of Mbem. In return, the sarki received a "dowry" worth 6 pounds, which the malam paid on his slave's behalf. But the woman loathed her marriage and ran home to her father, who responded by taking his daughter back to the husband. But after a month she ran away again, explaining in her own words: "The thing that prevent me from sitting at the [defendant's] house because the [defendant] have said that he bought me I became his conqubine [sic], and I told the [defendant] to pay back £6 dowry which my father paid to [his] master Mallam Tukur. ... I no like the [defendant] at all."[25] This time, the father could no longer refuse his daughter's wishes and hoped to end this ill-fated union.

For the daughters involved in these disputes, their parents' ability and willingness to act on their behalf had a profound impact on the state of their marriages and the treatment they could expect from their husbands. The relative proximity of the young women's consanguine relations within the diaspora afforded both of them some measure of protection when the intentions of their husbands overlapped too significantly with those of slave ownership. Such protections were not available to Hadija either before or after Alhaji Gashin Baki's death, making her much more vulnerable to those with local authority. On the other hand, the 65 kilometers that separated Ndop from Lassin had a dualistic effect: the distance was long enough for Musa and his brother to keep the girl separated from Shatu, but short enough for Shatu to make claims on behalf of her daughter's freedom. According to Kecia Ali, parents had reason to worry about their daughter's treatment and status once she was married off. When the early jurists of Islamic law compared marriage with slavery, they did not equate them but expressed "a cautionary sentiment: fathers should be careful about whom they marry their daughters off to, because their daughters will be like captives or slaves to their husbands. Husbands are exhorted to treat their wives kindly, with the vulnerability of the wives expressed in the notion that they are like slaves. This vulnerability is assumed even when the treatment due to a wife and to a slave is sharply distinguished."[26]

The role of the alkali court as both an enforcer of Islamic law and arm of the colonial government cannot be overestimated. Shatu did not have the means or enough power to pressure Musa into treating her daughter fairly, a struggle that endured for seven years. But just months after the alkali opened his doors, Shatu took the opportunity to speak for her family when apparently no one else would. In securing a long-overdue reunion with her daughter, Shatu also managed to publicly strip Musa and his brother of their domestic patriarchal privileges. Likewise, Sarkin Bambadawa attempted to use the alkali court to back his authority as a father who supported his daughter's desire to leave a marriage in which her status was insecure.

Whereas Shatu and Sarkin Bambadawa realized this predicament after their daughters had left their care, Alhaji Umaru of Bamali and his wife feared such a fate would befall their daughter Asmatu if they accepted only a small bridewealth for her marriage, an arrangement that was not of their doing. It was Asmatu's older brother, Alhaji Mohammadu, who in 1955 persuaded his parents to marry her off to the limam of Jakiri, Malam Muhammadu Limam. Alhaji Mohammadu was so adamant in his request that he threatened to leave his parents forever if the father refused to support the marriage. The precise reasons behind the brother's motivations are unknown, but he likely desired some kind of connection to the limam. The parents were worried, however, and did not want to "give the girl out for dash." Were they to do so, it might give the limam license to "look low on her." Finally, Alhaji Umaru capitulated and accepted 20 pounds as bridewealth. Then Asmatu left her family to live in seclusion (*auren kulle*) with the limam in Jakiri. Like Sarkin Bambadawa's daughter, Asmatu detested her marriage, which she viewed as "a forceful one." But she endured it for six years.

Asmatu was the limam's only wife. But according to her, he kept "many girl friends outside his compound and who always came to fight [her]." One of these women had been married to a malam, a friend and neighbor of the limam. The friendship between the malam and Asmatu's husband had been a close one, so much so that the malam asked his friend to care for his family after his death. After he died, the limam began a sexual relationship with the widow. He then started to purchase items in pairs: one for his wife and one for his mistress. When Asmatu confronted the limam and asked him to end his relationship with the widow, he retaliated by abusing her.

Adding insult to injury, the limam's sexual relations extended to "stranger" women as well, including one who stayed in their compound as a guest. The woman had traveled to Jakiri to look for her brother, and the limam offered his help. One evening when Asmatu encountered her husband in the compound, he told her he was on his way to the mosque. But when he left his wife he headed not for the mosque but for Asmatu's room, where the "stranger female" was staying. Later when Asmatu returned to her room, she found her husband "intercourcing [sic]" with the woman. In a start, the limam ran out of the compound toward the mosque with Asmatu grabbing at his robe. Asmatu decided to follow him and waited for him outside. Upon seeing her when exiting the mosque, the limam demanded to know why she "was out at such a time." In response, Asmatu told the court, "I approached him with anger, seized his [torch] and break it on the ground."[27] In so doing, an exasperated Asmatu succeeded in transforming a household affair into a public one.[28]

From Asmatu's perspective, the limam's relations with the widow and the "stranger female" were more than disrespectful—they were abusive. Asmatu believed that the limam's sexual promiscuity was a direct assault on her standing as his wife. But the widow and the "stranger female" may have also had their own motivations for linking themselves to the limam. The widow received some measure of local protection and material support from him. This support may have been essential, depending on the number of children she had, whether the malam had left her a livable inheritance, the amount of income she earned on her own, and whether she had any natal kin nearby to turn to upon the end of her marriage. Moreover, becoming a mistress or engaging in prostitution (karuwanci) had historically been acceptable forms of courtship and income generation for previously married women (zawarawa) in mid-century Hausa social worlds, even if some people in the community, like Asmatu, did not approve of it.

The situation of the "stranger female" is less clear, as is the nature of her relationship with the limam. As the stories below will illustrate, it was common for traveling Hausa women to stay in the compounds of local community leaders, such as wealthy patrons or Sarakunan Hausawa. The question remains, however, whether the woman was a willing participant in her sexual liaison with the limam. It is possible that she, too, was comfortable with some form of prostitution in exchange for lodging and protection, hoping to mitigate the vulnerability that her mobility caused. Given that it was common for court clerks in colonial Africa to code rape as adultery or some other kind of illicit sex in the law books, it is equally possible that the limam violently exploited the woman's isolation and temporary dependency on his power and connections.[29]

These three women form a living triptych that reflects how their unique experiences of isolation were ultimately connected. The widow lost the "rope of her marriage" and with it access to material resources that she and her children had difficulty earning on their own. To mitigate these challenges, she opted for pre-Islamic forms of Hausa relations that allowed her to engage in informal marriage or karuwanci with the limam. The "stranger female" and Asmatu were isolated by distance that separated them from consanguine relations, both of them vulnerable to the ways in which the limam exercised patriarchal privileges associated with his domestic and community authority. For Asmatu, this seemed to be compounded by the requirements of seclusion, a practice that is comparatively rare among Grassfields Hausas.[30] Through marriage, Asmatu belonged to the limam, but this was not Asmatu's ideal form of relation. However, none of these limitations stopped Asmatu from demanding better behavior from her husband and more respect for herself as a wife.

Eventually, Asmatu confided in her brother, explaining the nature of the limam's transgressions. Realizing his mistake in forcing the marriage on his sister, Alhaji Mohammadu informed his father, who then wrote letters to the limam requesting that he send Asmatu home to visit her family. The pretext for her return was to bid farewell to a sister leaving for Nigeria with her husband, but it also coincided with the Hausa custom of *ganin gida*, whereby secluded wives are expected to visit their parents after roughly five years of marriage. The limam hesitantly agreed and sent his wife to Bamali, accompanied by one of his boys. But after three days, the boy returned by himself with a message from Asmatu's father. Apparently her mother had become ill, so she needed to stay home longer than expected—a creatively spun tale also facilitated by distance. The limam eventually traveled to Bamali to retrieve his wife, but the family did not allow him to see her. He complained to the Sarkin Hausawa of Jakiri and other community leaders, but Asmatu remained with her family. Despite his many visits to Bamali, the couple's separation endured for two years, until at one point the father informed him that he and Asmatu were now divorced. The father did not have the legal authority to make this decision, and the limam sought justice against him by bringing the case to the alkali.[31]

In demanding better treatment and eventual escape from her husband, Asmatu concurrently reinforced patriarchal social structures and expected norms of masculine behavior while defying the patriarchal authority of her own husband.[32] Though Hausa norms sanctioned her husband's sexual promiscuity, Asmatu and the men of her natal family agreed that it compromised her respectability. That these sexual exploits placed her in an undesirable situation further underscored her family's perception that the limam abused his patriarchal privilege. They accordingly supported their kinswoman's desire to leave her marriage.[33]

In her work on domestic violence in colonial Sikasso, Emily Burrill has argued that women employed an "informal system of observation of male behavior." This neighborhood system pressured men to uphold their end of the bargain in marriage—to refrain from taking advantage of their patriarchal power especially through excessive physical abuse.[34] The Ndop alkali court records show that women also relied on male allies, such as fathers, brothers, neighbors, and community leaders, to support them in times of marital crisis.[35] With their backing, women like Asmatu could condemn their husbands while reinforcing expected norms of Hausa masculinity. This public role of men supporting other men's wives in their struggles for a peaceful married life also took form in its opposite: many men like Salimu defended the health, well-being, and respectability of their own wives against others' ill intentions or negligence.[36]

>>>•‹‹‹

Asmatu's father told the limam that their marriage had ended, but
according to Maliki Islamic law he did not have the right to make that
pronouncement. Marriage was a bilateral contract requiring the "consent of the wife, someone acting on her behalf, or both." By contrast,
divorce was first and foremost a unilateral act that only husbands could
perform. Citing the analogous relationship between marriage and slavery, Norman Calder has written, "Divorcing wives and freeing slaves are
peculiar problems because these are, in Islamic law, performative utterances: simply uttering the correct words in the correct form can produce
a change in the status of others."[37] A man can divorce a wife whenever he
chooses and in various ways. He might divorce his wife through multiple, usually three, repudiations at one time or spread across a matter of
days, weeks, or months. The intent behind these repudiations could be
very clear ("You are divorced") or allusive ("You are free"). He could also
pronounce divorce in a conditional manner ("If I take another wife, you
are divorced" or "You are divorced if you wish"). Sunnis, including those
of the Maliki school, claim that the presence of the wife is not necessary
and that no witnesses are required when the husband might decide to
utter those fateful words. Finally, a husband could state that the divorce
is revocable, meaning that he could take the wife back without contracting a new marriage or requiring her consent. The Malikis in particular
deemed that "in some cases action combined with intent was sufficient
for a husband to take back a wife," though they preferred—but did not
require—that his declaration be witnessed.[38]

Since Muslim men may divorce wives through triple repudiation,
nearly all divorce cases brought to the alkali court involved wives or
their natal families desiring a divorce or husbands trying to retrieve
wives or their bridewealth. Many cases demonstrate how the lack of
witnesses and variation in pronouncing triple repudiation could leave
room for confusion and contestation over whether a divorce had actually
taken place. As a result, both spouses could exploit the fragility of nuptial
bonds and the unobtrusiveness of repudiation in order to claim a status
as married or unmarried. A number of divorce cases involved allegations
of bigamy or adultery, as previously married women sought out new mar-

ital ties. Many repudiated women had become mobile in order to form these new relations. The distances separating diaspora settlements thus contributed to this landscape of contestation and belonging. In most cases, husbands stood before the alkali as plaintiffs accusing women and their lovers of adultery or bigamy, hoping to reclaim the women as wives.

Allegations of adultery pertained only to illicit relationships between married women and men other than their husbands. Similarly, the acceptability of polygyny and unlimited concubines meant that only married women and the men "enticing" them into unlawful marriages were found guilty of bigamy. In the 1950s, Baba of Karo referred to adultery as *sace jikinta*, whereby a woman "steals her own body." Because a Hausa husband gains control over his wife's sexual services through marriage, if she defies her husband's authority by engaging in illicit sex she has essentially "stolen her body" from him.[39] People could also be accused of these offenses if women, like Hadija, took part in marriages or sexual relations before completing idda or takaba. Adultery could also apply more broadly to any suspicious or inappropriate interactions between married women and male acquaintances.[40]

Court cases on divorce, adultery, and bigamy do not only illuminate tensions and misunderstandings between men, women, and their families in the diaspora. Trying bigamy as a criminal offense was a central element in legitimating the authority of the alkali. Unlike other areas of the Hausa world where Islamic judges rarely mediate marital disputes, the Grassfields alkali was the only official guarantor of divorce outside a husband's triple repudiation. Neither Sarakunan Hausawa nor limamai were officially vested with that authority, and alkalis were quick to point that out in a number of cases. In general, divorce, adultery, and bigamy were not uncommon features among the Islamic diasporas resident in the Grassfields. They constituted a considerable portion of cases over which the alkali of Ndop presided.[41]

In 1953, both Njidda of Babanke and Muhammadu of Nwa accused their wives and the wives' second husbands of bigamy.[42] Njidda had given his wife Nenne permission to travel, first to Bamenda to collect a debt and then to Santa where she wanted to "salute Mallam Muhammadu" regarding a death that occurred. But when Nenne arrived in Santa, she decided to stay with the sarkin pawa, the chief butcher, telling

him that she was a divorced woman. The sarkin pawa then took her
under his guardianship for five months and oversaw her marriage to a
Santa man named Idinsu. Believing that Nenne was indeed a divorced
woman—as no husband had come to look for her—the sarkin pawa approved Idinsu's marriage, and the new couple began living together as
husband and wife.

For Muhammadu of Nwa, his wife Azumi also traveled a fair distance, more than 50 kilometers to Dumbo, seeking a new form of male
guardianship as an unmarried woman. She soon attached herself to the
Hausa chief of Dumbo, residing in his compound where a man named
Umaru asked her to marry him. Both Nenne and Azumi claimed that
their husbands had severed their marital ties, while Muhammadu and
Njidda denied their wives' claims and desired their return. In the court
of the alkali, Nenne admitted that Njidda had never divorced her and
that she alone was guilty for entering into an illicit union with Idinsu.
Azumi, on the other hand, dared Muhammadu to swear on the Qur'an
that he did not divorce her. It appears that at least in her mind she was a
repudiated woman, but Muhammadu swore to the contrary and Azumi
was found guilty of bigamy.

Hausa women's lower social status situated their male lovers as the
sole instigators of illicit unions and were therefore deemed more cul-
pable and punished more severely in the courts.[43] The only apparent
exception to this rule occurred when the male acquaintance, lover, or
second husband, like Yusufu, could prove or swear on the Qur'an that
he had no knowledge of the woman's previous marriage. In both cases
above, the second husbands were acquitted, based on their ignorance of
their wives' marital status.[44]

In seeking out ties with new men and new Hausa communities, Nenne
and Azumi made use of the distances separating Hausa settlements in
the Grassfields, as well as the relative anonymity that such distances
caused. They also possessed the cultural knowledge that Hausa chiefs
and other community leaders often acted as temporary or even permanent guardians for stranger women traveling through enclaves in the
diaspora. Abner Cohen's research in Ibadan during the 1960s indicates
that it was advantageous for Hausa chiefs to attract women to their settlements and to keep them there through marriage. More women meant

more marriages, which in turn meant increased permanent settlement of men, more followers, and potentially greater political and economic power for the Hausa chiefs. A greater number of "stable" families also had repercussions on the local economy as housewives offered important services to the community through their petty trade in food items.[45] Hausa women, however, could exploit community leaders' competing demands for their social, economic, and reproductive capacities.

Women were also aware that the anonymity created by traveling between Hausa settlements allowed them to rewrite their biographies, which Hausa leaders seemed only happy to accept at face value on behalf of their growing communities and sometimes on their own behalf. In the late 1940s, Bakari of Banguna accused the Sarkin Hausawa of Bamessi of bigamy, believing that the Hausa leader had illicitly married his wife Hadija. The Sarkin Hausawa had indeed taken the woman in, but it was ambiguous whether the two had married. What did become clear in the court proceedings, however, is that Bakari and Hadija were never husband and wife to begin with: "No dowry or good marriage had been made at all. She has a husband at Bamum with two children there. The [plaintiff] had just kept the woman [temporarily]." Hadija thus succeeded twice in using distance and the demand for female dependents among Hausa men to create new relationships in multiple locations.[46]

Some of these relationships solidified in new marriages—licit and illicit—while others, including Hadija's ties to Bakari of Banguna and the Bamessi Sarkin Hausawa, ambiguously straddled informal marriage or karuwanci. The process of triple repudiation and marriage itself could be ambiguous within and between Hausa diaspora communities—social and geographical areas of gray men and women exploited to suit their needs and desires. But even in cases where triple repudiations occurred in the public eye, divorcées, their second husbands, and sometimes their family members were accused of contracting marriages before idda had run its course.[47]

Hadija's case and those analyzed in this chapter demonstrate that the business of marriage and divorce could be foggy and was often compounded by distances between Hausa settlements, competing patriarchal claims over women, and competing knowledge of what actually constituted a marriage, a divorce, or the observed length of idda.

Moreover, the breaking of marital bonds and arranging of allegedly illicit unions not only occurred at the behest of the very men and women involved in such relationships. They were also orchestrated by other individuals, namely parents concerned with the well-being and respectability of their daughters, as well as men of various rank and influence attempting to control the ways in which women related and created ties to men.

In an argument that arose between two community leaders, at issue was the question of whether one of the men had the authority to marry off the other man's daughter. Not all aspects of the story are clear, but it appears that the daughter capitalized on the distance separating the two men in order to marry the husband of her choice. Her father was the limam of Babanke, and he declared that the Sarkin Hausawa of Konnane "take my daughter and tied marriage to her without my knowing. . . . I got no relation with [him]." In the limam's mind, the Sarkin Hausawa had no right to act as the guardian to the limam's daughter because he did not have his permission to do so. The Sarkin Hausawa defended himself by pointing to the actions of the young woman. According to him, the daughter asked him to tie a marriage for her. She also brought a letter to him proving that "she got no marriage." Believing this letter to be sufficient evidence, the Sarkin Hausawa "tied the marriage for them." In the end, the alkali's judgment restored the limam's household authority and in so doing publicly reinforced his own power in indicating what defined the proper behavior of all individuals involved: "The father of the daughter said he do not like the marriage of the husband with the daughter. And in Muhammadan Law book the father is the man who is going to be (waliyi) of his daughter, and if not the father no body is fit to tie marriage for her. There fore [sic] when the father of the daughter refused the marriage, there is no marriage between them."[48]

Similar to the alkali court's first case in 1947 that was examined in Chapter 2, the authority of fathers and husbands over unmarried and married women, respectively, took precedence over the community authority of any Sarkin Hausawa or maigida since these roles were not recognized in Islamic law. Such debates highlight the important connections between kinship, community, law, and patriarchy that lay at the core of people's attempts to navigate and control family life in the diaspora. From the vantage point of the alkali, the limam's lawfully sanctioned authority over his daughter trumped the Hausa chief's power to incorporate stranger women into his community through marriage. Before the establishment of the alkali court in 1947, individual Hausa chiefs usually mediated such conflicts in their communities. As such, parents like the limam and husbands like Njidda and Muhammadu would have found it more difficult to reestablish their authority over autonomous women when the community-building interests of Hausa chiefs were at stake. Though the alkali's legal and religious authority over such matters appeared to have kept Hausa chiefs in check, sometimes entailing tighter constraints and tougher consequences for the women involved, the contestation between these various forms of patriarchy continued into the 1950s and beyond. Such conflicts reflected broader tensions among men regarding what it meant to act like a "proper Hausa," especially when it came to market affairs and relations with women. Sometimes these disputes stemmed from something as innocuous as miscommunication or competing notions of trust, but they often involved outright lying and cheating. The various alkalis seemed most annoyed when men displayed a lack of knowledge regarding Islamic principles, especially when those being reprimanded were Hausa community leaders.[49]

These debates over the control of women certainly left the door open —if only slightly—for women to exercise a modicum of power in how they created ties with Hausa communities. Geographical distance could help to widen that opening. Though the women and men discussed in this chapter were eventually made to abide by the alkali's judgments, many people in similar situations likely avoided such public scrutiny. People thus contended with multiple realms of patriarchy, sometimes employing them against one another to their advantage. Many women like Hadija of Lere took advantage of the multiple, coexistent patriarchies to geographically, socially, and sexually navigate the diaspora world, and they did so to exercise some form of control over their means of belonging. Such astute navigation often entailed simultaneously violating and supporting patriarchal privileges. But women did not often attempt this navigation alone: other women and men aided them, too, most often out

of their desires to ensure the fair treatment of female kin, for increased
followership, for friendship, and to acquire a wife, concubine, or slave
of one's own.

Distance and mobility could create spaces and moments where wom-
en lacked recognizable or meaningful forms of relation. It is within these
vicissitudes where the lack of social networks brought both constraints
and opportunities for Hausa women in the Grassfields. Shatu's kidnapped and apparently enslaved daughter, Asmatu in Jakiri with the
philandering limam, and perhaps even the female stranger staying at
Asmatu's home—all of these women experienced increased vulnerability primarily due to geographical isolation from their kin and the
related lack of local ties at new sites of dwelling or rest. These stories also
highlight the ways in which some women contended with shifting sites
of belonging: though marital ties for adult women were the norm, these
competed with the social capital women derived from their consanguine
relations which those with family in the diaspora cashed in during times
of marital strife.

But distance and mobility could have paradoxical effects for women.
They could present a woman with the possibility of power through
anonymity even as they heightened her vulnerability. Through travel,
women produced a lack of local collective memory in the places they
visited—a kind of "boundary crossing," which is not only physical but
also involved "shifts in identity, the creation of new identities, or the
familiarity and reconnections of old identities."[50] These circumstances
allowed women to take on new roles as personal storytellers. Female
strangers moving to new Hausa settlements lacked social networks, to
be sure, but they took on this risk in order to seek new status, new social
connections, and new ways of belonging or resonating with others. As
always, this search was influenced greatly by gender inequalities: the
logic of diasporic patrilineality meant that women had little choice but to
attach themselves to those social structures defined by male dominance
in the communities they journeyed to. But women like Nenne, Azumi,
Hadija of Bamum, and the daughter of Babanke's limam understood
the possibilities of travel just as they understood Hausa men's desires to
take on female dependents. Likewise, distance and the lack of knowledge about female strangers allowed men to ignore questions over their

marital status and later, in some instances, to plead ignorance on such matters before the alkali.[51]

This is not to say that all women traveled only to establish new connections with men in Hausa settlements. In 1952, for example, a Fulani or Huya (town Fulani) woman named Adda Petel traveled alone, operating beyond the control of a male guardian as she came upon the Hausa borough of Ntumbo. According to the Sarkin Hausawa, Adda Petel "abused all Ntumbo" and the sarki "about a pan," had sexual relations with another woman's husband, and caused general trouble by urging "people to put fire for [the sarki's] country."[52] Though one of Adda Petel's supposed offenses involved a sexual liaison with a married man, from the sarki's perspective this act, like the others, was meant to disrupt the order and well-being of the community rather than be a mechanism for her to attach herself to that community. A few years before the events above, the Sarkin Hausawa of Bikom physically abused his townswoman with "two slaps" and withheld money she had asked him to safeguard. He accused her of bringing two married women back with her from a trip to Mme-Bafumen without permission from their husbands.[53] It is not clear whether the women left their husbands indefinitely or merely wanted to visit the home of their female friend. Without knowing their intentions, the sarki understood these roaming women as operating outside and even in spite of male authority.

))))•((((

As with the case of Magajiya Dibino that opened this chapter, the proper site of belonging for women within the Grassfields Hausa diaspora was clearly under an acceptable form of male control, whether through marriage or some related form of dependency. For those women who were viewed as rejecting marriage or operating beyond a husband's influence, however temporarily, community leaders often feared such actions and in nearly all instances recorded by alkali court scribes, they attempted to reprimand such women through violence or legal action. Though Magajiya Dibino's case was unique, in large part due to the magnitude of her power, it speaks to the broader issues at stake for socially nonconforming women and men who sought acceptance in diaspora communities.

In the stories collected here, many women used distance, the passing of time, male desires for women, and imperfect collective memories to construct their own biographies—sometimes near to the truth, and sometimes "critical fictions" created with the participation of allies like Gashin Baki's son, Sanda, or male accomplices, especially new husbands or lovers.[54] As women traveled and encountered new kin networks and communities, they at once became navigators and storytellers. Whether in between marriages or in between Hausa settlements, women for a time lacked marriage as an easily recognizable mode of belonging. This impermanent, even transitory, lack of connections brought both opportunities and constraints for those women attempting to create ties with other individuals and families in ways personally favorable to them. Like many women in a number of diverse African diaspora contexts, the navigations of these Hausa women "reveal competing ways of realizing home and community," which were not always "celebratory spaces." In many cases, home and community could actually be "places of exile."[55]

Hadija of Lere may have certainly felt this way. Her lack of connections and the ambiguity over her social status made her vulnerable within Mme-Bafumen's Hausa community. The lack of knowledge about her past opened avenues for people like Malam Audu and Talle to contest her status as a wife and widow. But even before the trial began, the confusion surrounding Hadija's relationship with Gashin Baki combined with the importance Hausas placed on marriage to culminate in her impulsive marriage to Yusufu. And because Yusufu supposedly possessed incomplete knowledge about Hadija's past, he could claim ignorance over her status and whether she was in a position to marry him, as so many other men did before and after him.

For her part, Hadija used distance, travel, and anonymity to tell the story of how she came to belong in the Hausa diaspora as a woman worthy of a marital tie to the wealthiest of its members. She wanted to turn exile into inclusion, and she was not alone in this contestation. Many others chose to support her story of the past even though none of them, except for Talle perhaps, actually witnessed her exchange between the chief of Lere and the prosperous merchant. Finally, to evade responsibility for her actions, Hadija could point to her strangerhood in the Hausa diaspora world to claim a lack of cultural knowledge regarding the length of time constituting takaba. She violated Islamic law, yes, but she did so unwittingly. That women in general were held less accountable than their male counterparts for committing adultery or bigamy, or for knowing the rules of marriage and divorce, worked to Hadija's advantage in such a public forum. Her honor and social status were held intact and arguably improved upon with this admission.

Conclusion

Karfin mata sai yawan magana.
"The strength of a woman is in her talk."

HAUSA PROVERB

"THUS, AS AIR ABHORS A VACUUM, DIASPORA SEEMS TO ABHOR stasis or fixity. Conceptually or methodologically, fixities will never capture its deeper meanings and significance."[1] Thomas C. Holt wrote these words as he reflected on the implications of the diaspora framework for studying slavery and freedom in the Atlantic world, but their relevance extends beyond this particular context. This is nowhere more evident than with this history of Hausas in the Cameroon Grassfields. Despite the complexity of social relations that facilitated Hausa movement and settlement in the highlands, dominant ideologies produced narratives and structures that could be defined more simply—providing the illusion of stability. Though these ideologies emerged from different sources, they held in common the limitations of androcentrism, which ensured that women and their social ties with others were implicit, rather than explicit, factors in this history.

The Hausa diaspora concept of abakwa implies the participation of non-Muslim, non-Hausa women in founding settlements and facilitating the ramification of diaspora networks through marriage and their reproductive capacities, but in so doing it consequently reinforces the power of patrilineality to define how the diaspora and membership within it came into being. It also reinforces the power of Hausas to assimilate young women and girls as they entered their communities and compounds. The essential sex difference embedded in abakwa thus situates men as the primary migrants and bearers of Hausa culture and Islam. The Qur'an itself compounds this androcentrism, in that women consistently figure as passive participants in their relations with men.[2] Dominant Hausa narratives of dispersion imply that men traveled and settled because they sought out new means of wealth accumulation through long-distance trade, but this too relies on a narrow definition of wealth that excludes the importance of dependents in signifying ideal Hausa masculinity and social order.

The gendered lens through which German and British colonial officials understood Hausas in relation to Grassfielders similarly ignored the presence, much less the contributions, of women in the diaspora. This erasure represents the colonial state's early reliance on Hausa men to facilitate the economic and political goals of colonization through their roles as intermediaries between the state and "natives." Reorienting the definition of abakwa away from complex gender relations toward the marketplace is symbolic of these colonial perceptions, but this transformation in meaning also dovetailed with Hausa oral traditions in which men predominantly relate to each other as successful traders, fellow soldiers, and Muslim brothers from the savanna. This redefinition of abakwa further resonated with prevalent Grassfielder understandings of Hausas as a distinct group of commercially focused latecomers, even though Hausa communities influenced local societies through cultural borrowing and incorporated Grassfielders through patron–client relations, slavery, marriage, adoption, and religious conversion.

Hausas' in-between status eventually became institutionalized through the "native foreigner" legal category, which they shared with Fulanis, and through the consequent founding of the alkali court. The state established the court to shore up its understanding of social order in the Grassfields but also to placate Muslim African patriarchs who demanded better control over women through marriage. Gender relations were therefore central factors in constructing colonial governance structures demarcating Hausas as a distinct group of strangers, even as these multiple, dominant narratives of the past converged to deny women historicity.

As Holt notes, none of these dominant narratives captures the deeper complexities of the past, in large part because "studied ambiguities [lie] at the heart of the diasporan concept."[3] For Hausas in the Grassfields, ambiguities emerged from a variety of experiences, including the conceptual fuzziness separating marriage from concubinage, the anonymity, power, and vulnerability that travel created, competing notions of ideal gender relations, or the lack of precision in linking changes in clothing and naming to religious or ethnic affiliation. Some of these ambiguities were integral to the diaspora's dispersal, while others resulted from the precise historical context of settlement in the colonial Grassfields. Out of these ambiguities arose struggles that were "most often *interstitial* (that is, found in spaces and cracks within ostensibly hegemonic structures)." The alkali court was one of these structures: the convergence of colonial and Muslim African demands for social order and control through patriarchal authority in the household called it into existence. But it also became a space, like the "native foreigner" category itself, where instability was institutionalized—where litigants reproduced and undermined dominant gender roles and ideologies.

Referencing the Haitian slave revolt, Holt suggests that even though a specific diaspora community's struggles may be limited to a particular context, they have the ability to "cross international spaces and boundaries." The struggles examined here, by contrast, are much more intimate but are characteristically diasporic, for they surfaced as people navigated boundaries through social and geographical mobility—through peripeteia. This is particularly salient in a context where, unlike secular states, personal security or identification as a free person could not be defined by rights of citizenship but rather by belonging to a household or community through kinship, patronage, and other hierarchies of dependence and protection.[4] In one diaspora context, a person might struggle for belonging by claiming citizenship, while in the Grassfields Hausa or Hausa-ized individuals navigated shifting sites of belonging by relating to others variously and sometimes ambiguously as patrons, owners, husbands, parents, widows, wives, orphans, and lovers. Distance and travel both facilitated and impeded these intimate negotiations as people walked into and out of a patchwork of spaces and hierarchies. Death presented its own form of boundary crossing, too, prompting survivors to travel and struggle over claiming identities in relation to the dead.

Gender inequalities inflected each and every one of these struggles, so much so that Byfield, Denzer, and Morrison propose to view boundary crossing as "an entrée into overlapping meditations on race, gender, class, empire, and diaspora."[5] The encounter between Ernst Vollbehr and the Hausa dancer at Bamenda illustrates how the confluence of diasporic and colonial travel could generate similar meditations amongst historical actors themselves. The Hausa diaspora's early colonial status as a society marked by geographical, economic, and religious dynamism influenced the racialized way Vollbehr understood them vis-à-vis indigenous Grassfielders. If his travelogue is accurate, the Hausa dancer took advantage of the opportunity with Vollbehr to articulate a connection linking colonial violence against Africans with European society's cruelty toward women and the centrality of Christ's sacrifice in the symbolic imagery of the Christian faith. Perhaps this was how she defined whiteness. Through the assistance of a translator, her worldview crossed a linguistic and cultural boundary—racialized through colonialism—to prompt Vollbehr to reflect on the colony, European gender relations, and the various frames of reference people use to imbue images with meaning. As the painter internalized this new reality, he also rejected contemporary Orientalist narratives in Germany that would have had the Christian man liberate the "oppressed Muslim woman" from her inhumane surroundings.[6]

This encounter was but one episode, and it is one of the few where historical actors themselves voiced the significance of gender relations to empire and race. Most other tales examined in this book are of greater similarity to Hadija's—circumstances in which people debated the more intimate, yet no less political, details of household and community belonging from competing social positions and with conflicting memories of the past. Analyzing Hadija's experiences alongside so many others has demonstrated how gendered inequalities and anxieties over morality lay at the heart of diaspora and empire to inform struggles over social status, kinship affiliation, community acceptance, wealth accumulation, and "the will to identity" as people negotiated overlapping social and geographical spaces.[7]

Hadija's moments of peripeteia inspire us to rethink Hausa and other commercial diaspora histories. Her experiences and her testimony illuminate the ways in which gendered processes of separation and connection have been essential to diasporic conditions such as mobility, settlement, and those daily, interstitial struggles for belonging.[8] These factors were intimately intertwined with—not supplemental or secondary to—economic desires to expand markets and commercial networks. The story of her intimate relations thus offers a significant counterhistory of both global diasporas and colonialism.[9]

Hadija's fragile, fractured identity was situated in a shifting terrain marked by gender, race, and religion, as well as by distance, travel, and the passing of time.[10] She was a liminal diasporic figure whose primary ties to her host community were constructed through the ambiguous intentions of a propertied man who could have either offered her protection and social mobility or abused her powerlessness. With his death, Hadija's liminality intensified. But she took advantage of the time takaba allowed her to fashion a new tie to her community through Yusufu, an act that eventually jeopardized her social standing.

Despite these setbacks and hardships, and like women in other diaspora contexts around the world, Hadija employed what social and legal tools she had available to manage the discrimination she faced and to acquire new forms of wealth. She navigated the overlapping spheres of colonial governance and her host communities' legal customs to assert her status as a wife. As a nominal Muslim, Hadija capitalized on her access to the Islamic court and its embedded practice of mubahala. She also understood the significance of written documentation in supporting her claim as a wife to a deceased husband, for she weakened Malam Audu's position by pointing out he had no letter from Alhaji Gashin Baki that could prove she was unfree.[11]

This brings us to the most important tool of all—diasporic ambiguity. The nature of Hadija's tie to Gashin Baki was obscured in the public realm because of the distance she traveled and the vagueness distinguishing concubinage from marriage in mid-twentieth-century Hausa society. Distance through travel and the passing of time were therefore major factors in the ability to navigate locally for this woman of unknown origins and uncertain status. While these distances allowed some community members the latitude to marginalize Hadija, they also provided others the opportunity to accept and support her in her time of need, demonstrating the importance of local contacts and solidarity networks. The silence of a deceased husband or owner also meant that memory—or perhaps, invention—worked to resolve the uncertainties of the past. Hadija either told the version of events and affections as she understood or manipulated ambiguities in her favor. Those who supported her did likewise, creating "critical fictions" that became legal truths through oral testimony. Marriage as a social category of relation can often mislead us in understanding the various unions that facilitated and sustained the Hausa diaspora.[12] Nonetheless, Hadija recognized the significance of a particular kind of lawfully sanctioned wifehood that gave her access to new sources of wealth and a tie to her new community that would outlive the tie to her husband or owner.

Hadija may be a unique woman in the opportunities she had to navigate her world and how the various shards of her past made it into the archive. She was not a literate woman, but she had intimate relations with a man of considerable property and prominence who seemed to hold affections for her. This improved the odds that neighbors, associates, community leaders, or government officials might document some aspects of her life, however limited. Paternalistic constructions of law played their part, too. Hadija teaches us how the diasporic conditions of ambiguity and instability could combine with the power of selective storytelling to mitigate the daily impacts of social and legal inequality. This created the possibility for her and others, though certainly not all, to find "a freedom within particular surroundings"—to actively claim a place within a community and its historical memory.[13] Yet, despite her agency and what we learn from it, we also have to acknowledge the unknown. We will never be certain whether she ever felt these forms of belonging were ideal, just as we will never know whether she perceived the name Hadija as a representation of her incorporation or her erasure—or perhaps both.[14]

Glossary of Terms

Unless otherwise noted, all terms are in the Hausa language.

abakwa/abakpa	novice; the name, supposedly of Jukun origin, for Hausa settlements near or south of the Benue River
abakwan riga	descendants of mixed marriages between Hausa men and Tiv and other non-Hausa women (also *abakwariga*)
addini	religion
alhaji	title of a man who performed the pilgrimage to Mecca
alkali	Islamic judge (pl. *alkalai*)
Allah	God
amarya	bride
ardo	(Fulfulde) Fulani headman
asali	origin
aure	marriage
auren jin da'di	marriage for pleasure or temporary marriage
auren kulle	marriage of seclusion
auren takalmi	marriage of sandals
azahar	midday prayer
baiwa	gift, betrothal, or female slave
bori	spirit possession cult
budurwa	unmarried girl of marriageable age, virgin
cin rani	dry season migration or transhumance
'dan dandi	one who wanders seeking to avoid constraints in his community or to learn about the world (pl. *'yan dandi*)
fatauci	long-distance trading

fon	Grassfields "chief"
gadal	type of Hausa medicine
ganin gida	a woman's visit to her parents' home after roughly five years of marriage
gida	house, compound
hajiya	title of a woman who performed the pilgrimage to Mecca
Hausawa	Hausa people
idda	period of waiting for women whose marriages were dissolved by death or divorce
igiyar aure	rope of marriage
iskoki	spirits, winds
iya	title of an aristocratic senior woman who mediates domestic conflicts
Jam'iyyar Mutanen Arewa	Society of People of the North
jangali	cattle tax
jihad	conquest to spread Islam
jiki	body
kallabi	woman's head-tie (pl. *kalluba*)
karuwa	courtesan (pl. *karuwai*)
karuwanci	courtesanship, prostitution
'Kasar Hausa	Land of the Hausa, Hausa homeland
kasuwa	market
'kawa	bond friendship between women
kibam ke way ke fon	(Lamnso) royal market bag
kishiya	co-wife, lit. "jealous one"
kulle	seclusion
kunya	modesty, shame, self-consciousness, respect
kurwa	soul
la'ada	reward
lafiya	peace, well-being, order, fecundity, prosperity
laya	charm, amulet
limam, imam	Muslim priest (pl. *limamai*)
magajiya	"queen mother," elder sister, or heiress
mai duba	fortune teller
maigida	household or compound head, patron (pl. *masu gida*)
maita	witchcraft, "soul eating"
makaranta	Qur'anic school
malam	Qur'anic scholar, teacher, and often healer
masu sarauta	important office holders
milk	(Arabic) male authority or dominion over wives and female slaves
milk al-nikah	(Arabic) *milk* through marriage

milk al-yamin	(Arabic) *milk* through enslavement
mubahala	(Arabic) conditional curse and purifying oath sworn on the Qur'an
mufuti	court scribe, judicial assessor (pl. *mufutai*)
mutumin kirki	a good man
nki bu'	(Mankon) rope slave, license for dealing in slaves
nono	milk, female breast
rai	life
riga	gown
sabon gari	new town
sace jikinta	adultery, lit. to steal her body
sadaka	alms, charity
sadaki	bridewealth, money given by bridegroom to bride to legally bind the marriage
sarki or *sarike*	chief, lit. "snake slayer" (pl. *sarakuna*)
Sarkin Hausawa	Hausa chief
sarkin 'kasa	chief of the land
sarkin kasuwa	chief of the market
sarkin pawa	chief butcher
takaba	period of mourning performed by a widow
talakawa	commoners
tallafi	a child received for bringing up, adoption
ushira	tenth part paid as commission to court in cases involving debt
uwar gida	senior wife, lit. "mother of the home"
wahala	difficulty, trouble
wali/waliyi	guardian, empowered to give a woman in marriage
ya kamata	that one must do a certain act
yawon dandi	wandering to avoid constraints at home or to learn about the world
yawon kasuwanci	walk of marketing
yaye	fostering or weaning (fostering is also known as *'dauki renon*)
zane	woman's body cloth
zaure	entrance room to a compound
zawarawa	previously married women not presently married
zongo	a regular resting place on a journey, Hausa word for "stranger quarter"

Notes

INTRODUCTION

1. Northwest Alkali Court (NWAC), Ndop, Criminal Book 3/53, Suit No. 56/52, January 13, 1953.

2. Haour and Rossi, *Being and Becoming Hausa*, 4–8. This statement is as true today as it was two centuries ago, and it is as relevant for understanding Hausa society in the diaspora as it is in Northern Nigeria, the place that many Hausas in the Grassfields consider the site of their families' origins. Just as each scholar studying diasporas has had his or her own combination of criteria for determining which groups are diasporic, the same can be said for a number of scholars studying the Hausa world. In the 1970s, Mahdi Adamu pointed to four historical variables that the peoples across West Africa have used in establishing whether an individual may be considered Hausa. These include the use of the Hausa language, whether an individual could make historical claims to being Hausa, the location of residence for individuals or families, and, lastly, belief in Islam, though the tie between Islam and Hausaness has not been present at all times or with the same intensity. Within the context of his work in Kano, also in the 1970s, John N. Paden suggested that Hausa "individuals could be identified by layered categories of identity, including religion (*addini*), ancestral home (*asali*), family, urban place of residence, or shade of skin" (cited in Haour and Rossi, *Being and Becoming Hausa*, 5). However, even Adamu acknowledged at the time that a straightforward definition of Hausaness is next to impossible. See Mahdi Adamu, *The Hausa factor*, 3.

3. Haour and Rossi, *Being and Becoming Hausa*, 7.

4. On Wangaras, see for example Ivor Wilks, "Wangara, Akan and Portuguese." Oliver Bakewell suggests that the African continent is not home to many internal

diasporas, because sociocultural identification in Africa has traditionally been fluid. However, he agrees that the case of Hausas, like that of Wangaras and the Fulani pastoralist diaspora, diverges from this larger African pattern. Bakewell, "Diasporas within Africa," 22.

5. Cohen, "Cultural Strategies." With Robin Cohen's typology of global diasporas, the "trade and business diaspora" has become an "ideal type" for diaspora studies, a type into which many works on Hausa dispersal fall quite neatly. This is more than a coincidence, however, since he cites Abner Cohen as the first scholar to provide a convincing definition for the term: a "trade diaspora was 'a nation of socially interdependent, but spatially dispersed communities'" bounded together by a necessary "moral cohesion." See Cohen, *Global Diasporas*, 83.

6. Subrahmanyam, *Merchant Networks*, xiii. For scholars of Hausa diaspora history, the usual characteristics comprising the parameters for such internal cohesion range from language, devotion to Islam, and patrilineality, to location of residence and style of clothing, typically the donning of robes (the *riga*).

7. Adamu, *The Hausa Factor*; Arhin, *West African Traders*; Bovill and Hallett, *Golden Trade of the Moors*; Cohen, "Cultural Strategies"; Cohen, *Custom and Politics*; Levtzion, *Muslims and Chiefs in West Africa*; Lovejoy, *Caravans of Kola*; John Waterbury, *North for the Trade*.

8. According to Moses Ochonu, non-Muslim peoples north of the Grassfields, including those of the Nigerian Middle Belt where Hadija was exchanged, experienced a transformation in their relationships with Hausa traders as Sokoto extended its reach there in the nineteenth century. Hausa immigrants had once "engaged in trade and strategic sociopolitical communion with their non-Muslim hosts," but following the jihad that gave rise to the caliphate, their outposts came to represent Sokoto's economic and political influence. Hausa long-distance merchants then began to facilitate an institutionalized patronage system, whereby non-Muslim de facto vassals were obliged to transfer slaves and other forms of wealth as tribute to their new Muslim rulers. In the early twentieth century, the British further entrenched Hausa hegemony in these areas by placing Hausa officials as district heads ruling over non-Muslim peoples. In Lere of Kaduna State, the ruling head was a Muslim Hausa in the 1940s. Ochonu, *Colonialism by Proxy*, Chapter 2.

9. Haour and Rossi, *Being and Becoming Hausa*, 12; Pellow, "From Accra to Kano"; Pellow, *Landlords and Lodgers*; Schildkrout, *People of the Zongo*.

10. Pelican, "Getting along in the Grassfields," 279.

11. Clifford, "Diasporas," 302–338.

12. Adamu, *The Hausa Factor*, 16; Works, *Pilgrims in a Strange Land*, 104, 200. Paul Lovejoy critiques Abner Cohen on this account, stating that he had "missed a major dynamic of diaspora formation, namely the assimilation of immigrants within the metropolitan Hausa region at the same time that these immigrants and their descendants travelled on business elsewhere. Many of the kola merchants in Cohen's study trace their ancestry to these . . . groups." See Lovejoy, *Caravans of Kola*, 76.

13. Olofson, "The Hausa Wanderer"; Olofson, "'Yawon Dandi,'" 66.

14. Levtzion, *Muslims and Chiefs in West Africa*, 110–111.

15. Moses Ochonu shows how the Sokoto Caliphate and its Zazzau Emirate integrated the non-Muslim peoples of Southern Kaduna by converting some to Islam, while others became tribute-paying vassals or non-Muslim slave reservoirs. This history, especially pertaining to the town of Lere, Kaduna State, will be explored further in Chapter 3. Ochonu, *Colonialism by Proxy*, Chapter 2.

16. Ardener, *The Voice of Prophecy*, 75. John Middleton discussed similar tendencies among Swahilis regarding the significance of marriage in immigration patterns versus the more common historical narrative that highlights economy and politics: "Marriage is always mentioned as a means of absorption. The process is seen as that of autochthonous groups being 'swallowed' by immigrant patrilineal subclans, a privatization of resources by those able to acquire wealth by commerce. Demographically it is more likely that the swallowing was the other way, but the history is seen as one of commerce and political power." Middleton, *The World of the Swahili*, 98.

17. Ballantyne and Burton, *Moving Subjects*, 5. See also Bovill and Hallett, *Golden Trade of the Moors*; Brooks, *Landlords and Strangers*; Brooks, "The Signares of Saint-Louis and Gorée"; Anthony Reid's treatment of Portuguese "temporary marriages" in *Southeast Asia in the Age of Commerce*; Claude Markovitz's discussion of Shikarpuri traders keeping local Uighur women as concubines or common-law wives in Sinkiang [Xianjing], *Global World of Indian Merchants*; Sleeper-Smith, *Indian Women and French Men*; and Andaya, *Leaves of the Same Tree*.

18. Works in African and African diaspora studies redefining community narratives and identity formation that have historically privileged male experiences include Brown, *Dropping Anchor, Setting Sail*; Byfield, Denzer, and Morrison, *Gendering the African Diaspora*; and Scott and Hébrard, *Freedom Papers*.

19. Pittin, "Migration of Women in Nigeria."

20. Ibid., 1298; Bivins, *Telling Stories, Making Histories*, xii.

21. Paul Lovejoy has acknowledged the significance of marriage alliances, as such arrangements solidified common interests between the government and the commercial sector, strengthened Islamic influence, and led to the assimilation of immigrants as a privileged class. Lovejoy, "The Role of the Wangara," 177.

22. Launay, *Traders without Trade*, 66–67. For a recent and innovative account of the role of West African women in connecting the household to statecraft during the pre-colonial period, see Osborn, *Our New Husbands Are Here*.

23. Byfield et al., *Gendering the African Diaspora*. See also Gunning, Hunter, and Mitchell, *Dialogues of Dispersal*; Terborg-Penn, "Women in the African Diaspora."

24. Ballantyne and Burton, *Moving Subjects*, 11–12.

25. I thank Moses Ochonu for his invaluable insights, which greatly influenced the argumentative structure of this Introduction. On culture as a "site of difference and contestation," see the introductory chapter to Gupta and Ferguson, *Culture, Power, Place*.

26. Scott, "Gender: A Useful Category."

27. Abraham, *Dictionary*. G. P. Bargery defines *abakwanriga* as a Hausa child born to a "Pagan woman south of the river Benue." Bargery, *A Hausa–English Dictionary*.

28. In many respects, this transformation in meaning represents Frederick Cooper's contention that colonial officers failed to "[enter] into the social and cultural realm over which they presided." Cooper, *Africa since 1940*, 5.

29. Brown, *Dropping Anchor, Setting Sail*; Byfield, "Introduction: Rethinking African Diaspora"; Chivallon, "Beyond Gilroy's Black Atlantic," 359; Gilroy, *The Black Atlantic*; Hall, "Cultural Identity and Diaspora"; Miles, *Ties that Bind*; Morgan, *Laboring Women*.

30. Some scholars might question my usage of the term *diaspora*. After all, Hausas fail to meet all the criteria that some attribute to diasporas, including a shared history of persecution, the desire to return home, or a collective movement into some specific number of countries or continents. According to Robin Cohen, most scholars associated the term *diaspora* with Jewish history up until the 1960s, and as a result, scholars have often advanced theories extending from this "ideal type." See Cohen, *Global Diasporas*, 1; Safran, "Diasporas in Modern Societies." See James Clifford's *Cultural Anthropology* article, "Diasporas," for his critique of this "centered" model in which diasporas are comprised of people with a unified consciousness and similar (real or imagined) ties to a homeland.

31. Basel Mission Archives (BMA), E-5–2, 12, No. 69, "2. Tertial—Bericht 35, "Wir haben hier keine bleibende Stätte," January 10, 1936.

32. Cameroon National Archives, Buea (NAB), Ab/1/e, League of Nations Report, 1939, Bamenda Division, 5.

33. Geary, *Images from Bamum*, 127–128. See also Tardits, *Le royaume bamoum*.

34. Cohen, *Global Diasporas*, 1.

35. Sell, *Metaphor and Diaspora*, 3–5, 10.

36. Juliet Wagner and Helmut Walser Smith note that the term *diaspora* was regularly used in Germany in the late nineteenth century to describe Catholics and Protestants as well as Jews. Further research needs to be conducted to investigate the first use of the term in Germany, particularly in "non-religious," if not "non-Jewish" contexts (personal communication, February 12, 2014).

37. Sell, *Metaphor and Diaspora*, 3.

38. Some Europeans believed Grassfields Muslims had a "civilizing" effect on indigenous groups, while in other cases Hausas threatened the spread of Christianity or challenged European desires to see Africans through tribal distinctions.

39. All court records were written in English, even though hearings were usually heard in Hausa, Fulfulde, and Pidgin English (with some Arabic). Court scribes thus had to translate and transcribe simultaneously when hearing cases. All quotations from Islamic court cases in this text are taken directly from the record as written by court scribes. I had no hand in the translations.

40. See Pelican, "Getting along in the Grassfields," 279.

41. Barbara Cooper has suggested that historians using oral evidence need to include the performance context because such evidence is "essentially poetic and performative." These qualities are what—in part—distinguish oral sources from written ones, as the historian and the storyteller's friends and family in the audience take part in the production of this evidence. Cooper, "Oral Sources and the Challenge of African History," 202.

42. Luise White, Stephan Miescher, and David William Cohen have noted that many scholars entering the field of African history in the past twenty years have used "life history as a research modality and as a means to understanding," particularly to understand "how Africans saw their lives, their worlds, their histories." White, Miescher, and Cohen, *African Words, African Voices*, 19.

43. Most oral history interviews took place in Bamenda, the capital of the Northwest Province. I also interviewed participants in Sabga, Ndop, Fujua, Laikom, and Fumban.

44. Aristotle, *Poetics*, 30–31.

45. John Akomfrah, Symposium for the exhibit *Glyphs: Acts of Inscription*, Pitzer Art Galleries, Pitzer College, September 20, 2013. Akomfrah's exploration into his theorization of diaspora is depicted in his film *Peripeteia*, where he imagines the lives of a black man and woman who appear in sixteenth-century drawings by German Renaissance master Albrecht Dürer.

46. Glissant, *Poetics of Relation*, 18, 20.

1. "WORTHY SUBJECTS"

1. Vollbehr, *Mit Pinsel*, 67–72. Passage translated by Jade Finlinson.

2. Wilke, "Romantic Images of Africa," 294. Wilke cites quotes from Vollbehr's 1935 publication, Vollbehr, *Bunte leuchtende Welt*.

3. von Morgen (1893, 39), in Chilver and Röschenthaler, *Cameroon's Tycoon*, 54, n1.

4. Habermas, "Debates on Islam," 237.

5. Using his data of West African strangerhood to evaluate Georg Simmel's theory of strangers in world history, Elliot P. Skinner noted that the part of Simmel's thesis that held was the characterization of strangers, like Hausas here, as "mobile" and "opportunistic." However, Skinner noted "that this 'mobility' and 'opportunism' are limited by the structure of a society at any period of time." Such characterizations also reflect German understandings of Muslim populations as lacking agency, acting "either almost reflexively out of economic motives, or because they had fallen prey to a magical form of religious belief, not because they as Muslims were human beings endowed with intelligence and the ability to act rationally...." Habermas, "Debates on Islam," 237–238; Skinner, "Strangers in West African Societies," 319; Simmel, "The Stranger," 402–408. See also Rudin, *Germans in the Cameroons*, 234–236.

6. Vollbehr writes, "It is good that the German government of migrant business requires Hausas to have licenses and so at least Cameroon has a good income. They,

too, are seen at the English border at the Kentu post where the main trade route crosses the border. There, a white sergeant with 15 indigenous customs officers take 12,000–18,000 Mk. annually." Vollbehr, *Mit Pinsel*, 67–72. Passage translated by Jade Finlinson.

7. Chanock, *Law, Custom, and Social Order*, 172–173.

8. Pelican, "Getting along," 258. Pelican cites the dissertation of Awasom, "The Hausa and Fulani," 94–104.

9. BMA/QQ-30.027.0064, Ernst Vollbehr, watercolor, "Military station in Bamenda with a Hausa village in the foreground," 1912. This painting was published and distributed as a postcard by Basler Missionshandlung, Duala, Cameroon. The full caption for the postcard reads: "The Hausas are permanently on the move—the clever black merchants of Cameroon. They build themselves only very simple huts. They are very skilled in producing objects in leather or with bead decorations."

10. Warnier, *Échanges, développement et hierarchies*.

11. NAB/Cb/1916/10, Bamenda Division: Annual Reports 1916–1917, Quarterly Report 2, 1916–17, by G. S. Podevin. Two British officers died from the disease, prompting Podevin to take drastic measures. See NAB/Ab/1917/39 (also filed as Ba/1917/2), Diary, 1917–1920.

12. He also "put [the] Hausa settlement out of bounds for troops" and the civil staff. To ensure that no one trespassed the boundaries of that community, he went so far as to post guards on the hill, directly above the Hausa settlement. Eighteen days later, after the medical officer had examined all Hausas, the quarantine was removed from the Bamenda settlement.

13. In the dry season after crops were harvested it was common to participate in seasonal migration (*cin rani*) in search of work.

14. For a complete list of typical occupations in Hausaland during the pre-colonial period, see Smith, *Affairs of Daura*, 39.

15. Salamone, *The Hausa of Nigeria*, 111. One example of a female title for a senior woman of the aristocracy is *iya*. This woman mediates domestic conflicts among women of the *sarauta* class, as well as judges disputes for rural members of Hausa society, especially in matters pertaining to marriages. A detailed discussion on the role of the iya in Maradi, Niger, may be found in Cooper, *Marriage in Maradi*, 25–28.

16. Bivins, *Telling Stories*, 58.

17. Abaka, 'Kola Is God's Gift'; Lovejoy, *Caravans of Kola*.

18. Ochonu, *Colonialism by Proxy*, 24.

19. Some Hausas would never convert and came to be called Maguzawa, Hausa-speaking people who continued to practice polytheism and who placed fewer re-strictions on women's movement and social roles.

20. Hiskett, *The Development of Islam*, 158.

21. Salamone, *The Hausa of Nigeria*, 2; Polly Hill, *Rural Hausa*, 3.

22. Ochonu, *Colonialism by Proxy*, 24–25. Ochonu also asserts that equating Hausa identity with practicing Islam was coterminous with a new Islamic citizen-ship within the Sokoto Caliphate. The Fulani ruling the caliphate not only adopted

the language and culture of Hausa subjects but also the administrative infrastructure of the Hausa city-states. Through this process, "most of the urbanized Fulani *became* Hausa in linguistic and cultural terms."

23. Ochonu, *Colonialism by Proxy*, 26.

24. Haour and Rossi, *Being and Becoming Hausa*, 4.

25. Ochonu has argued, "Hausa is not just a language; it is a category synonymous with certain ways of acting, making a living, and worshipping God." Ochonu, *Colonialism by Proxy*, 27; Pierce, *Farmers and the State*, 27.

26. Haour and Rossi, *Being and Becoming Hausa*, 1. For further discussions on Hausa history, see Hogben and Kirk-Greene, *Emirates of Northern Nigeria*; Last, *The Sokoto Caliphate*.

27. Njeuma, "The Lamidates of Northern Cameroon," 17.

28. Chilver, *Zintgraff's Explorations*, 33.

29. Fardon, *Raiders and Refugees*.

30. See also Chapter 3 in Nkwi and Warnier, *Elements for a History*.

31. This agricultural activity has supported high population densities from ten to eighty people per square kilometer. For more information on the Grassfields environment, see Goheen, *Men Own the Fields*; Warnier, "Pre-Colonial Mankon"; Warnier, *Cameroon Grassfields Civilization*, 70.

32. Warnier, "The History of the Peopling of Western Cameroon," 395–410.

33. Warnier, *Cameroon Grassfields Civilization*, 42.

34. Goheen, *Men Own the Fields*, 47. Nso was variously estimated to have a population between 25,000 and 60,000. See also Warnier, "Pre-Colonial Mankon," 32.

35. Chilver and Röschenthaler, *Cameroon's Tycoon*, 107 n21.

36. Chilver notes that the effective end of the transatlantic slave trade from Cameroon occurred in the 1820s. Slave dealing was sustained and even enhanced over the course of the century due to northern slave markets, including the Sokoto Caliphate, and the coastal markets focused on palm oil plantations from the early 1800s onward. Chilver, "Nineteenth century Trade," 237, cited in Argenti, *The Intestines*, 281 n2. See also Austen and Derrick, *Middlemen of the Cameroons Rivers*.

37. Warnier asserts that the slave-gun cycle did not obtain in the Grassfields, for elites displayed guns to symbolize their wealth; they were not preferred weapons for battle. Warnier, *Cameroon Grassfields Civilization*, 78.

38. Men sported loincloths made of bark fiber while women wore a wisp of grass fiber. Warnier, *Échanges, développement et hierarchies*, 109.

39. Guyer, "Wealth in People"; Guyer and Beling, "Wealth in People as Wealth in Knowledge."

40. Nkwi, "Slavery and Slave Trade," 245.

41. Warnier, "Pre-Colonial Mankon," 162. Lovejoy and Hogendorn have noted that Hausas also employed drugs or objects that would make slaves, especially kidnapped children "forget their homes and relations." This likely "refers to some kind of amulet or local medication with a stronger psychological than medicinal impact." Lovejoy and Hogendorn, *Slow Death for Slavery*, 263–264.

42. Argenti, *Intestines*, 63, 281. Argenti also cites Bongfen Chem-Langhëë, who states that the kingdom of Nso had a slave market until the early 1920s. See Chem-Langhëë, "Slavery and Slave Marketing."

43. Nkwi, "Slavery and Slave Trade," 245.

44. Argenti, *Intestines*, 132.

45. Pelican notes that "the areas at the western fringes of the Bamenda Plateau, while rich in trade goods like palm oil and kernels," were particularly "dangerous and unsuitable for Hausa settlement." Pelican, "Getting Along," 256. George Sibbit Podevin also noted in his Touring Notes Diary that two Hausa men were murdered at Wum sometime during or before the war. He determined that the Hausa men were caught in a political game between the Chief of Wum and Esu people. NAB/Ab/1915/41, Touring Notes Diary, 1915–1916 by District Officer G. S. Podevin, Entries on January 17 and 19, 1916.

46. Warnier, *Cameroon Grassfields Civilization*, 72–73; Goheen, *Men Own the Fields*, 48–55.

47. Chilver, *Zintgraff's Explorations*, 16.

48. Chilver and Kaberry, *Traditional Bamenda*, 56–57.

49. Notably, such transformations did not occur in Mankon, which retained its clan-based structure. Nkwi and Warnier, *Elements for a History*, 86–87. Johannes Fabian coined the phrase "spectacular processes of change" to describe unprecedented changes in political and economic structures and connections in nineteenth-century Africa. See Fabian, *Out of Our Minds*, 47.

50. Skinner, "Strangers in West African Societies," 309.

51. Pellow, *Landlords and Lodgers*, 59.

52. Cohen, *Custom and Politics*, 9, 21.

53. Pelican, "Getting Along," 317. Becoming a successful and wealthy trader granted a man prestige. But he needed property in order to exercise the obligations and privileges that came with such stature. Obtaining property allowed Hausa men of means to become patrons or landlords to clients, be they settlers or peripatetic traders and strangers. One of these patrons, a *maigida*, would also come to be recognized by other Hausas and by the host society as the Sarkin Hausawa.

54. NAB/Aa/1, "Ethnological Notes on the Cameroons, 1916," translated from "Das Deutsche Kolonialreich (Meyer)." This description of the Hausa colony in Fumban is located in the section titled "The South Cameroon Uplands." See also BMA/QE-30.33.060, "In the Hausa Colony" (c.1905–1912). By 1917, one missionary estimated that the number had grown closer to two thousand. See BMA/E-30-0,6, Anna Wuhrmann, 1917, Commentaries to Slides from Bamum.

55. BMA/E-30-0,6/K 371, A. Wuhrmann, 1917, Commentaries to Slides from Bamum, Caption: "Hausa Chief and his attendants at the Sowing Festival," 1915. Anna Wuhrmann also believed "The Hausa king" to be "a friendly old man," but one who did not seem "to possess much power in his village. Nor [did] he impose much order."

56. BMA/E-30.33.058, Friedrich Lutz, "Hausa at Prayer," photograph, 1905–1906. The reference note for the photograph notes, "Haussa zum Gebet versammelt in Bamum auf dem Marktplatz vor dem alten Königspalast" (See BMA/QE-30.004.0005 and BMA/E-30-0,2). See also BMA/E-30.33.059.

57. BMA/E-30.33.044, Martin Göhring, "Hausa Butchers on the Market in Fumban," photograph, 1905–1912. Note accompanying the image: "Note the group of musicians with a drum on the right-hand side."

58. Goheen, *Men Own the Fields*, 211 n17, citing E. M. Chilver's field notes.

59. Geary, *Images*, 23, 59, 61.

60. Geary, *Images*, 78. BMA/QE-30.006.0045, Anna Wuhrmann, Untitled, photograph, 1911–1915.

61. BMA/QE-30.017.0027, 1912. It should be noted that the hairstyles of Bamum women were actually not archaic or Syrian in origin. This myth is derived from oral traditions claiming that Bamum people were not indigenous to the Grassfields but migrated to that region from the distant north. See Tardits, *Le royaume bamoum*.

62. Laya help bring lafiya. They can also be buried in the ground, especially for the purposes of protecting one's homestead. L. Lewis Wall, *Hausa Medicine*, 235–236.

63. BMA/E-5-2/15, Jahresbericht 1944 der Station Bafut; BMA/E-5-2/7/No. 50, Jahresbericht der Station Bali, 1934. These dynamics echo the use of amulets in Asante history as well. See Owusu-Ansah, *Islamic Talismanic Tradition*, 117–119.

64. BMA/QE-30.006.0160 and BMA/E-30.30.071, "Nzinzie, the Hausa Wife of King Ndjoya." Comments originated from BMA/E-30-0,6. K 348, Anna Wuhrmann, Commentaries to Slides from Bamum, 1917. Wuhrmann clearly held a biased opinion of Nzinzie and her relationship with the king: "Unfortunately this Muslim woman has no good influence on her royal husband. She uses every means at her disposal to estrange him from the Mission, and to damage the cause of Christianity. She is a gifted person but uses her capacities for intrigue and manipulation, and has already caused a lot of grief and unhappiness."

65. Abraham, *Dictionary*, 2. G. P. Bargery defines *abakwanriga* as a Hausa child born to a "Pagan woman south of the river Benue." Bargery, *A Hausa–English Dictionary*.

66. Adamu, *The Hausa Factor*, 39, 43.

67. Robinson, *Dictionary of the Hausa Language*, 3.

68. Adamu, *The Hausa Factor*, 3. This social context is quite different from what I observed in Bamenda and surrounding towns. True, Hausa people do emphasize patrilineality in order to claim an identity as Hausa. Unlike the Abakwariga that Adamu wrote about, most people I encountered in abakwa communities in the Grassfields consider themselves devout Muslims and fluent in the Hausa language, albeit with differences in dialect. See Adamu, *The Hausa Factor*, 3, 39, 43, 198. It should also be noted that none of the people I interviewed nor anyone else I came into contact with in Cameroon used the term *abakwariga* to classify Hausa quarters; *abakwa* or *abakpa* were used.

69. Interview with Buba Yerima et al., Sabga, November 9, 2006.

70. Helmreich, "Kinship, Nation, and Paul Gilroy's Concept of Diaspora," 245. See also Siu, "Queen of the Chinese Colony," 516. Jonathan P. A. Sell states, however, that we should be wary of diaspora's "sub-metaphors," which have been picked from the "etymological entrails of 'diaspora.'" These sub-metaphors refer to scholars' deployment of verbs such as *to sow* or *to scatter*. Sell, *Metaphor and Diaspora*, 6.

71. On kinship affiliation in mid-century Hausaland proper, see Smith, "The Hausa System of Social Status," 243; Smith, "Introduction," 13, 21.

72. Gopinath, "'Bombay, U.K., Yuba City,'" 305, 316.

73. Interview with Limam Alhaji Baba Malam Shuaibu, Bamenda, June 28, 2010.

74. Schmoll, "Black Stomachs, Beautiful Stones," 197.

75. See Lovejoy, *Caravans of Kola*, 31. Notably, both Adamu and Works argue that initial Hausa settlements and networks were not grounded in kinship relations. Adamu, *The Hausa Factor*, 16; Works, *Pilgrims in a Strange Land*, 114. Harold Olofson critiqued Abner Cohen's treatment of kinship within Hausa society, particularly his observations on the "estrangement" between parents and their firstborn children. Writing in 1981, Olofson called for scholars to "renew . . . investigations into . . . features of Hausa kinship and the existence of a Hausa diaspora." Olofson, "Hausa Kinship and Diaspora," 90.

76. Adamu, *The Hausa Factor*, 182; Lovejoy, *Caravans of Kola*, 31, 32,138; Works, *Pilgrims in a Strange Land*, 61, 70, 199.

77. Gopinath, "Bombay," 312, 315, 317, 319 n11.

78. The percentage of married women hailing from different chiefdoms ranged from 20 to 55 percent. Moreover, at every marriage a boy or girl between seven and twelve years of age was chosen among the relatives of the bride to accompany her to her new residence, to help her with chores, and to take care of her firstborn child. This meant that two people were exchanged with every marriage. Warnier, "Pre-Colonial Mankon," 8.

79. Warnier, "Pre-Colonial Mankon," 378–379.

80. Nkwi, "Slavery and Slave Trade," 245.

81. Warnier, *Cameroon Grassfields Civilization*, 43.

82. Goheen, *Women Own the Fields*, 52. See also: Kaberry, *Women of the Grassfields*.

83. Goheen, *Women Own the Fields*, 60.

84. Argenti, *Intestines*, xiii.

85. Paul Nchoji Nkwi similarly asserts that the Grassfields trading network "permitted *dealers within and outside the region* to establish friendship terms and protect the trade by special agreements" (my emphasis). Nkwi, "Slavery and Slave Trade," 244.

86. Whitehouse, *Migrants and Strangers in an African City*, 23. See also Geschiere, *The Perils of Belonging*; Igor Kopytoff, *The African Frontier*; Kuba and Lentz, *Land and the Politics of Belonging*.

87. Soon thereafter, other Hausa villages were established in Bali, Nso, Ndop, and Sabongari.

88. See also Pellow, *Landlords and Lodgers*, 46.

89. Adamu, *The Hausa Factor*; Levtzion, *Muslims and Chiefs*; Lovejoy, *Caravans of Kola*; Wall, *Hausa Medicine*. This statement does not mean, however, that women never act to reinforce this patriarchal order. Maintaining community hierarchies can and does also serve the interest of many women, especially post-menopausal women, mothers of masu gida, and senior wives.

90. Cooper, *Evangelical Christians*, 59; Wall, *Hausa Medicine*, 88.

91. Kirk-Greene, *Mutumin Kirkii*.

92. Morrell, "Of Boys and Men," 608.

93. Wall, *Hausa Medicine*, 112–113.

94. Ibid., 141–143. A woman who abides by these expectations, follows the way of Islam, and helps to maintain the peacefulness of the community through honesty is considered a "good woman," or *matan kirki*. Interview with Zainabu Mama, Bamenda, June 29, 2010.

95. Chilver, *Zintgraff's Explorations*, xi–xvii, 33.

96. Rudin, *Germans in the Cameroons*, 325.

97. German officers wrote about Hausas who accompanied them in their military expedition to Tibati, north of the Grassfields, and about the "voluntary spies of the Hausa quarter" in Banyo, who informed German forces of an impending insurrection as they attempted to establish a military station there. Cameroon National Archives, Yaoundé (NAY), TA-33, Extrait du Bulletin Colonial Allemand 1899–1900, Expédition Tibati, Rapport du Capitaine von Kamptz Commandant de la troupe, pp. 6–12; NAY/TA-31/2. La fondation de la station de Banyo en 1902 par le 1er Lt. Zickwolff, Bulletin Colonial Allemand, July 14, 1911, pp. 2–3; NAY/TA-24, La Soumission de Boubandjida, Rapport du Premier Lieutenant Radtke, December 1901, p. 3; NAY/TA-53, Rapport sur Banyo par Sandrock, Banyo, June 12, 1902, p. 3; and NAY/TA-26, Recit d'un voyage effectué dans le Nord Cameroun, 1903, Dominik, Premier Lieutenant à la suite, commandé par le Ministère des Affaires Etrangères, pp. 1, 11. All documents translated from German to French by Gisèle Lagrange.

98. NAY/TA-53, Rapport sur Banyo par Sandrock, Banyo, June 12, 1902, trans. Gisèle Lagrange, p. 7; NAY/TA-27, Rapport Rel. à la Marché de L'expédition Dominik de Yaoundé à Garoua, nd, trans. Gisèle Lagrange, p. 3. Dominik's report also notes that the Hausas were the primary merchants trading in livestock and kola (see p. 6). See also Andreas Eckert, "Slavery in Colonial Cameroon, 1880s to 1930s," 141.

99. Rudin, *Germans in the Cameroons*, 234.

100. NAY/TA-74, Le Cauri en Pays Bamoun, 1910, p. 3. Translated from German to French by M. Rohrbascher.

101. O'Neil, "Imperialisms at the Century's End," 84.

102. Chilver and Röschenthaler, *Cameroon's Tycoon*, 85.

103. Fomin, *A Comparative Study of Societal Influences on Indigenous Slavery in Two Types of Societies in Africa*, 77.

104. In 1901, Germans launched a punitive expedition against Bafut and Mankon of the Bamenda Plateau. More than 1,000 Bafut died, while Mankon lost 218 of its people. A further 575 Mankon and Bafut were taken as prisoners, and an additional 500 were levied as forced laborers. Mankon surrendered immediately, while Bafut continued its resistance. The Germans also organized a massive punitive expedition against Nso in 1906. See Warnier, "Pre-Colonial Mankon," 92; and Goheen, *Men Own the Fields*, 65.

105. Germans began to mistrust some of the fon's people, as some groups armed themselves with German weapons in order to raid their neighbors for slaves. Some Bali peoples also threatened German economic interests by engaging directly in trade.

106. Nkwi, "Slavery and Slave Trade," 247.

107. Pelican, "Getting Along," 255.

108. Cameroon Northwest Regional Archives (NWRA), Aa/1983/1, A Collection of Ethnography Notes, "History of Menda-Nkwe," November 1990. Today, this location is the cattle market at Up Station.

109. Awasom, "The Hausa and Fulani," 33–65, cited in Pelican, "Getting Along," 254. Historian Pius Bejeng Soh has suggested that the growth of the Hausa community at Bamenda occurred as men returned home or to former settlements. Upon returning they brought wives and children, as well as brothers or friends whom they encouraged to settle alongside them. Soh, *Abakpa, Mankon, Bamenda*.

110. Ernst Vollbehr, "Haussatänzerin (Bamenda)," gouache on paper, c. 1911 (Leipzig: Leibniz-Institute for Regional Geography, Archive for Geography).

111. Levine, "Why Gender and Empire?" 6–7.

112. Gorges, *The Great War in West Africa*; Moberly, *Togoland and the Cameroons 1914–1916*; Paice, *Tip and Run*; Strachan, *The First World War in Africa*.

113. BMA/E-4/1/No. 3, "Kriegsnachrichten aus Europa und ihre Folgen auf einer Inlands-Missionsstation in Kamerun," August 11, 1914–October 31, 1914, Besongabang, p. 31; NAB/Cb/1916/2, Report 1/1916, Bamenda Division, Cameroons Province, To His Honour, Lt-Gov, Southern Province, Lagos, Nigeria, from G. S. Podevin, D.O., Political Officer, Bamenda; BMA/E-4/2/No. 52, "Erlebnisse während des Krieges," January 16, 1915; BMA/E-4/1/No. 25, "Raubzug der Englisch. und Francosen nach Duala, Bericht," February 12, 1915, p. 7; BMA/E-4/1/No. 24, "Erlebnisse vor, bei und nach dem Raubzug der Engländer und Franzosen nach Duala," January 22, 1915, p. 2.

114. According to Bamenda's first district officer, G. S. Podevin, many of those Hausas who migrated to Fumban were "employed as carriers" by the Germans for their military campaigns. NAB/Cb/1916/6, Bamenda Division, Annual Report for Year Ended 31 December 1916, by District Officer G. S. Podevin.

115. Conflicts erupted when the Germans' Bali soldiers began occupying parts of Bamum territory, straining the once friendly relationship between these two chiefdoms. NAB/Ab/1915/41, Touring Notes Diary, 1915–1916 by District Officer G. S. Podevin, Entry, January 2, 1916.

116. NAB/Cb/1916/10, Annual Report of 1916.

117. Local oral traditions collected in Bamenda, Cameroon, indicate that all Hausas living near the German military station scattered, heading northward into Nigeria or toward Fumban. Some Hausas in Bamenda today believe that German officers wrote a letter to King Njoya of Bamum, asking him to allow Hausas to take refuge at Fumban. Though I did not collect any other evidence to corroborate the claim that a letter was written, British reports show that Hausas deserted the Western Grassfields during wartime hostilities. See NAB/Cb/1916/6, Bamenda Division Annual Report for Year Ended 31 December 1916, by District Officer G. S. Podevin.

118. NAB/Ab/1915/41, Touring Notes Diary, 1915–1916 by District Officer G. S. Podevin, Entry, March 8, 1916.

119. Vollbehr, *Mit Pinsel und Palette*, 67–72. Passage translated by Jade Finlinson.

2. "PEOPLE OF THE NORTH"

1. Interviews with Alhaji Zakari Mama, Hajiya Sa'adatu, and family, Bamenda, December 5 and 7, 2006.

2. Jacqueline Nassy Brown developed the concept of *diasporic resources* in "Black Liverpool, Black America," 291–325.

3. For more information on George Sibbit Podevin, see http://www.dover-warmemorialproject.org.uk/Casualties/WWI/SurnamesPigg.htm.

4. NAB/Ab/1915/41, Touring Notes Diary, 1915–1916 by District Officer G. S. Podevin, entry, January 6, 1916.

5. NAB/Ab/1915/41, entry, January 10, 1916.

6. NAB/Ab/1915/41, entry, January 7, 1916.

7. Soh, *Abakpa-Mankon-Bamenda*, 5.

8. NAB/Cb/1916/10, Bamenda Division: Annual Reports 1916–1917 by G. S. Podevin, D.O., Annual Report of 1916.

9. NAB/Ab/1915/41, entry, December 10, 1915.

10. Including women and children (eighteen men, five women, and ten children).

11. Hausas continued to increase their numbers in the vicinity, and Podevin persisted in directing all Hausas in the nearby area to join the community near the station. This desire was echoed in his instructions to a group of sixty-five Hausas who were staying in Bamendjing, near the Anglo-French border in the Grassfields. Podevin encountered them on his tour of that area. He seemed to view this particular group of Hausas rather contemptuously, recording in his journal that they "were a most awful collection of scallywags" and that "most of them have probably run west to escape the French." Podevin gave them six days to come and settle at Abakpa-Bamenda or otherwise clear out of his division. Over the next few months into May of 1916, Podevin encountered more and more Hausas who were arriving from Nigeria and French-mandated territory and hoping to return to the Grassfields settlements they had occupied before the war. One such community of Hausas asked

Podevin if they could return to Kentu in the northern part of the Grassfields where they were settled before the war. Five days later, a different delegation of Hausas from Fumban arrived in Bamenda and requested permission to settle there, which Podevin granted willingly. This deputation consisted of sixteen men and women and was led by a Mahamadu Kano. By the end of May 1916, the Hausa population at Abakpa-Bamenda likely totaled more than 250 people. NAB/Ab/1915/41, entries May 24, 1916 and May 29, 1916.

12. NAB/Cb/1916/10, Bamenda Division: Annual Reports 1916–1917 by G. S. Podevin, D.O., Annual Report of 1917. Podevin himself relied on Hausas for his personal needs. He sold a cow or two to Hausas for cash, and he also purchased onions, salt, and fowl at their market. NAB/Ab/1915/41, entry, March 6, 1916.

13. NAB/Cb/1916/4, Podevin remarked, "In the Bansso country Kolas are purchased by Hausas at from 10 to 20 marks per 1000. At Kentu and Banyo the price rises, 30 to 40 marks per 1000, being the usual rate."

14. This currency would then eventually replace German currency. This plan was supported by a test event in one specific locale, which, according to Podevin, was an "unqualified success." He further surmised that one particular group, the "Munchis" at Lake Bamendjing, would have not considered using the new coinage had it not been introduced to them by Hausas. Podevin suggested that in Bamenda, the proposition was slightly different, that "although the Hausa market will materially assist, [the coinage] will also be introduced through the Native courts." NAB/Cb/1916/10, Quarterly Report No. 1, 1917. Moreover, that Podevin referred to the group as *munchis* further suggests the extent to which Podevin relied on Hausas as facilitators of colonial rule. Ochonu has noted that some officers began using the Hausa "derogatory epithet" *munchi* to describe "less civilized" groups in the Middle Belt of Nigeria. See Ochonu, "Colonialism within Colonialism," 105. The reference to rubber is found in NAB/Cb/1916/4.

15. NAB/Ba/1920/5, Special annual report on the Cameroons Province, February 1920, by J. Davidson, pp. 30–31.

16. NAB/Ba/1916/3, "West Africa: Reports on Various Matters Relating to the Cameroons," Colonial Office, May 1916.

17. NWRA/Re/a/1921/1, Memorandum No.151/48/1921, Strangers Settlement, Ngemba, N.A. Area, Bamenda, the Divisional Officer, Bamenda, March 18, 1924.

18. NAB/Ha/7, Hausa Village Assessment (Malam Baba), Bamenda division, September 8, 1923. On this date, Hawkesworth, acting district officer, performed a surprise census of Malam Baba's "Hausa Town" in Bamenda. Not only did this census tabulate the men, women, and children of Hausa Town, but it also catalogued the numbers of huts, pigs, goats, sheep, cows, and fowl they possessed. In addition, Hawkesworth recorded the professions of all the men, from blacksmiths, traders, and tailors, to malams, teachers, and preachers, from magic men to those who were too sick, old, or poor to be taxed. The data shows that there were 309 men, 243 women, 103 boys, and 98 girls living in Hausa Town, a total of 753 inhabitants. Of the men living or visiting there, there were 4 blacksmiths, 152 traders, 9 tailors,

30 malams, 4 magic men, and 3 invalids or paupers. There were also 3 Protestants and 19 Catholics, but no preachers or teachers. These figures not only represent the permanent residents but also a large floating population. Fortunately, the records show the names of the "hamlets" where people resided, names that appear to correspond to men's places of origin. The names of these hamlets included Kano, Katsina, Borno, Yola, Takum, Ibi, Bauchi, Lafiya, and Ilorin, while others were named for local places such as Bamum, Bameta, Babanki, and Bali. Of all the names, that of Kano was the most frequently recorded.

19. Awasom in Pelican, "Getting along," 255.

20. NAB/Gd/I, Trade—Internal Report On, 1922, Doc. No. 50, date early: 1925; date late: 1926.

21. They were members of the Jaafun subgroup.

22. NAB/Cb/1938/3, League of Nations Report, 1938, Bamenda Division by M. H. W. Swabey, Esquire, District Officer. See also Pelican, "Mbororo Claims to Regional Citizenship," 540–560.

23. This second migration involved people belonging to the Aku group, a different subgroup from the Jaafun.

24. Pelican, "Getting along," 249, 256, and 295. Citing 1967 census data, Pelican states that the Grassfields Hausa population at that time comprised 2,700 inhabitants, "out of whom 1,350 lived in rural areas, 700 in major villages, and 650 in the urban centre of Bamenda."

25. Pelican, "Getting along," 265, 280.

26. Awasom has noted, for example, that rumors spread among Grassfielders about the ability of Mbororos to transform themselves into cattle: "On driving such a herd of cattle, they would, at an unexpected point of the journey, suddenly transform into humans each holding a long leather whip in his hand and mercilessly beat the drovers to death. Only Hausa who had special talismen could detect real cows from human-transformed cows. Such a rumour permitted only the Hausa to be engaged in the cattle trade. A cloud of suspicion therefore existed between the natives and the Fulani, and not between the natives and the Hausa, or the Hausa and the natives." Cited in Pelican, "Getting along," 265–266.

27. NAB/Aa/1915/86, Dr. Jeffreys' Note Book—compiled on his first tour, 1915. The document was written before August 8, 1915.

28. Mahmood Mamdani, "Beyond Settler and Native as Political Identities," 654; Mahmood Mamdani, "Beyond Settlers and Natives," W. E. B. Du Bois Lecture Series (Cambridge: Harvard University, November 18–21, 2008). For a comparative discussion on British attempts to define ethnic categories in the face of commercial diasporas and pan-ethnic identities in Africa, see works on Swahili history, including Horton and Middleton, *The Swahili*; Middleton, *The World of the Swahili*.

29. A number of scholars have argued that not only have historians of Africa oversimplified and overstated the power of colonial authorities to change African identities according to colonial categories, but they have also accepted, again incor-

rectly, the notion that concepts of race were imported into African lexicons rather than established from within prior to colonial rule. See Glassman, *War of Words, War of Stones*; Hall, *A History of Race in Muslim West Africa*.

30. NAB/Aa/1915/86, Dr. Jeffreys' Note Book.

31. J. N. D. Anderson, *Islamic Law in Africa*, 177.

32. The fons of Bali-Nyonga and Mankon were two such notables who benefited from these transformative intrusions. Paul Nchoji Nkwi and Jean-Pierre Warnier, *Elements for a History*, 71.

33. NAB/Ab/1915/41, Diary of 1915–1916 by Divisional Officers in Bamenda, Podevin Touring Notes, 1915–1916.

34. NAB/Ab/1917/39 (also catalogued as Ba/1917/2), Diary 1917–1920, Podevin, Crawford, and Duncan, June 21, 1917.

35. NAB/Ab/12, Assessment Report, Banso District, 1923, Report and Correspondence by E. G. Hawkesworth, Assistant District Officer, 27.

36. NAB/Ab/15, File E.P.16059.A, Index 118, "A Report on Tax Collection in the Banso Native Area, Bamenda Division," by F. R. Kay, Esquire, Assistant Divisional Officer, September 1937, 48. On historical relations between Hausas and Nchaney leadership in Misaje, see Pelican, "Getting along," 294.

37. NAB/Cb/1939, League of Nations Report 1939, Bamenda Division.

38. NAB/Ab/1, Bamenda Division, Native Customs—Report on, by W. E. Hunt, D.O., November 15, 1921.

39. NAB/Ad/4, File NO. 277/27, An Assessment Report of the Bum Area in the Bamenda Division, Cameroons Province, 1927.

40. Writing nine years later, Senior District Officer M. D. W. Jeffreys reported his understanding of the same phenomenon but left the door open as to whether clothing correlated directly to religious conversion. According to Jeffreys, "[Bum] women usually go naked. With the Mohammedan invasion, Mohammedan fashions have been adopted by certain tribes and two stages may be seen. Where pagan communities adopt the fashion it is the men who first begin and only later on do the women adopt the fashion." NAB/Cb/1936/1, File No. 2085, Bamenda Divisional and League of Nations Report, 1936, by M. D. W. Jeffreys, Senior District Officer.

41. Smith, *Baba of Karo*, 33.

42. Interview with Aishatu Ibrahim, Bamenda, February 13, 2007.

43. NAB/Ab/1915/41, Touring Notes Diary 1915–1916 by D.O. Podevin, Entry February 22, 1916. Even Podevin relied on Hausa expertise and trade in cloth. In February 1916, he advanced monies to Mallam Baba, the Hausa chief at Bamenda, to purchase cloth for the uniforms of office messengers.

44. Pelican, "Getting along," 263.

45. Cited in Pelican, "Getting along," 265.

46. According to the officer, "This man has shewn himself to be a suitable person and has been well-spoken of by District Officers in the past." NAB/Ab/1948/36, Bamenda Southwestern Federation, Letter from Bamenda Divisional Office to the Resident of the Cameroons, "Reorganised Ngemba Native Court," March 20, 1949.

47. NAB/Ab/1948/36, Bamenda Southwestern Federation, Petition addressed to the Resident of the Cameroons from Salah, Kieng, and Bango, three "settlers" from Santa. The letter was written by Mofor Gratis on March 23, 1949.

48. Pelican, "Getting along," 279.

49. NAB/Ab/1951/1h, Doc. No. 296/32, "New Abakpa," October 9, 1950.

50. NAB/Ab/1951/1h, Doc. No. 296/32, "New Abakpa," October 9, 1950, 5, 39.

51. NAB/Ab/1951/1h, Doc. 1188/51, "Planning of Mankon Abakpa," July 3, 1951.

52. The Native Authorities would then have the "say of whom the Joint Committee shall consist and in what manner its members shall be appointed." NAB/Ab/1951/1h, Doc. No. 23839/31, June 27, 1952.

53. NAB/Ab/1951/1h, Doc. No. 1188/137, December 22, 1952.

54. NAB/Ab/1951/1h, Doc. No. 1188/116, October 5, 1952.

55. NAB/Ab/1951/1h, Letter from the acting resident of the Bamenda Province, November 2, 1951; Letter from the fons of Mankon, Nkwen, and Manda, and from the secretaries of Tadkon-Widekum United Fondom and People and of the Bamenda Improvement Association, June 25, 1951.

56. NWRA/Fa/1950/1, Tours and Visit of Senior Officer to the Bamenda Province. Letter to the Chief Commissioner, Eastern Provinces, from Ngemba Clan, Moghamo Clan, Ngie Clan, Menemo Clan, Ngwaw Clan on behalf of the Bamenda South Western Native Authority, December 31, 1950.

57. Robin Cohen, *Global Diasporas*, 84.

58. Those interviewees who remarked on the history of Abakwa's cemetery and its relocation were Limam Alhaji Baba Malam Shuaibu, Bamenda, April 1, 2007; Aishatu Ibrahim, Bamenda, March 15 and 22, 2007; Sarkin Pawa Alhaji Adamu Audu Tunku, Bamenda, January 13, 2007; and Alhaji Zakari Mama, Bamenda, December 5, 2006.

59. The graveyard stretched from the heart of Abakwa toward Ayaba Stream, a length of about 600 meters.

60. People interviewed remember that the Sabon Gari (new town) that grew over both intact and disrupted graves began before the removal of the market from Abakwa but during the reign of Sarki Sule as the Sarkin Hausawa of Bamenda. As his reign lasted from 1945 to 1969, and since the transfer of the market took place in 1952–1953, we can conclude that Sabon Gari started to develop between the years of 1945 and 1952. It is also of note that Mary F. Smith stated that burials in Northern Nigeria in the 1950s took place on the outskirts of town rather than the center. Perhaps there were larger colonial directives among the British as they concerned themselves more and more with development and city planning during late colonial rule. See Smith, *Baba of Karo*, 264 n25.

61. Aishatu Ibrahim remembered that as Sabon Gari started to develop, Hausa malams found a new niche in their local market: "The Sabon Gari, when it started developing, the malams prepared laya as protection for us, to protect the compound. Because, as people sleep at night and something wakens them, something like spirits. So the malams prepared laya [which you buried in the ground] so that

one could avoid those things." Interview, Aishatu Ibrahim, Bamenda, March 22, 2007. Translation assistance from Aishatu Ibrahim's grandson, Jibril.

62. Abner Cohen, *Custom and Politics*, 185.

63. NAB/Ab/1951/1h; Awambeng, *Evolution and Growth of Urban Centres*; interviews with Adama Shuaibu Limam, March 28, 2007; Aishatu Ibrahim, January 18, 2007; Limam Alhaji Baba Mallam Shuaibu, December 12, 2006; Kungiyar Matan Musulman, December 25, 2006; Zainabu Mama, January 15, 2006.

64. Deeper in the Grassfields hinterland, a similar transition took place between the communities of Fundong and Fujua. Hausas and Fulanis had settled at Fujua with the permission of the fon of Laikom. The Hausa market there was an important center for trade. This changed in the 1950s, however, when the British decided to add another leg of the Bamenda–Fundong road connecting Fundong to the Ring Road at We. In this configuration, the dead-end road from Fundong to Fujua was relegated to secondary importance as more and more traffic passed through Fundong. The market at Fundong grew tremendously at the expense of the Hausa community in Fujua. All that remains of the Fujua market today are the overgrown remains of its foundation. Interviews with the fon of Laikom, and Abubakar Ismaila and Halima from Fujua, January 26, 2007.

65. Pelican, "Getting along," 293.

66. NWRA/Bb/1952/2, United Nations Organization and Visiting Missions, November 22, 1952.

67. In response to the claims of the Hausas, the resident assured the visiting mission that the colonial administration was "[keeping] very much in mind" the need to "safeguard the interests of strangers." NWRA/Bb/1952/2, Resident's comments on the welcome address by the Jam'iyyar Mutanen Arewa.

68. Interview with Alhaji Adamu Tunku, July 1, 2010, Bamenda. Into the 1930s, Sarakunan Hausawa and their trusted advisers ran informal hearings on disputes in their communities where "Hausa and Moselm law [were] concerned." NAB/Cb/1938/3, League of Nations Report, 1938, Bamenda Division, by M. H. W. Swabey, Esquire, District Officer, 15–16. For an extensive discussion of the relationship between the racialization of Islamic diasporas in the Grassfields and the founding of the Alkali court, see Harmony O'Rourke, "Native Foreigners and the Ambiguity of Order and Identity," 97–122. Martin Chanock also discusses the prevalence of adultery cases and attempts to criminalize adultery and control the movement of women in 1930s' Malawi and Zambia. See especially Chapter 10 and Chapter 11 of *Law, Custom, and Social Order*, 1998. On historical changes in Islamic law during imperial rule, see Rudolph Peters, "Shari'a and Colonial Public Policy"; Peters, *Islamic Criminal Law*; Peters, *Crime and Punishment*; Yadudu, "Substance and Form of Islamic Law," 17–47.

69. NAB/Mb/a/1943/1, Doc. N.A. 2334/43, "Alkali's Court," memo from the Bamenda divisional office to the senior resident of Cameroon in Buea, June 7, 1944.

70. NAB/Mb/a/1943/1, "Alkali's Court Bamenda," Letter from the resident of Cameroons, Buea, to the secretary's office, Eastern Provinces, Enugu, August 3, 1944.

71. NAB/Cb/1940/1, File No. 1084, Annual Report Part II, Bamenda Division, by Dr. M. D. W. Jeffreys, senior district officer, 1940.

72. NAB/Ab/1/e, League of Nations Report, 1939, Bamenda Division, 16. See also NAB/Cb/1939/3, 51; NAB/Ab/1/e, League of Nations Report, 1939, Bamenda Division, 4–5. In his Handing-Over Notes written in 1939 as well, M. D. W. Jeffreys reported a large influx of Fulani with cattle from French territory, which meant further tax revenue increases for the Native Treasury. See NAB/Ab/1/d, Handing-Over Notes, Bamenda Division, From M. D. W. Jeffreys, Snr. District Officer, to I. F. W. Schofield, Esq., District Officer, 1939, 7.

73. NAB/Mb/a/1943/1, Alkali's court, Bamenda Division.

74. The C-grade warrant is distinct from the A-grade warrant initially assigned to Islamic courts in Northern Nigeria decades prior to the establishment of the Alkali court in Ndop, Cameroon. For more information comparing British policies toward Islamic law in Nigeria and Cameroon, see O'Rourke "Native Foreigners." See also NAB/Ab/17/1, "Fulani in Bamenda Division—Reorganisation of." Letter from the Secretary at Enugu to the Chief Secretary, Government at Lagos, No. 19547/136, March 19, 1945. For an in-depth analysis on the history of criminal jurisdiction in British West Africa, see Roger Gocking, "British Justice and the Native Tribunals," 93–113.

75. BNA/Mb/a/1943/1, "Alkali's Court, Bamenda Division," No. N.A.1973/247, "Establishment of the Alkali's Court: Jurisdiction and Power," from Bamenda Divisional Officer to Resident of the Cameroons at Buea, July 6, 1947.

76. BNA/Mb/a/1943/1, "Alkali's Court and Status of Converted Muslims," to District Officer of Wum from J. Brayne Baker, Acting Resident, Bamenda Province. No.689/120, February 20, 1953.

77. NWRA/Kb/a/1940/1, Complaints, Alkali's Court, Bamenda, 1940–1964, 124.

78. NAB/Mb/a/1943/1, Correspondence from Bamenda NWNA Office, Wum (Agricultural District Officer, Wum), to the Resident, Bamenda. No. NW 496/49. "Alkali's Court and Status of Converted Muslims," February 10, 1953.

79. NAB/Ab/17/2, File No. 19547, Vol. II, Fulani in Bamenda Division—Reorganisation of (Correspondence). From resident of Cameroons Province to secretary at Enugu, "Alkali's Court in Bamenda Division," August 3, 1944.

80. By contrast, the British viewed the Grassfields Fulani as a people more strictly Muslim than Hausas. The fact that the population of the Fulani in most Grassfields locations had surpassed that of the Hausa by the early 1940s provided further grounds to create a judicial body that revolved more tightly around the needs of the Fulani. Fulani leaders no doubt underscored this idea, as they commonly viewed themselves as more faithful adherents to Islam, more knowledgeable of Qur'anic laws, and therefore more qualified than Hausas to serve as Islamic judges. NWRA/Ka/b/1966/1, Letter from Ardo Joda, Fundong, Kom Sub-District to the Secretary of State for Local Government in Buea, May 11, 1966.

81. Jeppie, Moosa, and Roberts, eds., Muslim Family Law, 21–22, 27, 33, 35, 41. See also Mann and Roberts, Law in Colonial Africa, and Stowasser, "Gender Issues," 30–44.

82. Motadel, *Islam and the European Empires*, 1, 5.

83. Hall, "Of Gender and Empire," 52.

84. Robinson-Dunn, *British Imperial Culture*, 206–207.

85. Marital contracts allow husbands access to their wives' domestic and sexual services, and in return for their wives' obedience, husbands are obliged to provide material maintenance in food and clothing. Not cooking for one's husband is a protest to that contract. Joseph and Najmabadi, *Encyclopedia of Women and Islamic Cultures*; see "Marriage Practice" in "Volume 3: Family, Body, Sexuality, and Health." See also Chapter 4 of this study for a discussion on the relationship between cooking, sexual intercourse, and husbands' "nocturnal access" to their wives.

86. NWAC, Civil Law Book 1947–1948, Civil Suit No. 1/47, March 24, 1947. "Not using his wife" refers to impotence or refusal to have sexual intercourse on the part of the husband.

87. NAB/Mb/a/1943/1, "Alkali's Court, Bamenda Division," Document No. N.A.1973/247, "Establishment of the Alkali's Court: Jurisdiction and Power," from Bamenda Divisional Officer to Resident of the Cameroons at Buea, July 6, 1947. Similar trends in the establishment of male-dominated customary law in British-controlled Malawi and Zambia are discussed in great detail in Chanock, *Law, Custom, and Social Order.*

88. NAB/Mb/a/1943/1, "Alkali's Court, Bamenda Division," Document No. 19547/187, "Alkali's Court, Bamenda Division," from the Secretary's Office at Enugu to Resident of the Cameroons at Buea, November 25, 1947.

89. Levine, *Gender and Empire*, 6.

90. NAB/Mb/a/1943/1, "Alkali's Court, Bamenda Division," Document No. N.A.1973/247. See also NAB/Mb/a/1943/1, "Alkali's Court, Bamenda Division," Document No. 19547/187, "Alkali's Court, Bamenda Division," from the Secretary's Office at Enugu to Resident of the Cameroons at Buea, November 25, 1947. This document confirms that sentencing for bigamy "shall not exceed six months' imprisonment with or without hard labour," while the sentence for contempt of court was either a fine not exceeding ten pounds "or imprisonment with or without hard labour for a term not exceeding one month." However, court records themselves indicate that the Alkali often tried cases beyond his purview, especially those dealing with public and domestic violence.

91. Levine, "Sexuality, Gender, and Empire," 154.

3. SLAVE OR DAUGHTER?

1. Mme-Bafumen is alternatively called Bafumai or Mmen.

2. As noted, widows must abstain from sexual relations for four months and ten days, while women whose marriages terminated through divorce or annulment must "observe a retreat of three lunar months." Bearman, *Encyclopedia of Islam*, accessed April 7, 2014. Note that *takaba* does not appear in the *Encyclopedia of Islam*, though it does appear in Hausa dictionaries.

3. NWAC, Criminal Book No. 2/51, Suit No. 56/52, October 8, 1952.

4. M. G. Smith, "The Hausa System," 244–245. See also: Smith, *Baba of Karo*; Barkow, "Hausa Women and Islam," 317–328.

5. Coles and Mack, *Hausa Women in the Twentieth Century*, 9.

6. Please see further discussion on the discursive relationship between marriage and female enslavement in Islamic law in Chapter 4, "First Reversal: Marriage and Enslavement."

7. I thank Moses Ochonu for this insight.

8. Note that when a female slave is married—not to her owner but to another man, perhaps himself a slave—and becomes widowed, her idda "should be half as long as that of a free woman. In other words, the *'idda* of a slave who is a widow would last for two months and five days, and that of a divorced woman not of menstruating age for one and a half months. As it is not possible to halve the period of three menstruations which is insisted on for the divorced free woman, it was decided that the *'idda* of a divorced slave who is of menstruating age should consist of two inter-menstrual periods (Shāfi'ī and Mālikī law) . . . the only exception being an *umm walad*, who as such is treated as a free woman." *Encyclopedia of Islam*, accessed April 7, 2014.

9. Reconvening of Suit No. 2/51, NWAC, Criminal Book 3/53, January 13, 1953.

10. Lere refers to a town in Kaduna State, Nigeria. There are also towns called Lere in Bauchi State, Nigeria, and near Lac de Léré in the Republic of Chad.

11. Alkali court clerks, or Scribe-Mufutis, often included the letter *F* after a name to indicate that the individual to whom the name referred was female.

12. According to Paul Lovejoy, one bag of cowry shells contained 20,000 cowries in 1906, a time when eight bags of cowries served as the redemption money for a female slave. However, the number of bags to purchase slaves changed considerably from 1906 to c.1950 when our story takes place, especially in light of the "great inflation" in cowries during these years. The other matter that complicates this interpretation is the decline in use of cowry as currency in the twentieth century. Marion Johnson suggested that cowries greatly declined in use after the First World War, though they both state that cowries continued to be used for bride-price payments and funeral offerings. Walter I. Ofonagoro argues, however, that cowries persisted as currency into the 1950s in various regions of Nigeria. Between 1939 and 1945/46, in southeast Nigeria, bride prices increased from 30 bags—containing only 1000 cowries each—to 432 bags; bride prices then rose again from 576 bags in 1948 to 720 bags in 1949. For further reference, see Marion Johnson's articles, "The Cowrie Currencies: Part I" and "The Cowrie Currencies: Part II"; Lovejoy, "Concubinage," 251; Ofonagoro, "From Traditional to British Currency," 623–654.

13. Hadija or Khadija was the name of the Prophet Muhammad's first wife. Khadīja bint Khuwāylid was also the Prophet's employer and chief sponsor in his caravanning business. Ghislaine Lydon has noted that "the Muslim cult of domesticity generally portrays the younger, betrothed 'Āisha as Muhammad's model wife

while systematically relegating the status of Khadīja, the entrepreneur, to a pre-Islamic era." Lydon, *On Trans-Saharan Trails*, 233.

14. Lovejoy and Hogendorn, *Slow Death for Slavery*, 251.

15. For those girls of low status who did not have parents, the Sultan of Sokoto declared in 1921 that "an Emir, District Head or other tribal Head or Chief" be the guardian to oversee their transfers. Lovejoy and Hogendorn, *Slow Death for Slavery*, 251–258.

16. Ochonu, *Colonialism by Proxy*, Chapter 2.

17. Lovejoy and Hogendorn, *Slow Death for Slavery*, 259.

18. Ochonu, *Colonialism by Proxy*, 55–56, 75.

19. Ali, *Marriage and Slavery in Early Islam*, 167. Prophet Mohammed did this himself when he freed and then married Safiyya.

20. NWRA/Kb/a/1940/1, N.W.496/69, "Alkali's Court: Inheritance Case," Bamenda N.W.N.A. Office, Wum, June 21, 1953. According to Malikite norms, free women received half of the male share of estates. See also Lovejoy, "Concubinage," 247.

21. See Jumare, "The Late Treatment of Slavery," 303–322; Lovejoy and Hogendorn, *Slow Death for Slavery*, 238–239.

22. BNA/Mb/a/1943/1, "Alkali's Court, Bamenda Division," Document No. N.A.1973/247; and BNA/Mb/a/1943/1, "Alkali's Court, Bamenda Division," Document No. 19547/187, "Alkali's Court, Bamenda Division," from the secretary's office at Enugu to resident of the Cameroons at Buea, November 25, 1947. Sentencing for contempt of court was significantly less than for bigamy: an individual found guilty of contempt of court was either fined an amount not exceeding 10 pounds or imprisoned "with or without hard labour for a term not exceeding one month."

23. The word for *to borrow* is the same as *to lend* in the Hausa language (*ranta*).

24. Moses Ochonu notes that Hausas were the district heads in Lere, including in the 1940s, and that they collected taxes and rounded up labor for public works projects. Notably, Chawai peoples organized many protests against the British-sanctioned "emirate rule" of the Lere district head in this decade. Ochonu, *Colonialism by Proxy*, 71.

25. Barkow, "Hausa Women and Islam," 322: "From a [Hausa] man's point of view, the burden of polygyny is that of diplomacy: he must not show favoritism. Thus, wives cook and share their husband's sleeping room in strict rotation, regardless of whether one is age 15 and the other 50. . . ."

26. Ruxton, *Maliki Law*, 118.

27. Ali, *Marriage and Slavery*, 101–102, 117. Everyone I interviewed also stated that husbands should spend two nights with a wife and only one with a concubine.

28. Lovejoy, "Concubinage," 247, citing from Abraham, *Spoken Hausa*, 120, 150–153.

29. Miers and Kopytoff, *Slavery in Africa*.

30. Cooper, *Marriage in Maradi*, 2, 8–11, 13. Though the transformation of slave labor in Maradi may shed some light onto Talle's motivations for damaging Hadija's social status in the Hausa diaspora, the information should be treated delicately

since Maradi's cultural and historical context vary greatly from that of the Grass-fields. During the nineteenth-century jihad that created the Sokoto Caliphate, the Maradi Valley was home to the resistant Hausa forces of Kano, Katsina, and Gobir states, and later the Katsinawa aristocracy settled there. The Grassfields, on the oth-er hand, lay beyond the direct influence of the jihad and Sokoto Caliphate, as well as Hausa culture until the latter part of the nineteenth century. Whereas domestic slave labor was outlawed in Maradi, causing a shift to senior wives' control of junior wives' labor, domestic slave labor in Northern Nigeria persisted under the British until 1936 legally, and, as this chapter shows, as late as 1953 tacitly.

31. Cooper, *Evangelical Christians*, 212.

32. Interview with Hajja Buba, July 5, 2010, Tchabbal, Sabga, Northwest Prov-ince, Cameroon.

33. *Encyclopedia of Islam*, accessed April 7, 2014.

34. "Costs" refer to court fees. The symbol /- refers to shillings. The standard court fee for the Northwest Province Alkali Court was 10 shillings, which was most commonly paid by the guilty party.

35. NWRA/Kb/a/1940/1, N.W.496/69, "Alkali's Court: Inheritance Case," re-sponse from Bamenda Senior District Officer to the Wum District Officer, Septem-ber 10, 1953.

36. I thank Anthony Lee for his insightful comments on mubahala and how it relates to this case. Personal communication, January 8, 2014.

4. FIRST REVERSAL

1. Rebekah Lee and Megan Vaughan suggest that "the migrant labour system imposed a necessary mathematics of distance upon the delicate calibrations of so-cial and kinship relations." Lee and Vaughan, "Death and Dying in the History of Africa since 1800," 356.

2. These nine markings represent Kanuri heritage more specifically. Though Malam Baba possessed Kanuri heritage, intermarriage between Hausas and Kanuris, along with Malam Baba's origins and early life in Kano, together meant that Malam Baba identified with the Hausa culture more strongly. Today, none of Malam Baba's descendants identify as Kanuri, nor do they speak the Kanuri lan-guage. They identify themselves as Hausa with origins in Kano State.

3. Levtzion, *Muslims and Chiefs*, xxv, 160.

4. Ibid., 23. Levtzion references Lander, *Records of Captain Clapperton's Last Expedition*, 274–275.

5. Levtzion, *Muslims and* Chiefs, 110–111.

6. Ibid., 100.

7. Interview with Hajiya Sa'adatu, Bamenda, January 9, 2007.

8. The act of renaming in particular may be read as signifying a change in one's identity as both a continuation of earlier forms of African and Islamic naming tradi-tions (Hadija and its variations refer to the first wife of Prophet Muhammad), and

as a way for individuals to reshape their identities in light of particular openings created through modernity. Emmanuel Akyeampong, for example, has written that an "important dimension of modernity is its ability to reshape social identity," and that the names people chose for themselves and for others were an important part of this reshaping. Akyeampong, "Seizing Modernity," 97, 103.

9. Brown, "Black Liverpool, Black America," 301.

10. A. W. Banfield (1905) in Abaka, "Kola is God's Gift," 71.

11. Abner Cohen cites J. Rouch's 1956 study titled "Migration au Ghana" found in *Journal de la société des africanistes*. Cohen, *Custom and Politics*, 52.

12. Interview with Aishatu Ibrahim, Bamenda, January 18, 2007.

13. Trimingham, *Islam in West Africa*, 168–169, cited in Duffill and Lovejoy, "Merchants, Porters, and Teamsters," 137–167. The Qur'anic passage referenced is Surat an-Nisa, verse 28.

14. The deployment and breaking of marital bonds as part and parcel of Hausa men's long-distance commercial activity are revealed in many family histories in the Grassfields and beyond. In earlier versions of this chapter, and in my dissertation, I labeled this strategy as trading-post polygyny. However, this characterization reinforces the androcentrism of the trading diaspora narrative and is rather unsympathetic to the individuals involved in these unions.

15. Hausa women in Hausaland and in the diaspora are known for conducting trade and producing their own capital. This cottage industry usually entails the production of snacks and other foodstuffs that women's biological, adopted, or foster children sell daily in the local markets. Abner Cohen viewed married women's ability to earn their own income as a stabilizing factor in Ibadan's Hausa community. To him and the men he interviewed, that women could steadily increase their wealth by being married stabilized marriages and stabilized Sabo's female population. Cohen, *Custom and Politics*, 69. My observations in the Hausa community of Bamenda show a negative side, however, to Hausa men's reliance on their wives' ability to earn their own income. Some women felt that their husbands shirked their economic responsibility to their families, expecting their wives to feed and clothe their children and themselves. Failing to feed and clothe one's wife is considered grounds for divorce under Islamic legal norms. One may thus conclude that Hausa wives' traditional practice of "trading from behind the purdah" in some cases allows Hausa husbands to evade the Islamic tenet that they feed and clothe their wives.

16. Olofson, "The Hausa Wanderer," 62, and Smith, *Baba of Karo*, 52–53, 288 n2.

17. Interview with Alhaji Gambo, Sabga, December 19, 2006.

18. Interview with Mariam Muhamed, Bamenda, January 15, 2007.

19. Abner Cohen, *Custom and Politics*, 35.

20. Interview with Limam Alhaji Baba Malam Shuaibu, Bamenda, July 7, 2010.

21. In M. G. Smith's words, "Marriage [placed] women in an indeterminate kinship position. Wives [were] neither full members of their husband's family nor of that into which they were born." Smith, "The Hausa System," 246.

22. Robertson, *Sharing the Same Bowl*; Cooper, "Chronic malnutrition," 8.

23. Cooper, *Marriage in Maradi*, xxiii–xxvi. Cooper has also shown that many Hausa women consider the institution of marriage to be central to their lives and find it easier to discuss than politics or formal history encountered through schooling.

24. On returning to a father's house after the termination of a marriage, see Callaway, *Muslim Hausa Women*, 42. Others lived out their temporary status as karuwai, or courtesans, in order to earn an income and to establish relationships with potential suitors. While past authors have glossed karuwai as "prostitutes," "courtesans" is the preferred translation given that, first, usually men of means are the clients of karuwai, second, karuwai could as likely be daughters of nobleman and malams as they could be of commoners, and third, most karuwai are women in between marriages (zawarawa) who work temporarily in this capacity.

25. While some authors have suggested that kinship incorporation through marriage and slavery are two ends of the same spectrum, others have suggested that slavery is the very antithesis of kinship. Miers and Koptyoff in *Slavery in Africa* have argued for the slavery–kinship continuum model to understand enslavement in Africa's history, while Claude Meillassoux has asserted that a slave is always an outsider. See Meillassoux, *The Anthropology of Slavery*.

26. See Cooper, *Marriage in Maradi*, 10. See also Abraham, *Dictionary*, 60, 947. Mohammed Bashir Salau has also noted that in the context of nineteenth-century Northern Nigeria, "For female slaves, a route toward mobility in emiral Kano was concubinage. Islam allowed a free man to marry a maximum of four wives simultaneously and also to possess as many concubines as his means allowed. Largely under the influence of this injunction, concubinage became widespread in Birnin Kano. Once a slave woman became a concubine her status approximated that of a free-born wife in many respects, as was the case in other Muslim societies." See Salau, "Slaves in a Muslim City," 91–101.

27. Lovejoy, "Concubinage," 245–248. On the British misunderstanding or ambivalence regarding domestic slavery in Northern Nigeria, see also Jumare, "The Late Treatment of Slavery," 303–322.

28. Lovejoy and Hogendron, *Slow Death*, 258–259. See also Jumare, "The Late Treatment of Slavery in Sokoto," 303–322.

29. Fomin notes that for the Grassfields' centralized societies, a slave was one who was both acquired and alien. Fomin, *A Comparative Study*, 20.

30. Argenti, *Intestines*, 281 n2; Fomin, *A Comparative Study*, 34.

31. Fomin, *A Comparative Study*, 75 and 95. See also Njiasse-Njoya, "Slavery in the Bamum Kingdom in the 19th and 20th Centuries," 230; Nkwi, "Slavery and Slave Trade," 243.

32. Fomin, *A Comparative Study*, 73.

33. Brain, *Bangwa Kinship and Marriage*, 98–99, cited in Warnier, *Cameroon Grassfields Civilization*, 77. According to Fomin, in Bangwa society, "When a female slave was given out in marriage tabs were kept on her children, and . . . the patri-group of the original slave-owner possesse[d] . . . rights on the matrilineal descen-

dants of these slaves. This system became known as the tangap [or Ngkap] system." These women were usually absorbed as wives whose slave status was rarely passed on to their children, with some exceptions. Many children of slave women went to work for notables as retainers, and slaves' daughters could be transferred to settle indebtedness or to be used as gifts to chiefs and as payments for society fees and death dues. Men could also collect bridewealth "derived from the offspring of slave wives," an economic venture that produced significant income. See Fomin, *A Comparative Study*, 78. See also Warnier, *Cameroon Grassfields Civilization*, 77.

34. Nkwi, "Slavery and Slave Trade," 245.

35. Buell, *The Native Problem in Africa*, vol. 2, 314, cited in Argenti, *Intestines*, 281 n2.

36. Fomin, *A Comparative Study*, 45.

37. Argenti, *Intestines*, 44. According to Eugenia Shanklin, "The next child to be born was surnamed 'maize grain' since the cereals obtained by the sale of his elder sibling had probably saved his life." Cited in Warnier, *Cameroon Grassfields Civilization*, 76. No evidence suggests that this form of exchange was practiced anywhere else in the Grassfields.

38. A question remains as to whether Grassfields associations with the slave-rope as a license and tool of amnesia in slave dealing framed women's understanding of their marriages with Hausa men and the related idioms of rope tying and severing in the Hausa language they came to learn.

39. Meredith Terreta, personal communication, December 15, 2010.

40. Ali, *Marriage and Slavery*, 8, 39–40, 52, 63. This is similar to Margaret Strobel's assertion that "slavery and male dominance converged in the institution of concubinage." Strobel, *Muslim Women in Mombasa*, 48, cited in Klein and Robertson, *Women and Slavery in Africa*, 9.

41. Ali, *Marriage and Slavery*, 6, 53–54, 171. See also Ali, *Sexual Ethics and Islam*, 4, 6. Al-Shafi'i and other jurists even referred to dower as "the vulva's price," *thaman al-bud'a*.

42. Calder, "Hinth, Birr, Tabarrur, Tahannuth," 216, cited in: Ali, *Marriage and Slavery*, 136.

43. Rapoport, *Marriage, Money, and Divorce*, cited in Ali, *Marriage and Slavery*, 136–140. Notably, freeing a slave was always a final act that was irrevocable, whereas divorce could be either irrevocable or revocable.

44. Lovejoy, "Concubinage," 245–248.

45. Ali, *Marriage and Slavery*, 6, 22, 53, 100. Hanbal and Shafi'i were also slaveholders.

46. Ali, *Marriage and Slavery*, 5.

47. Willis, "Jihad and the Ideology of Enslavement," 23.

48. Wright, *Strategies of Slaves and Women*, 26, 31, 35.

49. Schmoll, "Black Stomachs, Beautiful Stones," 209–210.

50. Interview with Hajiya Hajera, Bamenda, January 13, 2007.

51. Abraham, *Dictionary*, 748.

52. Interview with Alhaji Adamu Audu Tunku, Bamenda, January 13, 2007.

53. Interview with Limam Alhaji Baba Malam Shuaibu, Bamenda, June 28, 2010.

54. Cooper, *Evangelical Christians*, 207.

55. Pellow, *Landlords and Lodgers*, 48.

56. For her discussion on the "production of diasporic space" in Liverpool, see Brown, "Black Liverpool, Black America," 301.

57. Interview with Alhaji Adamu Audu Tunku, Bamenda, January 13, 2007.

58. This sentiment applies to Hausa communities throughout West Africa. Deborah Pellow's research on the story of one Hausa woman and her relocation from Accra to Kano illustrates this tension superbly by focusing on the gendered dynamics of these references. Hajiya was born and raised in Ghana. She married a Hausa trader, Alhaji, and they had five children together. In 1984, when Hajiya was pregnant with her sixth child, Alhaji decided to leave Ghana to seek better fortunes in Kano and desired that his entire family move with him. But going to Kano was not a "return" experience for Hajiya, even though her father also lived there. She told Pellow that she longed for her life in Accra. Though Kano's greater restrictions on women's liberties were at issue, a large part of her concern was caused by the separation from her maternal relations. Hajiya's knowledge of her family ties, her memory of being raised by her maternal kin, and the affinities she felt as a result, fly in the face of formulations that venture to cast her Hausaness in terms of succeeding lines of traveling Kano men. Hajiya's Hausaness is much more the product of three generations of temporary unions between women and men from Ghana and Northern Nigeria. Pellow, "From Accra to Kano," 54, 68.

59. Interview with Adama Shuaibu Limam, Bamenda, July 7, 2010.

60. Interview with Adama Shuaibu Limam, Bamenda July 14, 2010.

61. This theme of shame is not unique to Hausa diaspora narratives. Emmanuel Akyeampong has discussed that "the nightmare of Ghanaian migrants is to return home empty-handed," effectively being "denied the 'hero's welcome.'" Akyeampong, "Africans in the Diaspora," 207. He notes that this theme is also central to migrant traditions in the following works: Diawara, *In Search of Africa* and Manchuelle, *Willing Migrants*.

62. Merrick, *Hausa Proverbs*, 32.

5. SECOND REVERSAL

1. NWAC, Criminal Book 2/51, Suit No. 62/51, November 5, 1951.

2. van Gennep, *Rites of Passage*. See in particular his chapter on funerals, 146–165.

3. Hertz, *Death and the Right Hand*.

4. Rosaldo, "Grief and a Headhunter's Rage," 1–21.

5. De Witte, *Long Live the Dead!*, 9.

6. Appiah, *In My Father's House*, 181–192, 209–210; Brown, *Reaper's Garden*; Cohen and Odhiambo, *Burying SM*.

7. For discussions of death, gender, ritual, and mourning in the Islamic world, see Abu-Lughod, "Gendered Discourses of Death," 187–205; Smith and Haddad, *Islamic Understanding of Death and Resurrection*.

8. NWRA/Kb/a/1940/1. Letter from the Wum district officer to the senior district officer at Bamenda, "Alkali's Court: Inheritance Case," June 21, 1953. Reply letter from the senior district officer at Bamenda to the Wum district officer, September 10, 1953. Page 4 of the file is missing.

9. A limitation of the present study is the extent to which these court cases are representative of the kinds of mediation involved in inheritance matters. Polly Hill, for instance, noted that in the Kano City Settled Zone in the 1970s "few disputes were referred to alkali's courts, . . . considering that most disputes are dealt with informally by unimportant *dagatai*—thus, very few inheritance or land cases (in relation to the size of the population), in fact, reach an alkali's court at the District capital." That there were fewer individuals in the Grassfields who would utilize the alkali court in Ndop, at least, increases the percentage of the total Muslim population that found their way into his court. Hill, *Population, Prosperity and Poverty*, 63.

10. Hill, *Population, Prosperity and Poverty*, 147.

11. Exceptions to this understanding might be, for example, mentally ill and homosexual adult men.

12. Hertz, *Death and the Right Hand*, 48.

13. Smith, *Baba of Karo*, 212.

14. Shipton, *The Nature of Entrustment*, 173.

15. Within Sunnī Islamic law, "gender, marital status, kin relation, and the presence of contending heirs impact upon inheritance rights. The Sunnī Islamic law of inheritance is prescriptive and strongly partible; it restricts the right of testation and stipulates allotments to a large number of heirs, divided into two categories. First in line are the Qur'ānic heirs . . . who are entitled to a fixed percentage of the estate, varying from one-half to one-sixth. This category mainly consists of close kin, such as the father, mother, daughter, and sister of the deceased, and the widow or widower. The remainder is divided amongst the male agnatic heirs . . . with the nearer agnate excluding the farther. Certain categories of women, such as the daughter and the sister, turn from [Qur'ānic to agnatic] heirs if there are male heirs of the same category; in that case they receive one-half of the share of their male counterparts. A widow is entitled to a fixed share of one-eighth of her late husband's estate if he had children (not necessarily by her) and one-quarter if not. A widower in a similar situation would take twice as much: one-quarter and one-half of his wife's estate respectively. Daughters receive a fixed share if the deceased has no sons: one daughter is entitled to half the estate, two or more sharing two-thirds of it. Thus, if a man dies without leaving sons, a considerable part of the estate goes to his male agnates, usually his brothers. If, on the other hand, there are sons, these are the first heirs and daughters turn into agnatic heirs, entrusted with one-half the share of a son." Joseph and Najmabadi et al., *Encyclopedia of Women and Islamic Cultures*. See "Inheritance: Contemporary Practice" in vol. 2: Family, Law and Politics.

16. A similar motive was employed by the British in Northern Nigeria in the 1920s. See Steven Pierce, "Farmers and 'Prostitutes," 467. Polly Hill explains that "much property, such as small livestock and trains, is sold on death, partly to avoid embarrassment arising from valuation, but also to meet *ushira* (the 10% death duty)" collected by the alkali for the Native Affairs Treasury. Hill, *Rural Hausa*, 270.

17. Polly Hill, *Rural Hausa*, 270.

18. Aishatu Ibrahim of Bamenda also understood widows' options in this manner. Interview, June 28, 2010.

19. See Schildkrout, "Widows in Hausa Society." Cooper notes in her study in Maradi, Niger, that even though divorced and widowed women are both called zawarawa and their situation considered a temporary, ritual phase, 58.5 percent of Cooper's informants who were widowed remarried as compared to 74.8 percent of divorcées. This contrast results mainly from the nearly certain possibility that widows will lose their children to their in-laws should they remarry, whereas divorced women can often "negotiate with their former husbands to keep some of the children." Cooper also asserts that this is "not a function of old age," but rather "the younger women whose husbands die have a greater interest in remaining unmarried because their children are still dependent." Cooper, *Marriage in Maradi*, 67. Additionally, implicit in being a "good man" in Hausa society is the capacity and obligation of men to provide for women. As Kenda Mutongi artfully illustrated in her study on widows in Maragoli, Kenya, many women who were largely reliant on their sons pressured the men in their families to support them through public displays of grief and vulnerability, attempting and often succeeding in forcing patriarchy to work for them. Mutongi, *Worries of the Heart*, 7–8, 35, 43, 116.

20. The name of the village is illegible.

21. NWAC, 1947–1948 Civil Law Book, Civil Suit No. 128/47, December 1, 1947.

22. Barbara Cooper addresses similar inheritance issues, especially among Hausa women who lived in Maradi's urban environment. According to her study, Maradi's urban women in the 1990s "tend, when they inherit property, to inherit a house from their husband, which they hold in a sense for their children by him." *Marriage in Maradi*, 82.

23. Enid Schildkrout deems the Hausa practice of separating the widow or divorcée from her children as "more severe" than Islamic law, the latter of which stipulates that women may "keep their children after marriage termination until children reach puberty." One important exception to this practice is the uxorilocal marriage (as opposed to the more commonly practiced virilocal marriage pattern) in which a woman—usually an older woman or widow—may live with her kin or on her own while her husband resides elsewhere with his other wife or wives. In these arrangements, in Hausa called *auren daukisandanka* ("marriage of take up your staff"), women do not have to give up their children from previous marriages. Schildkrout, "Widows in Hausa Society," 145–146.

24. Schildkrout, "Widows in Hausa Society," 144, 149.

25. NWAC, Case Book of February 1959, Suit No. 107/59, October 27, 1959.

26. The defendant gave the equivalent of forty-one cows to Diddi's son, not the total of forty-three given previous payments he made to the cowboys for their labor and as jangali (cattle tax).

27. NWAC, Civil Law Book May 1959, alkali's "traveling court," Suit No. 44/60, June 19, 1960. This trial was held in Bamenda, one of the many stops of the alkali's traveling itinerary, which he began in the latter part of the 1950s. Colonial officials were concerned about the court's accessibility, so they encouraged the alkali to hold court in various locations throughout the year.

28. The alkali then used this opportunity to distribute Magaji Aska's inheritance. Since the compound was worth 250 pounds, the alkali court claimed the customary one-tenth for arbitration fees. Twenty pounds were given to Kuku Makeri, as he had paid out-of-pocket to maintain the compound. Thirty pounds were distributed among Magaji Aska's two sons and another man, as they had invested in the compound over the years, building more rooms for the family. Garuwa, as the widow, was entitled to one-eighth of her deceased husband's entire estate, a total amounting to just over 21 pounds. Her two sons, Isma'ila and Adamu, each received half-shares.

29. Shipton, Nature of Entrustment, 186.

30. Itinerant Muslim trading networks, generally speaking, place a great premium on trust among Muslim migrant communities. This pattern may thus not be peculiar to the Hausa. For an early example, see Michael Brett, "Islam and Trade in Bilad al-Sudan," 431–40.

31. NWAC, 1954–1955 Civil Law Book, Civil Suit No. 110/55, April 13, 1955. Garba Na Kirki left behind Hausa gowns woven from red, white, and black threads ('barage), and from "native weaves" (fanin bullam). He left behind embroidered trousers, white and blue gowns, women's cloth, a pair of leather shoes, his hat, three pans, and a basket. These items were all that he owned. For other cases involving sons' and brothers' travel to claim inheritance for themselves and other agnatic relations, see NWAC, 1954–1955 Civil Law Book, Civil Suit No. 279/54, November 1, 1954; NWAC, Case Book of February 1959, Case No. 70/59, March 23, 1959.

32. NWAC, Book of March 1953, Civil Suit No. 75/53, April 29, 1953.

33. NWAC, Civil Law Book 1955–1957, Civil Case No. 222/56, August 28, 1956.

34. The letter was supposedly written by the Sarkin Hausawa of Kibiya to the Sarkin Hausawa of Bamenda. The original letter was written in Arabic. Though the English translator is unknown, it was likely someone in the alkali's court. Both Arabic and English versions are included with Civil Case No. 222/56 in the Alkali's 1955–57 law book.

35. Abner Cohen also noted in his study in Ibadan that a number of times, when a man died and left no heirs in the area, "after a time—in some cases after many years—someone may come from the North and claim to be an heir." Cohen, Custom and Politics, 33.

36. This letter was written on January 8, 1958 and is included with Civil Case No. 222/56 in the alkali's 1955–1957 law book.

37. NWAC, Case Book 1955–1957, Case No. 302/55, October 22, 1955.

38. Olofson, "'Yawon Dandi,'" 66–79.

39. Many inheritance cases beyond those analyzed directly in the text form the basis for this discussion. Other cases considered include the following: NWAC, Civil Law Book 1947–1948, Civil Suit 16/47, April 13, 1947; Civil Law Book 1947–1948, Civil Suit 58/47, May 7, 1947; Criminal Book 3/53, Suit No. 53/53, 23 March 1953; Criminal Book 3/53, Suit No. 54/53, March 24, 1953; Criminal Book 3/53, Suit No. 55/53, March 24, 1953; Criminal Book 3/53, Suit No. 68/53, May 23, 1953; Civil Law Book 1954–1955, Civil Suit No. 279/54, November 1, 1954; Civil Law Book 1954–1955, Civil Suit No. 340/54, December 2, 1954; Civil Law Book 1954–1955, Civil Suit No. 125/55, April 23, 1955; Civil Law Book 1954–1955, Case No. 202/55, July 28, 1955; Civil Law Book 1954–1955, Case No. 235/55, August 24, 1955; Case Book beginning October 1955, Civil Suit 50/56, February 19, 1956; Case Book beginning October 1955, Civil Suits 24/56 and 25/56, May 22, 1956; Case Book of February 1959, Case No. 70/59, March 23, 1959; Case Book of February 1959, Case No. 45/60, April 28, 1960.

40. Abner Cohen, *Custom and Politics*, 65 and 87. Both men and women foster children throughout Hausa societies across Africa.

41. Fostering is known as *yaye*. The term *tallafi* is used only when a child's parents are both dead. Fostered children, on the other hand, remain the legal children of their legal parents.

42. The story about Bobo and his family, especially his two children, Ali Bobo and Mommy Nono, is derived from interviews with three individuals: Hajiya Sa'adatu, Bamenda, February 13, 2007; Aishatu Ibrahim, Bamenda, March 15, 2007; and Ali Bobo himself, Bamenda, March 21 and March 26, 2007.

43. The sequence of events during the birth and childhood of Mommy Nono differ depending on the memory of different persons interviewed and the stories or rumors they transmitted. One of my sources thought that Bobo was driven from Bafunge because people there believed he, as a witch, caused the death of his second wife as she gave birth to Mommy Nono. Given the contrasting views of two others who had more personal contact with Bobo and his family, it is unlikely that these events of Bobo's life collapsed into one episode as this one individual suggested.

44. Abraham, *Dictionary*, 846.

45. Perhaps "bun" refers to the Hausa word *'buna*, meaning both a "farm already worked where soil is therefore fertile," or a word to describe that someone got something "easily or cheaply." Abraham, *Dictionary*, 119.

46. Interview with Aishatu Ibrahim, Bamenda, March 15, 2007.

47. Paul Lovejoy noted similar circumstances among the Tokarawa, Agalawa, and Kambarin Beriberi kola traders in the nineteenth century. Though their origins were not Hausa, and though they would reference those origins within Hausaland, they often emphasized their Hausaness and Islamic faith in their travels. Accordingly, along the diaspora's many frontiers, indigenous peoples would view them as Hausa. Lovejoy, *Caravans of Kola*, 76.

6. THIRD REVERSAL

1. Hirsch, *Pronouncing and Persevering*, 3.

2. This is distinct from a number of works on Hausa diaspora communities that have analyzed one particular settlement, usually in a large town or city, such as Ibadan, Accra, or Kumasi. The dispersed nature of Grassfields Hausa settlement that contributed to this landscape of travel and conflict emerged from the nature of Grassfields political structures and geography. The hierarchically organized chiefdoms throughout the region meant multiple sites of potential integration for Hausas. Colonial attempts to influence the process of Hausa settlement also played a significant role, especially in founding entirely new centers of political authority and economic activity such as Bamenda. The second alkali court was established at Nkambe in 1957. See Pelican, "Getting along," 273.

3. This definition was provided by Aishatu Ibrahim, Interview, June 28, 2010.

4. We can deduce from the court records that Magajiya Dibino was indeed physically abused. The court acknowledged that she appeared to be the victim of assault when she originally came to issue the court summons. The alkali asked Magajiya Dibino, "Have I not told you to go to Hospital in order the [*sic*] [dispensary] to examine you? . . . What prevent from [*sic*] going to hospital and you are [beaten] by the accuseds?" "Pape," as it is written in the text, refers to "pe-pe," which is comprised of hot peppers or dried and ground hot peppers.

5. NWAC, Criminal Book No. 2/51, Criminal Case No. 78/52, December 15, 1952, and Criminal Case No. 79/52, November 17, 1952. Continuation of these cases may be found in Criminal Book 3/53. Verdicts were reached on February 18, 1953.

6. NWAC, Criminal Book 3/53, Case No. 80/53, February 18, 1953.

7. See Wall, *Hausa Medicine* and Schmoll, "Black Stomachs, Beautiful Stones."

8. Schmoll, "Black Stomachs, Beautiful Stones," 199. The soul is also connected to a person's shadow; therefore, if one's shadow or body is even touched by a soul-eater, the soul can be captured. Soul-eaters may also transform themselves into animals, who may frighten their victim enough to cause the soul to jump out of the body, leaving itself vulnerable to being "caught" by the soul-eater.

9. Schmoll, "Black Stomachs, Beautiful Stones," 200–203.

10. Some authors have maintained that twentieth-century bori belief and practice were located almost exclusively within the domain of karuwai and other persons socially marginalized among Hausas, including homosexuals. In contrast, Abner Cohen found no statistical correlation between those diasporic women who practiced prostitution and those who were bori mediums in 1960s' Ibadan. Most scholars do agree, however, that membership in the spiritual group offers a sense of social cohesiveness to the lives of individuals marginalized in Muslim Hausa society. See the following references on the history of the magajiya office and other female titles: Abraham, *Dictionary*, 632; Callaway, *Muslim Hausa Women*, 3–6; Christelow, "Women and the Law," 140; Masquelier, "Narratives of Power, Images of Wealth"; Smith, *Baba of Karo*; Wall, *Hausa Medicine*, 152, 158; Cooper, *Marriage*

in Maradi, 27. For information on tensions between bori practitioners and Islamic malams in the diaspora, see Abner Cohen, *Custom and Politics*, 10, 58, 163–164; Works, *Pilgrims in a Strange Land*, 4, 152.

11. Interview with Hajiya Sa'adatu at her home in Bamenda, January 9, 2007; interview with Zainabu Mama at her home in Bamenda, January 15, 2007. Zainabu confirmed that Magajiya and her husband had no children, but she did not know the reason behind their relocation to Sabga. In her mind, sometimes Hausa people just decide to leave for one reason or another: "I don't know why [they left]. We get up and we leave. . . ." The Northwest Alkali Court records confirm that a man named 'Dan Dumbu resided in Sabga at least by June of 1953. Reference: NWAC, Criminal Book No. 3/53, Suit No. 46/53, and Book of March 1953, Suit No. 102/53. Interview with Alhaji Amadu Audu Tunku, Sarkin Pawa of Bamenda, Bamenda, January 13, 2007. *Yam bori* refers to bori practitioners, literally "children of bori." NWAC, Criminal Book 3/53, Suit No. 46/53, June 9, 1953.

12. Interview with Limam Alhaji Baba Mallam Shuaibu, Bamenda, June 28, 2010.

13. Ibid.

14. Austen, "Moral Economy of Witchcraft," 91.

15. Ibid., 91, 99, 100, 104. Beyond the court case detailed here, other alkali court cases on witchcraft allegations include Civil Law Book 1947–1948, Case No. 51/47, July 3, 1947; Criminal Book 3/53, Case No. 76/53, August 17, 1953, and Case No. 48/53, June 22, 1953; Criminal Book 8/61, Case No. 29/62, October 10, 1962, and Case No. 63/63, July 7, 1963.

16. From the alkali court records, it may be determined that even in the small village of Sabga to which the couple was exiled, 'Dan Dumbu could not escape community ostracism. In June 1953, 'Dan Dumbu supposedly accused a man named 'Dan Biyu of surreptitiously harming him by placing bad medicine in his home and killing his horse. 'Dan Biyu turned the tables, however, and brought 'Dan Dumbu to court for "spoiling" his good name by spreading such rumors. NWAC, Criminal Book 3/53, Suit No. 46/53, June 9, 1953. Murray Last has stated that butchers are "a particularly low-status, if very rich, group" in Hausa society. "Social Exclusion in Northern Nigeria," 228.

17. Pamela Schmoll noticed similar trends in the Maradi region of Niger during her fieldwork in the mid-1980s. "Black Stomachs, Beautiful Stones," 213.

18. Beyond the court cases detailed in this chapter, other alkali court cases on witchcraft allegations include: Civil Law Book 1947–1948, Suit No. 51/47, July 3, 1947; Criminal Book 3/53, Suit No. 76/53, August 17, 1953, and Suit No. 48/53, June 22, 1953; Criminal Book 8/61, Suit No. 29/62, October 10, 1962, and Suit No. 63/63, July 7, 1963.

19. Wall, *Hausa Medicine*, 148–149.

20. Kandiyoti, "Islam and Patriarchy: A Comparative Perspective," 23–42, 27, 40 n22. For further discussion of the "patriarchal bargain" in West African contexts, see Burrill, "Disputing Wife Abuse."

21. Iliffe, *Honour in African History*, 262. See also Mack and Boyd, *One Woman's Jihad*.

22. Ali, *Marriage and Slavery*, 6.

23. Cooper, *Marriage in Maradi*, 21.

24. NWAC, Civil Book No. 1/47, Civil Suit No. 78/47, August 5, 1947.

25. NWAC, Civil Book No. 1/47, Civil Suit No. 72/48, July 3, 1948.

26. Ali, *Marriage and Slavery*, 166.

27. NWAC, Criminal Book No. 8/61, Criminal Case No. 90/64, July 10, 1964.

28. See Barbara Cooper's discussion on Hausa women's use of the "neighborhood forum" in Maradi, Niger. *Marriage in Maradi*, 22–25.

29. For commentary on court clerks marking rape cases as adultery or omitting them from court records altogether, see Beidelman, "Kaguru Justice and the Concept of Legal Fictions," 10.

30. Some women lived much more secluded lives, however, as this was often a sign of the husband's wealth and prestige. This may have been the case for Asmatu given that her husband was a local religious leader. This type of marriage is known as *auren kulle*.

31. Though the court case record is incomplete, I found a letter from the solicitor of Asmatu's father, Alhaji Umaru, to the sub-division officer of Bamenda. In this letter, Asmatu's father states he was arrested and taken to Banso, where he was detained and kept without trial for eight days for divorcing Asmatu from the limam and later remarrying her to a man named Yusufu. He asks the officer to order the alkali to conduct the trial at once. NWRA/Kb/a/1940/1/B3081, May 26, 1964.

32. For examples of other cases in which women reinforced a community's patriarchal structures through violating their own husbands' authority, see the following: NWAC, Civil Law Book 1947–1948, Civil Suit No. 1/47, March 24, 1947; and NWAC, Casebook 1955–1957, Civil Suit No. 301/55, October 31, 1955.

33. For examples of court cases where parents intervened to extract daughters from disadvantageous or abusive marriages, see NWAC, Civil Book No. 1/47, Civil Suit No. 3/47, April 1, 1947; NWAC, Civil Book No. 1/47, Civil Suit No. 4/47, April 12, 1947; and NWAC, Casebook 1955–1957, Civil Suit No. 23/56, July 28, 1956.

34. Burrill, "Disputing Wife Abuse," 604.

35. See for example: NWAC, Civil Law Book 1947–48, Suit 51/47, July 3, 1947; NWAC, Criminal Book 2/51, Suit 46/51, November 8, 1951; and NWAC, Casebook beginning October 1955, Suit 301/55, October 31, 1955.

36. See for example: NWAC, Casebook 1947–1948, Civil Suit 6/48, January 9, 1948; NWAC, Casebook starting November 11, 1954, Suit 260/54, November 13, 1954.

37. Calder, "Hinth, Birr," cited in Ali, *Marriage and Slavery*, 136.

38. Ali, *Marriage and Slavery*, 136, 140.

39. Smith, *Baba of Karo*, 261 n12.

40. Barbara Callaway also found this to be the case in her research conducted in Nigeria in the 1980s. See Callaway, *Muslim Hausa Women*, 44. Ismail Abdallah has also noted that the act of secluded wives mixing freely with strangers compromises husbands' social status among the Hausa. Abdalla, "Neither Friend nor Foe," 44.

41. According to the present alkali of Ndop, the same may be said for Grassfields Muslims today. Interview with Alkali Alhaji Mohamadu Bello, Alkali Courthouse, Ndop, January 15, 2007.

42. NWAC, Criminal Book No. 3/53, Criminal case 21/53, March 17, 1953, and NWAC, Criminal Book No. 3/53, Criminal case 35/53, June 24, 1953.

43. For a similar discussion on women's legal status and nature of culpability in such cases among the Asante, see Jean Allman, "Adultery and the State in Asante."

44. During his fieldwork in Ibadan, Nigeria in the mid-1960s, Abner Cohen witnessed a similar trend, but one occurring between place of settlement and homeland instead of between multiple diaspora settlements. In these cases, the women involved were born in Northern Nigeria; and, therefore, he attributed women's mobility entirely to their attachment to their parents, especially their mothers. He stated that a number of Sabo housewives pressed their husbands to let them visit their families in the North: "In many cases which I recorded the wife had extended her visit and even stayed indefinitely, sometimes insisting that the husband should move back to the North. Sometimes the wife contracted a lover and finally divorced the husband." Cohen, *Custom and Politics*, 36.

45. Abner Cohen, *Custom and Politics*, Chapters 1 and 2.

46. NWAC, Civil Book No. 1/47, Civil Suit No. 29/47, May 28, 1947. For other cases dealing with confusion over divorce, see: Civil Book No. 1/47, Civil Suit 67/47, August 5, 1947; NWAC, Criminal Book No. 2/51, Criminal Case No. 57/51, November 1, 1951; Criminal Book 2/51, Suit 46/51, November 8, 1951.

47. NWAC, Criminal Book No. 2/51, Criminal Case No. 73/51, December 8, 1951 and January 5, 1952.

48. NWAC, Civil Book No. 1/47, Civil Suit No. 70/48, July 2, 1948.

49. See for example: NWAC, Civil Book No. 1/47, Suit 20/47, April 28, 1947; NWAC, Civil Law Book 1947–1948, Suit 48/47, June 16, 1947; NWAC, Civil Book No. 1/47, Suit 62/47, September 4, 1947; NWAC, Civil Book No. 1/47, Unknown suit number, pages 129–130, December 19, 1947; NWAC, Criminal Book No. 2/51, Suit number unknown, January 1, 1952; NWAC, Criminal Book No. 2/51, Suit 31/52, May 16, 1952; NWAC, Criminal Book No. 3/53, Suit 82/53, September 9, 1953, case incomplete; and NWAC, Casebook beginning November 11, 1954, Suit 117/55, September 17, 1955.

50. Byfield et al., *Gendering the African Diaspora*, 9. In this passage, the authors reference the work of Davies, *Black Women, Writing, and Identity*.

51. There are many examples in which distance was a factor in matters of adultery and bigamy: NWAC, Civil Law Book 1947–48, Suit 3/47, April 1, 1947; NWAC, Civil Book No. 1/47, Suit 4/47, April 12, 1947; NWAC, Civil Book No. 1/47, Suit 29/47, May 28, 1947; NWAC, Civil Book No. 1/47, Suit 38/47, July 23, 1947; NWAC, Civil Book No. 1/47, Suit 67/47, August 5, 1947; NWAC, Criminal Book 2/51, Suit 57/51, November 1, 1951; NWAC, Criminal Book 2/51, Suit 73/51, December 8, 1951; NWAC, Criminal Book 2/51, Continuation of Suit 73/61; NWAC, Criminal Book 2/51, Suit 13/52, January 5, 1952; NWAC, Criminal Book 3/53, Suit 23/53, February 16, 1953; and NWAC, Criminal Book 3/53, Suit 35/53, June 24, 1953.

52. NWAC, Criminal Book No. 2/51, Criminal Case No.25/52, June 21, 1952. Though this issue of "abusing" with a pan appears to be one of violence, it may actually be an issue of theft. This is evident in Adda Petel's defense, where she describes how she paid for the pans. The threat of setting the sarki's country on fire, however, was a physical threat to Ntumbo. There is no verdict in this case: the court adjourned, and on the day it continued, neither party was present.

53. NWAC, Civil Book No. 1/47, Civil Case No. 96/47, October 6, 1947.

54. Tiya Miles borrowed this concept from Philomena Mariani to describe how Cherokee witnesses tacitly agreed not to reveal the slave status of Doll Shoeboots in a 1858 court case where she acquired property owing to her status as widow to Shoeboots, a Cherokee man. Mariani, *Critical Fictions*, cited in Miles, *Ties that Bind*, 185.

55. Byfied et al., *Gendering the African Diaspora*, 9.

CONCLUSION

1. Holt, "Slavery and Freedom," 33–44, 37. The proverb in the epigraph was found in Merrick, *Hausa Proverbs*, 38.

2. Ali, *Islamic Sexual Ethics*, 112–113.

3. Holt, "Slavery and Freedom," 37.

4. Lee, "Enslaved African Women in Nineteenth-Century Iran."

5. Byfield et al., *Gendering the African Diaspora*, 9. Here the authors reference the works of Maryse Condé and Paule Marshall.

6. Wildenthal, *German Women for Empire*, 111.

7. Glissant, *Poetics of Relation*, 18, 20.

8. For a discussion of "diaspora" as process and condition, see Sturtz, "Mary Rose: 'White' African Jamaican Woman?"

9. Ballantyne and Burton suggest that historians not capture intimacy and mobility for the sake of imperial history but rather "to suggest some of the counter-histories of colonialism that attention to the intimate domains at the interstices of political economy and cultural life can yield...." *Moving Subjects*, 25.

10. Many of the insights shared in this last part of the conclusion arose out of discussions I had with a particularly talented and diverse group of undergraduate students in my "Diaspora, Gender, and Identity" course at Pitzer College. I would like to thank the following former students in particular for their keen insights and creativity: Caleb Castaneda, Abby Deliz, Leonardo Flores, Ayanna Harris, Louie Lemus-Mogrovejo, Gina Magnuson, Tarquin Schwartz, Emma Shorr, and Angie Tyler. Our discussions on gender and diaspora grew out of a comparative framework that analyzed Hadija's experiences alongside other diasporic contexts throughout world history and literature, including those found in the following works: Brown, "Black Liverpool, Black America"; Brown, *Reaper's Garden*; Ghosh, *Sea of Poppies*; McKeown, "Conceptualizing Chinese Diasporas"; Miles, *Ties that Bind*; Mohapatra, "'Restoring the Family'"; Pellow, "From Accra to Kano"; Scott and Hébrard, "Rosalie of the Poulard Nation"; Siu, "Diasporic Cultural Citizenship."

11. Linda L. Sturtz discusses the "tools" that an eighteenth-century "white" African Jamaican woman, Mary Rose, used to combat her racial and gendered discrimination, including letters (she was literate), contacts, legal petitions, and economic agency. See Sturtz, "Mary Rose," 77. Rebecca Scott and Jean Hébrard also trace how the Tinchant family, beginning with "Rosalie, Black Woman of the Poulard Nation" during the Haitian Revolution, used "the power and legitimacy of documents to help secure freedom and respect." See also Scott and Hébrard, *Freedom Papers*.

12. Miles, *Ties that Bind*, 184; Ann Marie Plane, *Colonial Intimacies*, 6.

13. Glissant, *Poetics of Relation*, 18, 20.

14. For a similar discussion on the relationship between naming, incorporation, and erasure, see Miles, *Ties that Bind*, 27.

Bibliography

INTERVIEWS

All interviews were digitally recorded and conducted in either English, French, Fulfulde, Hausa, or Pidgin English, or a combination of languages. For most interviews conducted in Fulfulde, Hausa, or Pidgin English, a research assistant supported me in translating and transcribing the interviews.

Abubakar Ismaila, Fujua: January 26, 2007.

Adama Shuaibu Limam, Bamenda: January 15, 2007; March 28, 2007; July 7, 2010; July 14, 2010; with her mother on July 11, 2010.

Aishatu Ibrahim, Bamenda: January 18, 2007; January 23, 2007; February 13, 2007; March 15, 2007; March 22, 2007; March 27, 2007; June 28, 2010; July 7, 2010.

Alhaji Gambo, Sabga: December 19, 2006.

Alhaji Zakari Mama, Bamenda: December 5, 2006.

Alhaji Zakari Mama, Hajiya Sa'adatu, and family, Bamenda: December 5, 2006; December 7, 2006.

Alkali Alhaji Mohamadu Bello, Alkali Courthouse, Ndop: January 15, 2007; July 2, 2010.

Ali Bobo, Bamenda: March 21, 2007; March 26, 2007.

Buba Yerima and friends, Sabga: November 9, 2006.

Fon of Laikom, Laikom: January 26, 2007.

Hajiya Adama Bako dan Pollu, Bamenda: November 28, 2006.

Hajiya Hajera, Bamenda: January 13, 2007; March 27, 2007.

Hajiya Sa'adatu, Bamenda: December 7, 2006; January 9, 2007; January 16, 2007; February 13, 2007; March 14, 2007; June 28, 2010.

Hajja Buba, Tchabbal, Sabga: July 5, 2010.

Halima, Fujua: January 26, 2007.

Kungiyar Matan Musulman, Bamenda: December 25, 2006.

Limam Alhaji Baba Malam Shuaibu, Bamenda: December 12, 2006; April 1, 2007; June 28, 2010; July 7, 2010.

Mariam Muhamed, Bamenda: January 15, 2007; June 30, 2010.

Sarkin Hausawa, Fumban: February 15, 2007.

Sarkin Pawa Alhaji Adamu Audu Tunku, Bamenda: January 13, 2007; July 1, 2010.

Zainabu Mama, Bamenda: January 15, 2007; April 2, 2007; June 29, 2010.

ARCHIVAL SOURCES

Basel Mission Archives, mission 21, Basel, Switzerland (BMA)

E-4/1: I. Kamerun Berichte, 1914–1915, Stationen Kriegserlebnisse Internierung.

E-4/2: II. Kamerun Berichte, 1914–1915, Stationen Kriegserlebnisse Internierung.

E-5-2/4: Berichte, 1925–1930, Bali und Mbengwi.

E-5-2/7: (III. Kamerun) Berichte, Jan 1931–Dez 1934 von Bali.

E-5-2/12: (IV. Kamerun) Berichte: Jan 1935–Dez 1939, Besongabang, Fotabe, Bafut, Kishong, We.

E-5-2/15: Jahresberichte 1944.

E-30-0,6/K 371: Anna Wuhrmann, Commentaries to Slides from Bamum, 1917.

E-30.26.035: Gottleib Friedrich Spellenberg, "Fo Nyonga, King in Bali (Cameroon), Wearing a Hausa Robe," photograph, Bali, 1902–1903.

E-30.30.071: Anna Wuhrmann, "Nzinzie, the Hausa wife of King Ndjoya," photograph, Bamum, 1911–1915.

E-30.31.055: Anna Wuhrmann, "Hausa Chief and His Attendants at the Sowing Festival," photograph, Bamum, 1915.

E-30.33.044: Martin Göhring, "Hausa Butchers on the Market in Fumban," photograph, Bamum, 1905–1912.

E-30.33.058: Friedrich Lutz, "Hausa at Prayer," photograph, 1905–1906.

E-30.33.062: Anna Wuhrmann, "A Hausa Musician outside the Mission House in Fumban," Bamum, photograph, 1911–1915.

E-30.85.164: Wilhelm Zürcher, "Haussas on trek with donkeys," photograph, Grassfields, 1932–1939.

QE-30.006.0045: Anna Wuhrmann, "Untitled," photograph, Bamum, 1911–1915.

QE-30.017.0027: Ernst Vollbehr, "8. Bamum girls have an archaic old-assyrian [*sic*] hair-style. In their ears they have tubular glass beads with a circular section. At the back of their heads they have small leather envelopes introduced by the Hausa as magical protection," watercolor, Bamum, c. 1912.

QQ-30.027.0064: Ernst Vollbehr, "Military station in Bamenda with a Hausa village in the foreground," watercolor, Bamenda, c. 1912.

Cameroon National Archives, Buea (NAB)

Aa/1: Ethnological notes on the Cameroons, 1916.

Aa/1915/86: Dr. Jeffrey's Note Book—compiled on his first tour, 1915.

Aa/1934/16: Notes on Witchcraft: Relation to Administrative Problems; General Question of Cameroons Province.

Ab/1: Bamenda Division Native Customs–Report on, 1921.

Ab/1/d: Handing-over notes, Bamenda Division, from Dr. Jeffreys to Schofield, 1939.

Ab/1/e: League of Nations Report, 1939, Bamenda Division.

Ab/3/c: Bafut Intelligence Report, 1934.

Ab/12: Assessment Report, Banso District, 1923.

Ab/17/1: Fulani in Bamenda Division—Reorganisation of.

Ab/17/2: Fulani in Bamenda Division—Reorganisation of (Correspondence).

Ab/1915/41: Diary of 1915–1916 by Divisional Officers in Bamenda.

Ab/1917/39: Diary, 1917–1920.

Ab/1948/36 and 37: Bamenda Southwestern Federation.

Ab/1951/1h: Abakpa Settlement, Bamenda Province, 1950.

Ad/4: An Assessment Report of the Bum Area in the Bamenda Division, Cameroons Province, 1927.

Ba/1916/3: West Africa Confidential Reports on Various Matters Relating to the Cameroons, May 1916.

Ba/1920/5: Special Annual Report on the Cameroons Province, February 1920.

Cb/1916/2: Report No. 1/1916, Bamenda Division, Cameroons Province, 1916.

Cb/1916/4: Report No. 3/1916, Bamenda Division, 1916.

Cb/1916/6: Bamenda Division, Annual Report for Year Ended 31.12.1916.

Cb/1916/10: Bamenda Division: Annual Reports 1916–1917.

Cb/1924/1: Annual Report, Bamenda Division, 1924.

Cb/1934/1: Bamenda Division Annual Reports, 1934–1935.

Cb/1936/1: Bamenda Divisional and League of Nations Report, 1936.

Cb/1938/3: League of Nations Report 1938, Bamenda Division.

Cb/1939: League of Nations Report 1939, Bamenda Division.

Cb/1940/1: Bamenda Division: Annual and League of Nations Report, 1940.

Gd/I: Trade–Internal Report on, 1922.

Ha/7: Hausa Village Assessment (Malam Baba), Bamenda Division, September 8, 1923.

Ma/a/1965/1: Alkali Courts.

Mb/a/1943/1: Alkali's Court, Bamenda Division.

Mc/a/1952/1: Proposed Alkali Court in Nkambe.

Cameroon National Archives, Yaoundé (NAY)

TA-24: La Soumission de Boubandjida, 1901.

TA-26, Recit d'un voyage effectué dans le Nord Cameroun, 1903.

TA-27, Rapport Rel. à la Marché de L'expédition Dominik de Yaoundé à Garoua, nd.
TA-31/2: La fondation de la station de Banyo en 1902 par le 1er Lt. Zickwolff, Bulletin Colonial Allemand, July 14, 1911.
TA-33: Extrait du Bulletin Colonial Allemand, 1899–1900, Expédition Tibati.
TA-53: Rapport sur Banyo par Sandrock, 1902.
TA-74: Le Cauri en Pays Bamoun, 1910.

Cameroon Northwest Alkali Court, Ndop (NWAC)

Civil Book No. 1/47
Civil Law Book of March 1953
Civil Law Book beginning November 11, 1954
Civil Law Book 1954–1955
Civil Law Book beginning October 1955
Civil Law Book 1955–1957
Civil Law Book February 1959
Civil Law Book May 1959
Criminal Book 2/51
Criminal Book 3/53
Criminal Book 8/61

Cameroon Northwest Regional Archives, Bamenda (NWRA)

Aa/1983/1, A Collection of Ethnography Notes.
Bb/1952/2, United Nations: Organization's Second Visiting Mission, Bamenda, 1951–1952.
Fa/1950/1, Tours and Visits of Senior Officers to the Bamenda Province, Touring Notes and Addresses, 1950–1954.
Ka/b/1966/1, Application for Employment, Alkali Court, Bamenda, 1966.
Kb/a/1940/1, Complaints, Alkali's Court, Bamenda, 1940–1964.
Re/a/1921/1, Abakpa (Strangers Settlement), Ngemba N.A. Area, Bamenda, 1921–1944.

The Dover War Memorial Project, Dover, United Kingdom

http://www.doverwarmemorialproject.org.uk/Casualties/WWI/SurnamesPigg.htm. Visited February 6, 2009, August 2, 2013, and May 31, 2016.

Leibniz-Institute for Regional Geography, Archive for Geography, Leipzig, Germany (LIL)

Ernst Vollbehr, "Haussatänzerin (Bamenda)," gouache on paper, 26,6 x, 26,4 cm, ca 1911, Leibniz-Institute for Regional Geography, Archive for Geography, Vollbehr0656.

Private Photograph Collection, Aishatu Ibrahim, Bamenda, Cameroon

Private Collection, Alhaji Zakari Mama and Hajiya Sa'adatu, Bamenda, Cameroon

"'Old Town Abakpa-Bamenda Originated as an Independent Village',—Alhaji Zakari Mama," *The Watchdog: Watching the Nation*, Issue No. 0053, Friday, February 3, 2006.

UNPUBLISHED LECTURES, PAPERS, AND PRESENTATIONS

Akomfrah, John. Symposium. *Glyphs: Acts of Inscription.* Claremont, Calif.: Pitzer Art Galleries, Pitzer College, September 20, 2013.

Lee, Anthony A. "Enslaved African Women in Nineteenth-Century Iran: The Life of Fezzeh Khanom of Shiraz." American History Association Annual Meeting. Washington, D.C., 2014.

Mamdani, Mahmood. "Beyond Settlers and Natives." W. E. B. Du Bois Lecture Series. Cambridge, Mass.: Harvard University, November 18–21, 2008.

Peters, Rudolph. "Shari'a and Colonial Public Policy: Criminal Law in British India and Colonial Nigeria." Islamic Legal Studies Program. Cambridge, Mass.: Harvard University, April 2, 2008.

WORKS CITED

Abaka, Edmund. *"Kola Is God's Gift": Agricultural Production, Export Initiatives and the Kola Industry of Asante and the Gold Coast, c.1820–1950.* Athens: Ohio University Press, 2005.

Abdalla, Ismail H. "Neither Friend nor Foe: The *Malam* Practitioner–*Yan Bori* Relationship in Hausaland." In *Women's Medicine: The Zar-Bori Cult in Africa and Beyond*, ed. I. M. Lewis, Ahmed Al-Safi, and Sayyid Hurreiz, pp. 37–48. Edinburgh: Edinburgh University Press, 1991.

Abraham, R. C. *An Introduction to Spoken Hausa and Hausa Reader for European Students.* London: Crown Agents for the Colonies, 1940.

———. *Dictionary of the Hausa Language.* London: University of London Press, 1962 [1949].

Abu-Lughod, Lila. "Islam and the Gendered Discourses of Death." *International Journal of Middle East Studies* 25 (1993): 187–205.

Adamu, Mahdi. *The Hausa Factor in West African History.* Zaria/Ibadan: Ahmadu Bello University Press, 1978.

Akomfrah, John. *Peripeteia.* HD video, colour, sound, 18:12 min. A Smoking Dogs Films Production, in association with Carroll/Fletcher and the European Cultural Foundation, 2012.

Akyeampong, Emmanuel. "Africans in the Diaspora: The Diaspora and Africa." *African Affairs* 99 (2000): 183–215.

———. "Seizing Modernity: Migrant Aspirations and Social Conflict in Early Colonial Keta (Gold Coast)." In *The "Traditional" and the "Modern" in West African*

(Ghanaian) History: Case Studies on Co-Existence and Interaction, ed. Per Hernæs, pp. 93–104. Trondheim: Norwegian University of Science and Technology, 2005.

Ali, Kecia. *Sexual Ethics and Islam*. Oxford: Oneworld Publications, 2006.

———. *Marriage and Slavery in Early Islam*. Cambridge, Mass.: Harvard University Press, 2010.

Allman, Jean. "Adultery and the State in Asante." In *The Cloth of Many Colored Silks: Papers on History and Society, Ghanaian and Islamic, in Honor of Ivor Wilks*, ed. John Hunwick and Nancy Lawler, pp. 27–65. Evanston, Ill.: Northwestern University Press, 1996.

Andaya, Leonard Y. *Leaves of the Same Tree: Trade and Ethnicity in the Straits of Melaka*. Honolulu: University of Hawai'i Press, 2008.

Anderson, J. N. D. *Islamic Law in Africa*. London: Frank Cass, 1970 [1954].

Appiah, Anthony. *In My Father's House: Africa in the Philosophy of Culture*. Oxford: Oxford University Press, 1993.

Ardener, Edwin. *The Voice of Prophecy: And Other Essays*. New York: Berghahn Books, 2006.

Argenti, Nicolas. *The Intestines of the State: Youth, Violence, and Belated Histories in the Cameroon Grassfields*. Chicago: University of Chicago Press, 2007.

Arhin, Kwame. *West African Traders in Ghana in the Nineteenth and Twentieth Centuries*. London and New York: Longman, 1979.

Aristotle. *Poetics*. Trans. Anthony Kenny. Oxford: Oxford University Press, 2013.

Austen, Ralph. "The Moral Economy of Witchcraft." In *Modernity and Its Malcontents: Ritual and Power in Postcolonial Africa*, ed. Jean Comaroff and John Comaroff, pp. 89–110. Chicago: University of Chicago Press, 1993.

———, and Jonathan Derrick. *Middlemen of the Cameroons Rivers: The Duala and their Hinterland, c.1600–c.1960*. Cambridge: Cambridge University Press, 1999.

Awambeng, Christopher M. *Evolution and Growth of Urban Centres in the North-West Province (Cameroon): Case Studies, Bamenda, Kumbo, Mbengwi, Nkambe, Wum*. Bern and New York: Peter Lang, 1991.

Awasom, Nicodemus Fru. "The Hausa and Fulani in the Bamenda Grasslands 1903–1960." Ph.D. dissertation, University of Yaoundé, 1984.

Bakewell, Oliver. "In Search of the Diasporas within Africa." *African Diaspora* 1 (2008): 5–27.

Ballantyne, Tony, and Antoinette Burton, eds. *Moving Subjects: Gender, Mobility, and Intimacy in an Age of Global Empire*. Urbana: University of Illinois Press, 2009.

Bargery, G. P. *A Hausa–English Dictionary and English–Hausa Vocabulary*. London: Oxford University Press, 1934.

Barkow, Jerome H. "Hausa Women and Islam." *Canadian Journal of African Studies* 6, no. 2 (1972): 317–328.

Bearman, P. et al. *Encyclopedia of Islam (Second Edition) Online*, www.brill.com. Leiden: Koninklijke Brill, 2012.

Beidelman, Thomas O. "Kaguru Justice and the Concept of Legal Fictions." *Journal of African Law* 5 (1961): 5–21.

Bivins, Mary Wren. *Telling Stories, Making Histories: Women, Words, and Islam in Nineteenth-Century Hausaland and the Sokoto Caliphate*. Portsmouth: Heinemann, 2007.

Bovill, E. W., and Robin Hallett. *The Golden Trade of the Moors: West African Kingdoms in the Fourteenth Century*. London: Oxford University Press, 1968.

Brain, Robert. *Bangwa Kinship and Marriage*. Cambridge: Cambridge University Press, 1972.

Brett, Michael. "Islam and Trade in Bilad al-Sudan, Tenth-Eleventh Century A D." *Journal of African History* 24, no. 4 (1983): 431–440.

Brooks, George. "The Signares of Saint-Louis and Gorée: Women Entrepreneurs in Eighteenth-Century Senegal." In *Women in Africa: Studies in Social and Economic Change*, ed. Nancy Hafkin and Edna Bay, pp. 19–44. Stanford: Stanford University Press, 1976.

———. *Landlords and Strangers: Ecology, Society, and Trade in Western Africa, 1000–1630*. Boulder, Colo.: Westview Press, 1993.

Brown, Jacqueline Nassy. "Black Liverpool, Black America, and the Gendering of Diasporic Space." *Cultural Anthropology* 13, no. 3 (August 1998): 291–325.

———. *Dropping Anchor, Setting Sail: Geographies of Race in Black Liverpool*. Princeton, N.J.: Princeton University Press, 2005.

Brown, Vincent. *The Reaper's Garden: Death and Power in the World of Atlantic Slavery*. Cambridge, Mass.: Harvard University Press, 2008.

Buell, Raymond Leslie. *The Native Problem in Africa*. London: Frank Cass, 1965 [1928].

Burrill, Emily. "Disputing Wife Abuse: Tribunal Narratives of the Corporal Punishment of Wives in Colonial Sikasso, 1930s." *Cahiers d'études africaines* 47, no. 187 (2007): 603–622.

Byfield, Judith. "Introduction: Rethinking African Diaspora." *African Studies Review* 42, no. 1 (April 2000): 1–9.

———, LaRay Denzer, and Anthea Morrison, eds. *Gendering the African Diaspora*. Bloomington: Indiana University Press, 2010.

Calder, Norman. "Hinth, Birr, Tabarrur, Tahannuth: An Inquiry into the Arabic Vocabulary of Vows." *Journal of the School for Oriental and African Studies* 51, no. 2 (1998): 214–239.

Callaway, Barbara J. *Muslim Hausa Women in Nigeria: Tradition and Change*. Syracuse, N.Y.: Syracuse University Press, 1987.

Chanock, Martin. *Law, Custom, and Social Order: The Colonial Experience in Malawi and Zambia*. Portsmouth: Heinemann, 1998.

Chem-Langhëë, Bongfen. "Slavery and Slave Marketing in Nso' in the Nineteenth Century." *Paideuma* 41 (1995): 177–190.

Chilver, Elizabeth M. "Nineteenth-century Trade in the Bamenda Grassfields," *Afrika und Übersee* 45, no. 4 (1961): 233–258.

———. *Zintgraff's Explorations in Bamenda: Adamawa and the Benue Lands 1889–1892*, ed. E. W. Ardener. Buea: Government Printer, 1966.

————, and Phyllis M. Kaberry. *Traditional Bamenda: The Pre-colonial History and Ethnography of the Bamenda Grassfields*. Cameroon: Ministry of Primary Education and Social Welfare and West Cameroon Antiquities Commission, 1968.

————, and Ute Röschenthaler, eds. *Cameroon's Tycoon: Max Esser's Expedition and Its Consequences*. New York: Berghahn Books, 2001.

Chivallon, Christine. "Beyond Gilroy's Black Atlantic: Experience of the African Diaspora." Trans. Karen E. Fields. *Diaspora* 11, no. 3 (2002): 359–382.

Christelow, Allan. "Women and the Law in Early-Twentieth-Century Kano." In *Hausa Women in the Twentieth Century*, ed. Catherine Coles and Beverly Mack, pp. 130–144. Madison: University of Wisconsin Press, 1991.

Clifford, James. "Diasporas." *Cultural Anthropology* 9, no. 3 (August 1994): 302–338.

Cohen, Abner. *Custom and Politics in Urban Africa: A Study of Hausa Migrants in Yoruba Towns*. Los Angeles: University of California Press, 1969.

————. "Cultural Strategies in the Organization of Trading Diasporas." In *The Development of Indigenous Trade and Markets in West Africa*, ed. Claude Meillassoux, pp. 266–281. London: Oxford University Press, 1971.

Cohen, David, and Atieno Adhiambo. *Burying SM: The Production of Knowledge and the Sociology of Power in Africa*. Portsmouth: Heinemann, 1992.

Cohen, Robin. *Global Diasporas: An Introduction*. 2nd edition. London/New York: Routledge, 2008.

Coles, Catherine, and Beverly Mack, eds. *Hausa Women in the Twentieth Century*. Madison: University of Wisconsin Press, 1991.

Cooper, Barbara M. *Marriage in Maradi: Gender and Culture in a Hausa Society in Niger, 1900–1989*. Portsmouth: Heinemann, 1997.

————. "Oral Sources and the Challenge of African History." In *Writing African History*, ed. Edward Philips, pp. 191–215. Rochester, N.Y.: University of Rochester Press, 2005.

————. *Evangelical Christians in the Muslim Sahel*. Bloomington: Indiana University Press, 2006.

————. "Chronic Malnutrition and the Trope of the Bad Mother: Reflections on the 2005 Crisis in Niger." Paper delivered at the African Studies Association Conference, Chicago, 2008.

Cooper, Frederick. *Africa since 1940: The Past of the Present*. Cambridge: Cambridge University Press, 2002.

Curtin, Philip D. *Cross-Cultural Trade in World History*. Cambridge: Cambridge University Press, 1984.

Davies, Carol Boyce. *Black Women, Writing, and Identity: Migrations of the Subject*. New York: Routledge, 1994.

Diawara, Manthia. *In Search of Africa*. Cambridge, Mass.: Harvard University Press, 2000.

De Witte, Marleen. *Long Live the Dead! Changing Funeral Celebrations in Asante, Ghana*. Amsterdam: Aksant Academic Publishers, 2001.

Duffill, M. B., and Paul E. Lovejoy. "Merchants, Porters, and Teamsters in the Nineteenth-Century Central Sudan." In *The Workers of African Trade*, ed. Catherine Coquery-Vidrovitch and Paul E. Lovejoy, pp. 137–167. Beverly Hills: Sage Publications, 1985.

Eckert, Andreas. "Slavery in Colonial Cameroon, 1880s to 1930s." In *Slavery and Colonial Rule in Africa*, ed. Suzanne Miers and Martin A. Klein, pp. 133–148. London: Routledge, 2004 [1999].

Fabian, Johannes. *Out of Our Minds: Reason and Madness in the Exploration of Central Africa*. Berkeley and Los Angeles: University of California Press, 2000.

Fardon, Richard. *Raiders and Refugees: Trends in Chamba Political Development, 1750 to 1950*. Washington: Smithsonian Institution Press, 1988.

Fomin, Denis E. S. *A Comparative Study of Societal Influences on Indigenous Slavery in Two Types of Societies in Africa*. Lewiston, N.Y.: Edwin Mellen Press, 2002.

Fowler, Ian, and David Zeitlyn, eds. *African Crossroads: Intersections between History and Anthropology in Cameroon*. New York: Berghahn Books, 1996.

Geary, Christraud M. *Images from Bamum: German Colonial Photography at the Court of King Njoya, Cameroon, West Africa, 1902–1915*. Washington: National Museum of African Art, Smithsonian Institution Press, 1988.

Geschiere, Peter. *The Perils of Belonging: Autochthony, Citizenship, and Exclusion in Africa and Europe*. Chicago: Chicago University Press, 2009.

Ghosh, Amitav. *Sea of Poppies*. New York: Farrar, Straus and Giroux, 2009.

Gilroy, Paul. *The Black Atlantic: Modernity and Double-Consciousness*. Cambridge, Mass.: Harvard University Press, 1993.

Glassman, Jonathon. *War of Words, War of Stones: Racial Thought and Violence in Colonial Zanzibar*. Bloomington: Indiana University Press, 2011.

Glissant, Édouard. *Poetics of Relation*. Trans. Betsy Wing. Ann Arbor: University of Michigan Press, 1997.

Gocking, Roger. "British Justice and the Native Tribunals of the Southern Gold Coast Colony," *Journal of African History* 42, no. 1 (1993): 93–113.

Goheen, Miriam. *Men Own the Fields, Women Own the Crops: Gender and Power in the Cameroon Grassfields*. Madison: University of Wisconsin Press, 1996.

Gopinath, Gayatri. "'Bombay, U.K., Yuba City': Bhangra Music and the Engendering of Diaspora." *Diaspora* 4, no. 3 (1995): 303–321.

Gorges, E. Howard. *The Great War in West Africa*. Uckfield: Naval & Military Press, 2004.

Gunning, Sandra, Tera Hunter, and Michele Mitchell, eds. *Dialogues of Dispersal: Gender, Sexuality, and African Diasporas*. Oxford: Blackwell, 2004.

Gupta, Akhil, and James Ferguson, eds. *Culture, Power, Place: Explorations in Critical Anthropology*. Durham, N.C., Duke University Press, 1997.

Guyer, Jane I. "Wealth in People, Wealth in Things—Introduction." *Journal of African History* 36, no. 1 (1995): 83–90.

———, and Samuel M. Eno Beling. "Wealth in People as Wealth in Knowledge: Accumulation and Composition in Equatorial Africa." *Journal of African History* 36, no. 1 (1995): 91–120.

Habermas, Rebekka. "Debates on Islam in Imperial Germany." In *Islam and the European Empires*, ed. David Motadel, pp. 213–253. Oxford: Oxford University Press, 2014.

Hall, Bruce S. *A History of Race in Muslim West Africa, 1600–1960*. New York: Cambridge University Press, 2011.

Hall, Catherine. "Of Gender and Empire: Reflection on the Nineteenth Century." In *Gender and Empire*, ed. Philippa Levine, pp. 46–76. Oxford: Oxford University Press, 2004.

Hall, Stuart. "Cultural Identity and Diaspora." In *Identity: Community, Culture, Difference*, ed. Jonathan Rutherford, pp. 222–237. London: Lawrence & Wishart, 1990.

Hamilton, Carolyn. *Terrific Majesty: The Powers of Shaka Zulu and the Limits of Historical Invention*. Cambridge, Mass.: Harvard University Press, 1998.

Haour, Anne and Benedetta Rossi, eds. *Being and Becoming Hausa: Interdisciplinary Perspectives*. Leiden: Brill, 2010.

Helmreich, Stefan. "Kinship, Nation, and Paul Gilroy's Concept of Diaspora." *Diaspora* 2, no. 2 (1992): 243–249.

Hertz, Robert. *Death and the Right Hand*. Trans. Rodney and Claudia Needham. London: Cohen & West, 1960 [1907].

Hill, Polly. *Rural Hausa: A Village and a Setting*. Cambridge: Cambridge University Press, 1972.

———. *Population, Prosperity and Poverty: Rural Kano, 1900 and 1970*. Cambridge: Cambridge University Press, 1977.

Hirsch, Susan F. *Pronouncing and Persevering: Gender and the Discourses of Disputing in an African Islamic Court*. Chicago: University of Chicago Press, 1998.

Hiskett, Mervyn. *The Development of Islam in West Africa*. New York: Longman, 1984.

Hogben, S. J., and Anthony H. M. Kirk-Greene. *The Emirates of Northern Nigeria: A Preliminary Survey of Their Historical Traditions*. London: Oxford University Press, 1966.

Holt, Thomas C. "Slavery and Freedom in the Atlantic World: Reflections on the Diasporan Framework." In *Crossing Boundaries: Comparative History of Black People in Diaspora*, ed. Darlene Clark Hine and Jacqueline McLeod, pp. 33–44. Bloomington: Indiana University Press, 1999.

Horton, Mark, and John Middleton. *The Swahili: The Social Landscape of a Mercantile Society*. Malden: Blackwell, 2000.

Iliffe, John. *Honour in African History*. Cambridge: Cambridge University Press, 2005.

Jeppie, Shamil, Ebrahim Moosa, and Richard Roberts, eds. *Muslim Family Law in Sub-Saharan Africa: Colonial Legacies and Post-colonial Challenges*. Amsterdam: Amsterdam University Press, 2010.

Johnson, Marion. "The Cowrie Currencies of West Africa: Part I." *Journal of African History* 11, no. 1 (1970): 17–49.

———. "The Cowrie Currencies of West Africa: Part II." *Journal of African History* 11, no. 3 (1970): 331–353.

Joseph, Suad, Afsaneh Najmabadi et al., *Encyclopedia of Women and Islamic Cultures.* Leiden and Boston: Brill, 2003–2007.

Jumare, Ibrahim M. "The Late Treatment of Slavery in Sokoto: Background and Consequences of the 1936 Proclamation." *International Journal of African Historical Studies* 27, no. 2 (1994): 303–322.

Kaberry, Phyllis M. *Women of the Grassfields: A Study of the Economic Position of Women in Bamenda, British Cameroons.* London: Her Majesty's Stationery Office, 1952.

Kandiyoti, Deniz. "Islam and Patriarchy: A Comparative Perspective." In *Women in Middle Eastern History,* ed. N. Keddie and B. Barton, pp. 23–44. New Haven, Conn.: Yale University Press, 1991.

Kirk-Greene, Anthony H. M. *Mutumin Kirkii: The Concept of the Good Man in Hausa.* Bloomington: Indiana University Press, 1974.

Klein, Martin, and Claire Robertson, eds. *Women and Slavery in Africa.* Madison: University of Wisconsin Press, 1983.

Kopytoff, Igor, ed. *The African Frontier: The Reproduction of Traditional African Societies.* Bloomington: Indiana University Press, 1987.

Kuba, Richard, and Carola Lentz, eds. *Land and the Politics of Belonging in West Africa.* Leiden and Boston: Brill, 2006.

Lander, Richard L. *Records of Captain Clapperton's Last Expedition.* London: H. Colburn and R. Bentley, 1830.

Last, Murray. *The Sokoto Caliphate.* London: Longmans, Green, and Co, 1967.

———. "Social Exclusion in Northern Nigeria." In *Madness, Disability, and Social Exclusion: The Archaeology and Anthropology of "Difference,"* ed. Jane Hubert, pp. 217–240. New York: Routledge, 2000.

Launay, Robert. *Traders without Trade: Response to Change in Two Dyula Communities.* New York: Cambridge University Press, 1982.

Lee, Rebekah, and Megan Vaughan. "Death and Dying in the History of Africa since 1800." *Journal of African History* 49 (2008): 1–19.

Levine, Philippa, ed. *Gender and Empire.* Oxford: Oxford University Press, 2004.

Levtzion, Nehemia. *Muslims and Chiefs in West Africa: A Study of Islam in the Middle Volta Basin in the Pre-colonial Period.* Oxford: Clarendon Press, 1968.

Lovejoy, Paul E. *Caravans of Kola: The Hausa Kola Trade, 1700–1900.* Zaria: Ahmadu Bello University Press, 1980.

———. "Concubinage and the Status of Women Slaves in Early Colonial Nigeria." *Journal of African History* 29, no. 2 (1988): 245–266.

———. "The Role of the Wangara in the Economic Transformation of the Central Sudan in the Fifteenth and Sixteenth Centuries." In *Merchant Networks in the Early Modern World,* ed. Sanjay Subrahmanyam, pp. 29–49. London: Valdove, 1996.

———, and Jan S. Hogendorn. *Slow Death for Slavery: The Course of Abolition in Northern Nigeria, 1897–1936.* New York: Cambridge University Press, 1993.

Lydon, Ghislaine. *On Trans-Saharan Trails: Islamic Law, Trade Networks, and Cross-Cultural Exchange in Nineteenth-Century Western Africa*. Cambridge: Cambridge University Press, 2009.

Mack, Beverly B., and Jean Boyd. *One Woman's Jihad: Nana Asma'u, Scholar and Scribe*. Bloomington: Indiana University Press, 2000.

Mamdani, Mahmood. "Beyond Settler and Native as Political Identities: Overcoming the Political Legacy of Colonialism." *Comparative Studies in Society and History* 43, no. 4 (October 2001): 651–664.

Manchuelle, François. *Willing Migrants: Soninke Labor Diasporas, 1848–1960*. Athens: Ohio University Press, 1997.

Mann, Kristin, and Richard Roberts, eds. *Law in Colonial Africa*. Portsmouth, N.H.: Heinneman, 1991.

Mariani, Philomena, ed. *Critical Fictions: The Politics of Imaginative Writing*. Seattle: Bay Press, 1991.

Markovitz, Claude. *Global World of Indian Merchants, 1750–1947: Traders of Sind from Bukhara to Panama*. Cambridge: Cambridge University Press, 2000.

Masquelier, Adeline. "Narratives of Power, Images of Wealth: The Ritual Economy of Bori in the Market." In *Modernity and Its Malcontents: Ritual and Power in Postcolonial Africa*, ed. Jean Comaroff and John Comaroff, pp. 3–33. Chicago: University of Chicago Press, 1993.

Mbuagbaw, Tambi Eyongetah, Robert Brain, and Robin Palmer. *A History of the Cameroon*. Harlow: Longman Group, 1987.

McKeown, Adam. "Conceptualizing Chinese Diasporas, 1842 to 1949." *Journal of Asian Studies* 58, no. 2 (May 1999): 306–337.

Meillassoux, Claude. *The Anthropology of Slavery: The Womb of Iron and Gold*. Trans. Alide Dasnois. Chicago: University of Chicago Press, 1991.

Merrick, George. *Hausa Proverbs*. New York: Negro Universities Press, 1969 [1905].

Middleton, John. *The World of the Swahili: An African Mercantile Civilization*. New Haven, Conn.: Yale University Press, 1992.

Miers, Suzanne, and Igor Kopytoff, eds. *Slavery in Africa: Historical and Anthropological Perspectives*. Madison: University of Wisconsin Press, 1977.

Miles, Tiya. *Ties that Bind: The Story of an Afro-Cherokee Family in Slavery and Freedom*. Berkeley and Los Angeles: University of California Press, 2006.

Moberly, F. J. *Togoland and the Cameroons 1914–1916*. London: Her Majesty's Stationery Office, 1931.

Mohapatra, Prabhu. "'Restoring the Family': Wife Murders and the Making of a Sexual Contract for Indian Immigrant Labour in the British Caribbean Colonies, 1860–1920." *Studies in History* 11 (August 1995): 227–260.

Morgan, Jennifer L. *Laboring Women: Reproduction and Gender in New World Slavery*. Philadelphia: University of Pennsylvania Press, 2004.

Morrell, Robert. "Of Boys and Men: Masculinity and Gender in Southern African Studies." *Journal of Southern African Studies* 24, no. 4, Special Issue on Masculinities in Southern Africa (1998): 605–630.

Motadel, David, ed. *Islam and the European Empires*. Oxford: Oxford University Press, 2014.

Mutongi, Kenda. *Worries of the Heart: Widows, Family, and Community in Kenya*. Chicago: University of Chicago Press, 2007.

Njeuma, Martin, ed. *Introduction to the History of Cameroon: Nineteenth and Twentieth Centuries*. London: Macmillan, 1989.

———. "The Lamidates of Northern Cameroon, 1800–1894." In *Introduction to the History of Cameroon: Nineteenth and Twentieth Centuries*, ed. Martin Njeuma, pp. 1–31. London: Macmillan, 1989.

Njiasse-Njoya, Aboubakar. "Slavery in the Bamum Kingdom in the 19th and 20th Centuries." *Paideuma* 41 (1995): 227–237.

Nkwi, Paul Nchoji. "Slavery and Slave Trade in the Kom Kingdom of the 19th Century." *Paideuma* 41 (1995): 239–249.

———, and Jean-Pierre Warnier. *Elements for a History of the Western Grassfields*. Yaoundé: University of Yaoundé, 1982.

Ochonu, Moses E. "Colonialism within Colonialism: The Hausa-Caliphate Imaginary and the British Colonial Administration of the Nigerian Middle Belt." *African Studies Quarterly* 10, nos. 2 & 3 (Fall 2008): 95–127.

———. *Colonialism by Proxy: Hausa Imperial Agents and Middle Belt Consciousness in Nigeria*. Bloomington: Indiana University Press, 2014.

Ofonagoro, Walter I. "From Traditional to British Currency in Southern Nigeria: Analysis of a Currency Revolution, 1880–1948." *The Journal of Economic History* 39, no. 3 (1979): 623–654.

Olofson, Harold. "'Yawon Dandi': A Hausa Category of Migration." *Africa* 46, no. 1 (1976): 66–79.

———. "Hausa Kinship and Diaspora." *Ethnos: Journal of Anthropology* 46, nos. 1–2 (1981): 80–91.

———. "The Hausa Wanderer and Structural Outsiderhood: An Emic and Etic Analysis." In *Circulation in Third World Countries*, ed. R. Mansell Prothero and Murray Chapman, pp. 54–74. London: Routledge and Kegan Paul, 1985.

O'Neil, Robert. "Imperialisms at the Century's End: Moghama Relationships with Bali-Nyonga and Germany, 1889–1908." In *African Crossroads: Intersections between History and Anthropology in Cameroon*, ed. Ian Fowler and David Zeitlyn, pp. 81–100. New York: Berghahn Books, 1996.

O'Rourke, Harmony. "Native Foreigners and the Ambiguity of Order and Identity: The Case of African Diasporas and Islamic Law in British Cameroon." *History in Africa: A Journal of Method* 39 (2012): 97–122.

———. "Beyond the World of Commerce: Rethinking Hausa Diaspora History through Marriage, Distance, and Legal Testimony." *History in Africa: A Journal of Method* 43 (June 2016): 141–167.

Osborn, Emily. *Our New Husbands Are Here: Household, Gender, and Politics in a West African State from the Slave Trade to Colonial Rule*. Athens: Ohio University Press, 2011.

Owusu-Ansah, David. *Islamic Talismanic Tradition in Nineteenth-Century Asante.* Lewison, N.Y.: Edwin Mellen, 1991.

Paice, Edward. *Tip and Run: The Untold Tragedy of the Great War in Africa.* London: Weidenfeld & Nicolson, 2007.

Pelican, Michaela. "Getting along in the Grassfields: Interethnic Relations and Identity Politics in Northwest Cameroon." Ph.D. dissertation, Martin-Luther-Universität Halle-Wittenberg, 2006.

———. "Mbororo Claims to Regional Citizenship and Minority Status in North-West Cameroon." *Africa* 78, no. 4 (2008): 540–560.

Pellow, Deborah. "From Accra to Kano: One Woman's Experience." In *Hausa Women in the Twentieth Century,* ed. Catherine Coles and Beverly Mack, pp. 50–68. Madison: University of Wisconsin Press, 1991.

———. *Landlords and Lodgers: Socio-Spatial Organization in an Accra Community.* Chicago: University of Chicago Press, 2002.

Peters, Rudolph. *Islamic Criminal Law in Nigeria.* Ibadan: Spectrum Books Limited, 2003.

———. *Crime and Punishment in Islamic Law: Theory and Practice from the Sixteenth to the Twenty-first Century.* Cambridge: Cambridge University Press, 2005.

Pierce, Steven. "Farmers and 'Prostitutes': Twentieth-Century Problems of Female Inheritance in Kano Emirate, Nigeria." *Journal of African History* 44 (2003): 463–486.

———. *Farmers and the State in Colonial Kano: Land Tenure and the Legal Imagination.* Bloomington: Indiana University Press, 2005.

Pittin, Renée. "Migration of Women in Nigeria: The Hausa Case." *International Migration Review* 18, no. 4 (1984): 1293–1314.

Plane, Ann Marie. *Colonial Intimacies: Indian Marriage in Early New England.* Ithaca, N.Y.: Cornell University Press, 2000.

Rapoport, Yossef. *Marriage, Money, and Divorce in Medieval Islamic Society.* Cambridge: Cambridge University Press, 2007.

Reid, Anthony. *Southeast Asia in the Age of Commerce.* New Haven, Conn.: Yale University Press, 1988.

Robertson, Claire. *Sharing the Same Bowl: A Socioeconomic History of Women and Class in Accra, Ghana.* Ann Arbor: University of Michigan Press, 1984.

———, and Martin A. Klein, eds. *Women and Slavery in Africa.* Madison: University of Wisconsin Press, 1983.

Robinson, Charles H. *Dictionary of the Hausa Language.* Cambridge: Cambridge University Press, 1925.

Robinson-Dunn, Diane. *The Harem, Slavery and British Imperial Culture: Anglo-Muslim Relations in the Late Nineteenth Century.* Manchester: Manchester University Press, 2006.

Rosaldo, Renato. "Introduction: Grief and a Headhunter's Rage." In *Culture and Truth: The Remaking of Social Analysis,* ed. Renato Rosaldo, pp. 1–21. Boston: Beacon Press, 1993 [1989].

Rudin, Harry R. *Germans in the Cameroons 1884–1914: A Case Study in Modern Imperialism*. London: Jonathan Cape, 1938.

Ruxton, F. H. *Maliki Law: Being a Summary from French Translations of the Mukhtasar of Sidi Khalil*. Westport, Conn.: Hyperion Press, 1980 [1916].

Safran, William. "Diasporas in Modern Societies: Myths of Homeland and Return." *Diaspora* 1, no. 1 (1991): 83–99.

Salamone, Frank A. *The Hausa of Nigeria*. Lanham, Md.: University Press of America, 2010.

Salau, Mohammed Bashir. "Slaves in a Muslim City: A Survey of Slavery in Nineteenth-Century Kano." In *Slavery, Islam and Diaspora*, ed. Paul E. Lovejoy, Behnaz Mirzai, and Ismael Montana, pp. 91–101. Trenton: Africa World Press, 2009.

Schildkrout, Enid. *People of the Zongo: The Transformation of Ethnic Identities in Ghana*. Cambridge: Cambridge University Press, 1978.

———. "Widows in Hausa Society: Ritual Phase or Social Status?" In *Widows in African Societies: Choices and Constraints*, ed. Betty Potash, pp. 131–152. Stanford, Calif.: Stanford University Press, 1986.

Schmoll, Pamela. "Black Stomachs, Beautiful Stones." In *Modernity and Its Malcontents: Ritual and Power in Postcolonial Africa*, ed. Jean Comaroff and John Comaroff, pp. 193–220. Chicago: University of Chicago Press, 1993.

Scott, Joan W. "Gender: A Useful Category of Historical Analysis." *The American Historical Review* 91, no. 5 (December 1986): 1053–1075.

Scott, Rebecca J., and Jean M. Hébrard. "Rosalie of the Poulard Nation: Freedom, Law, and Dignity in the Era of the Haitian Revolution." In *Assumed Identities: The Meanings of Race in the Atlantic World*, ed. John. Garrigus and Christopher Morris, pp. 116–143. Arlington: University of Texas Press, 2010.

———. *Freedom Papers: An Atlantic Odyssey in the Age of Emancipation*. Cambridge, Mass.: Harvard University Press, 2012.

Sell, Jonathan P. A., ed. *Metaphor and Diaspora in Contemporary Writing*. New York: Palgrave Macmillan, 2012.

Shipton, Parker. *The Nature of Entrustment: Intimacy, Exchange, and the Sacred in Africa*. New Haven, Conn.: Yale University Press, 2007.

Simmel, Georg. "The Stranger." In *The Sociology of Georg Simmel*, ed. and trans. K. Wolff, pp. 402–408. London: Free Press, 1950.

Siu, Lok. "Diasporic Cultural Citizenship: Chineseness and Belonging in Central America and Panama." *Social Text* 69, Cultural Citizenship (Winter 2001), 7–28.

———. "Queen of the Chinese Colony: Gender, Nation, and Belonging in Diaspora." *Anthropological Quarterly* 78, no. 3 (2005): 511–542.

Skinner, Elliott P. "Strangers in West African Societies." *Africa* 33, no. 2 (October 1963): 307–320.

Sleeper-Smith, Susan. *Indian Women and French Men: Rethinking Cultural Encounter in the Western Great Lakes*. Amherst: University of Massachusetts Press, 2001.

Smith, Jane Idleman, and Yvonne Yazbeck Haddad. *The Islamic Understanding of Death and Resurrection*. Oxford: Oxford University Press, 2002.

Smith, Mary F. *Baba of Karo: A Woman of the Muslim Hausa*. New Haven, Conn.: Yale University Press, 1981 [1954].

Smith, M. G. "The Hausa System of Social Status." *Africa* 29, no. 3 (July 1959): 244–245.

———. *The Affairs of Daura*. Berkeley: University of California Press, 1978.

———. "Introduction." In *Baba of Karo: A Woman of the Muslim Hausa*, by Mary F. Smith, pp. 11–34. New Haven, Conn.: Yale University Press, 1981 [1954].

Soh, Pius Bejeng, *Abakpa, Mankon, Bamenda: Creation and Evolution of an Urban Centre in a Traditional Milieu*. Cameroon: Delegation generale a la recherche scientifique et technique, 1983.

Sonbol, Amira El Azhary. "Introduction," *Women, the Family, and Divorce Laws in Islamic History*, ed. Amira El Azhary Sonbol, pp. 1–22. Syracuse, N.Y.: Syracuse University Press, 1996.

Stowasser, Barbara, "Gender Issues and Contemporary Quran Interpretation." In *Islam, Gender, and Social Change*, ed. Yvonne Yazbeck Haddad and John L. Esposito, pp. 30–44. Oxford: Oxford University Press, 1998.

Strachan, Hew. *The First World War in Africa*. Oxford: Oxford University Press, 2004.

Strobel, Margaret. *Muslim Women in Mombasa, 1890–1975*. New Haven, Conn.: Yale University Press, 1979.

Sturtz, Linda L. "Mary Rose: 'White' African Jamaican Woman? Race and Gender in Eighteenth-Century Jamaica." In *Gendering the African Diaspora Gendering the African Diaspora*, ed. Judith Byfield et al., pp. 59–87. Bloomington: Indiana University Press, 2010.

Subrahmanyam, Sanjay. *Merchant Networks in the Early Modern World*. London: Valdove, 1996.

Tardits, Claude. *Le royaume bamoum*. Paris: A. Colin, 1980.

Terborg-Penn, Rosalyn. "Women in the African Diaspora: An Overview of an Interdisciplinary Research Conference." In *Women in Africa and the African Diaspora: A Reader*, ed. Rosalyn Terborg-Penn and Andrea Benton, pp. xvii–xxvi. Washington, D.C.: Howard University Press, 1996.

Thomas, Lynn. *Politics of the Womb: Women, Reproduction, and the State in Kenya*. Berkeley and Los Angeles: University of California Press, 2003.

Trimingham, J. S. *Islam in West Africa*. Oxford: Oxford University Press, 1959.

van Gennep, Arnold. *Rites of Passage*. Chicago: University of Chicago Press, 1964 [trans. 1960]).

Vollbehr, Ernst. *Mit Pinsel und Palette durch Kamerun: Tagebuchaufzeichnungen und Bilder*. Leipzig: List & von Bressensdorf, 1912.

———. *Bunte leuchtende Welt: Die Lebensfahrt des Malers*. Berlin: Ullstein, 1935.

Wall, L. Lewis. *Hausa Medicine: Illness and Well-being in a West African Culture*. Durham, N.C.: Duke University Press, 1988.

Warnier, Jean-Pierre. "Pre-Colonial Mankon: The Development of a Cameroon Chiefdom in Its Regional Setting." Ph.D. dissertation, University of Pennsylvania, 1975.

———. "The History of the Peopling of Western Cameroon and the Genesis of its Landscapes." *Journal of African History* 25 (1984): 395–410.

———. Échanges, développement et hierarchies dans le Bamenda pré-colonial (Cameroun). Stuttgart: Franz Steiner Verlag Wiesbaden GmbH, 1985.

———. *Cameroon Grassfields Civilization*. Mankon, Bamenda: Langaa Research & Publishing Common Initiative Group, 2012.

Waterbury, John. *North for the Trade; The Life and Times of a Berber Merchant.* Berkeley: University of California Press, 1972.

White, Luise, Stephan F. Miescher, and David William Cohen, eds. *African Words, African Voices: Critical Practices in Oral History.* Bloomington: Indiana University Press, 2001.

Whitehouse, Bruce. *Migrants and Strangers in an African City: Exile, Dignity, Belonging.* Bloomington: Indiana University Press, 2012.

Wildenthal, Lora. *German Women for Empire, 1884–1945.* Durham: Duke University Press, 2001.

Wilke, Sabine. "Romantic Images of Africa: Paradigms of German Colonial Paintings." *German Studies Review* 29, no. 2 (May 2006): 285–298.

Wilks, Ivor. "Wangara, Akan and Portuguese in the Fifteenth and Sixteenth Centuries I. The Matter of Bitu." *Journal of African History* 23, no. 3 (1982): 333–349.

Willis, John Ralph, ed. *Slaves and Slavery in Muslim Africa.* Vol. 1: *Islam and the Ideology of Enslavement.* London: Frank Cass, 1985.

Works, John. *Pilgrims in a Strange Land: Hausa Communities in Chad.* New York: Columbia University Press, 1976.

Wright, Marcia. *Strategies of Slaves and Women: Life-Stories from East/Central Africa.* New York: Lilian Barber Press, 1993.

Yadudu, Auwalu Hamsxu. "Colonialism and the Transformation of the Substance and Form of Islamic Law in the Northern States of Nigeria." *Journal of Law and Religion* 9 (1991): 17–47.

Index

Harmony O'Rourke is an Associate Professor of History at Pitzer College, where she teaches courses on African history, world and diaspora histories, gender and feminist studies, and oral history methodology. She earned her B.A. in History and International Studies from Macalester College and her Ph.D. in African History from Harvard University. For her research on the Hausa diaspora, she was awarded the Fulbright-Hays Doctoral Dissertation Research Award from the U.S. Department of Education. Her articles have appeared in the journals *History in Africa: A Journal of Method* and *The Journal of West African History*.